Muslims in America

Recent Titles in Contemporary Debates

MUSLIMS IN AMERICA

Examining the Facts

Craig Considine

Contemporary Debates

ABC-CLIO ™

An Imprint of ABC-CLIO, LLC
Santa Barbara, California • Denver, Colorado

Copyright © 2018 by ABC-CLIO, LLC

Library of Congress Cataloging-in-Publication Data

Names: Considine, Craig, author.
Title: Muslims in America : examining the facts / Craig Considine.
Description: Santa Barbara : ABC-CLIO, 2018. | Series: Contemporary debates |
    Includes bibliographical references and index.
Identifiers: LCCN 2018008406 (print) | LCCN 2018020515 (ebook) |
    ISBN 9781440860546 (ebook) | ISBN 9781440860539 (alk. paper)
Subjects: LCSH: Muslims—United States | Islam—United States.
Classification: LCC BP67.U6 (ebook) | LCC BP67.U6 C66 2018 (print) |
    DDC 297.0973—dc23
LC record available at https://lccn.loc.gov/2018008406

ISBN: 978-1-4408-6053-9 (print)
      978-1-4408-6054-6 (ebook)

22 21 20 19 18   1 2 3 4 5

This book is also available as an eBook.

ABC-CLIO
An Imprint of ABC-CLIO, LLC

ABC-CLIO, LLC
130 Cremona Drive, P.O. Box 1911
Santa Barbara, California 93116-1911
www.abc-clio.com

This book is printed on acid-free paper ∞

Manufactured in the United States of America

Contents

How to Use This Book

Muslims in America: Examining the Facts is part of ABC-CLIO's Contemporary Debates reference series. Each title in this series, which is intended for use by high school and undergraduate students as well as members of the general public, examines the veracity of controversial claims or beliefs surrounding a major political/cultural issue in the United States. The purpose of this series is to give readers a clear and unbiased understanding of current issues by informing them about falsehoods, half-truths, and misconceptions—and confirming the factual validity of other assertions—that have gained traction in the political and cultural discourses of the United States. Ultimately, this series has been crafted to give readers the tools for a fuller understanding of controversial issues, policies, and laws that occupy center stage in American life and politics.

Each volume in this series identifies 30 to 40 questions swirling about the larger topic under discussion. These questions are examined in individualized entries, which are in turn arranged in broad subject chapters that cover certain aspects of the issue being examined, for example, history of concern about the issue, potential economic or social impact, or findings of latest scholarly research.

Each chapter features 4 to 10 individual entries. Each entry begins by stating an important and/or well-known **Question** about the issue being studied—for example, "Do Muslims in the United States condemn the radical beliefs and actions of militant groups such as ISIS and Al-Qaeda?" or "Is Islamophobia on the rise in the United States?"

The entry then provides a concise and objective one- or two-paragraph **Answer** to the featured question, followed by a more comprehensive, detailed explanation of **The Facts**. This latter portion of each entry uses quantifiable, evidence-based information from respected sources to fully address each question and provide readers with the information they need to be informed citizens. Importantly, entries will also acknowledge instances in which conflicting data exists or data is incomplete. Finally, each entry concludes with a **Further Reading** section, providing users with information on other important and/or influential resources.

The ultimate purpose of every book in the Contemporary Debates series is to reject "false equivalence," in which demonstrably false beliefs or statements are given the same exposure and credence as the facts; to puncture myths that diminish our understanding of important policies and positions; to provide needed context for misleading statements and claims; and to confirm the factual accuracy of other assertions. In other words, volumes in this series are being crafted to clear the air surrounding some of the most contentious and misunderstood issues or our time—not just add another layer of obfuscation and uncertainty to the debate.

Introduction

There has never been an America without the presence of Muslims. Yet, American Muslims have been increasingly branded as an "un-American" and unassimilable population that poses a societal and security threat to the United States. The faith of American Muslims—Islam—has also come under scrutiny for allegedly condoning violence against non-Muslims, oppressing women, and stifling freedom of speech and freedom of religion. Accusations against American Muslims, whether resulting from differences in religion or culture (or a combination of the two), have focused public attention on the state and lives of Muslims as well as the Islamic religion.

The attacks of September 11, 2001 (henceforth 9/11), had a significant impact on perceptions of American Muslims and even those in the United States who might be perceived to be Muslim. For some Americans, the utter indifference to the value of human life and the hostility shown toward the United States by Muslims came as a great surprise. Other Americans were confirmed in their beliefs that the United States is undergoing a civilization war between "Western civilization" and the "Muslim world." This perceived war is rooted in a struggle against *terrorism*, a term often linked to Muslims, even though the overwhelming majority of violent attacks on American soil have been perpetrated by non-Muslims.

The 9/11 attacks also initiated social and institutional responses that resulted in the marginalization of Muslims in the United States. Some of these processes led to hate crimes against Muslims, surveillance of Muslim communities and mosques, racial profiling, and immigration policies that are widely regarded as discriminatory toward Muslims. American Muslims have responded to these measures by speaking out against anti-Muslim racism and standing firmly for American values, such as the separation of church and state, equal rights for all, freedom of speech, and freedom of religion.

Despite the integration of Muslims into mainstream "American culture," they remain under the microscope. Media outlets, religious leaders, far-right organizations, and politicians have depicted Muslims as a "foreign" and threatening religious minority population. The term *Islamophobia*, which refers to a dislike of or prejudice against Islam or Muslims, especially as a political force, is now part of the American lexicon. Some chart the popularization of this term to the Runnymede Trust, a liberal British think tank that, in 1997, published a report entitled "Islamophobia: A Challenge for Us All." Edward Said, the postcolonial theorist, is regarded as the first scholar to reference the term in the English language, claiming in his article "Orientalism Reconsidered" that "hostility to Islam in the modern Christian West has historically gone hand in hand with, has stemmed from the same source, has been nourished at the same stream as anti-Semitism." Critics of the term *Islamophobia*, as Nathan Lean (author of *The Islamophobia Industry*) points out, "often lambast it on the basis of an etymological deficiency, insisting that it thwarts the possibility of critiquing Islam as a religion while simultaneously suggesting the presence of a mental disorder on the part of those who do."

A community of individuals and organizations across the United States has dedicated time and energy to convincing Americans that Muslims adhere to "anti-American" views and that Muslims should be marginalized in the United States. The network of bloggers, activists, politicians, religious leaders, and think tanks has been popularly referred to as the Islamophobia industry, a lucrative and well-coordinated network of anti-Muslim personalities that help to fuel the anti-Muslim and anti-Islam sentiments across the United States. The effects of the Islamophobia industry have contributed to an environment in which American Muslims are subject to increased scrutiny, negative public framing, physical attacks, verbal abuse, and institutional discrimination.

The relationship between the Islamic faith and American national identity has come to a boiling point. In the context of the rhetoric toward American Muslims, deciphering fact from fiction is more important than ever.

"Muslims have lived on American soil before the United States existed."

"The Founding Fathers of the United States welcomed the migration of Muslims."

"American Muslims are among the most diverse populations in the country."

"Muslims are among the most educated populations in American society."

"Islamic organizations in the United States regularly participate in interfaith dialogue."

"Muslims are not responsible for the majority of terrorist attacks on American soil."

"American Muslims do not prefer to be governed by Islamic law (sharia)."

All of the preceding statements are facts. The American Muslim population is racially, ethnically, culturally, and religiously diverse, with groups from the Middle East, Africa, and South and Southeast Asia, as well as a very significant African American community represented across the country. For the most part, American Muslims are happy living in the United States and are happier with conditions in American society compared to the broader U.S. population. Despite questions on the degree of their assimilation or integration, American Muslims are quite mainstream and "moderate."

Yet, like religious and ethnic minority populations before them, Muslims have faced significant challenges in American society. Media outlets, religious leaders, and politicians share their views on American Muslims and Islam, which are then transmitted to the U.S. public. Terms such as *radical Islamic terrorism*, which often appears on television and computer screens, shape how Americans view their Muslim neighbors and the Islamic faith. In response to these developments, American Muslims are working to define their own narratives and create identities that are simultaneously *American* and *Muslim*.

Muslims in America: Examining the Facts is a resource to all who are interested in separating fact from fiction as it concerns Muslims living in the United States. Written as part of a series of books that address controversial current event topics in American society, this book is an effort to empower and equip readers with facts about American Muslims through the presentation of historical documentation, empirical research, and hard data. As it weaves through the commonly misunderstood myths and realities about American Muslims and the Islamic faith, this book answers familiar and controversial questions with research-driven facts. Ultimately, after examining various Muslim-related issues through facts and statistics, it is up to the reader to decide how the data shapes his or her questions about such topics.

It is hoped that the data and information presented in this book will dispel myths about American Muslims and encourage deeper reflection on the actual realities and lived experiences of Muslims in the United States.

1

History of Muslims on American Soil

Q1. DID THE FIRST AMERICAN MUSLIMS ARRIVE AS SLAVES?

Answer: Yes. The first American Muslims were slaves from West Africa who were brought to the Americas during the transatlantic slave trade. Between 10 and 20 percent of the enslaved West Africans were Muslims, and historians believe the figure could be as high as 30 percent.

The Facts: Unbeknownst to many Americans today, the United States has never existed without the presence of Muslims. Several studies elaborate on how the history of Muslims in America was immeasurably augmented by the transatlantic slave trade. As many as 15 million West Africans were enslaved by Europeans beginning in the 16th century (Diouf, 1998). Among those West Africans, approximately 10 to 20 percent were Muslim (Austin, 1997). Other scholars have suggested that upward of 30 percent of all enslaved Africans were Muslims (Ahmed, 2003).

The Muslims who were enslaved and brought to the Americas are thought to have been mostly well learned and literate. Consistent with the basic teachings of Islam, education was paramount to the West African civilizations. Timbuktu, in modern-day Mali, was one of the great centers of learning in the world, with libraries having up to 700 volumes and numerous schools (well over 150 during the 16th century) (Dirks, 2006). Most of the Muslim slaves from West Africa were literate in at least Arabic, and it has been estimated that the percentage of literacy in Arabic among African slaves was actually higher than the percentage of literacy in English among their Christian owners (Dirks, 2006).

Al Haj Omar Ibn Said, a notable American Muslim slave with family roots in West Africa, is said to have been born and educated in the modern country of Senegal, where he served as an Islamic scholar of the Fula people. He is known for 14 documents that he wrote in Arabic, including an autobiography that detailed his life as a trader, soldier, and faithful Muslim. Said wrote that he performed the *hajj*, an Arabic word referring to the annual pilgrimage to Mecca, Saudi Arabia, required by all Muslims (Considine, 2017: 185), and studied the Qur'an for 25 years before being sold into slavery in 1807 (The Pluralism Project, n.d.). Said's handwritten works are now part of the North Carolina Collection in the Wilson Library at the University of North Carolina–Chapel Hill. Today, in Fayetteville, North Carolina, the Omar Ibn Said mosque on Southern Avenue stands as a testament to his legacy. A nearby historical marker notes that Said was a slave, scholar, and African-born author who penned in autobiography in Arabic. Other details of his life on the marker show that he lived in Blady County and worshipped with local Presbyterians.

Muslims from the territories of North Africa and the Ottoman Empire are considered to be the second group of Muslims to arrive on U.S. soil. One European Christian, the English sea captain and privateer Sir Francis Drake, commanded 25 to 30 English ships, whose shipmen liberated approximately 500 prisoners at Saint Augustine in Florida between 1585 and 1586. Dirks (2006) notes that about 300 or more of these liberated slaves were North African and Turkish galley slaves. North African and Ottoman captives from the Mediterranean region, usually called Moors and Turks, respectively, were needed to perform menial duties for their Spanish overlords in places such as Saint Augustine. Further evidence of Muslim galley slaves in the Americas is documented by the Smithsonian, which estimated that many of the Colombian city of Cartagena's slave population were Muslims. In 1586, Drake besieged and captured the town, instructing his men to treat Frenchmen, Turks, and black Africans with respect (Lawler, 2017).

Edward D. Neill, an historian of early American history, wrote in his book *The Virginia Carolorum* that several shipments of Turkish and Armenian indentured servants, both men and women, were present in the British colony of Jamestown, Virginia, in the early 17th century, meaning that the slaves Drake captured were likely of Turkish and Armenian descent (Neill, 1886). These hypotheses are confirmed in recordings by *The Virginia Carolorum*, which note that several of the Turks in Jamestown included the names "Mehmet the Turk," "Ahmad the Turk," "Joseph the Armenian," and "Sayyan Turk" (Neill, 1886). A 1652 colonial document also refers to a "Turk" in Virginia, who wrote in the Turkish language. In the same year, Governor William Boyd of Virginia referred to a Turkish merchant in a letter (Dirks, 2006).

An obscure group known as the Melungeons also had a presence in pre-colonial and colonial America. Of mixed racial background, the Melungeons settled in the Appalachian region as early as the 17th century (Dirks, 2006). According to Wayne Winkler (2004), the Melungeons are a hybrid group with African, Middle Eastern, and Mediterranean ancestry. A DNA study published in the *Journal of Genetic Genealogy* in 2012 found that Melungeon families are the offspring of sub-Saharan African men and white women of northern or central European origin. Further details about the ancestry of the Melungeons are provided by Kathy Lyday, a researcher based at Elon University. Lyday claims that a Spanish influence is likely, given that the Southwest and the mountains were explored and settled by Spaniards as far back as Hernando de Soto, a conquistador who marched through the region in 1540 (Neal, 2015). These Spaniards likely brought African Muslim slaves with them, and they probably intermarried with Natives.

FURTHER READING

Ahmed, Zahir. (2003). *Islam: Africa to America*. Rancho Palos Verdes: Islamic Research and Publications.

Austin, Allan D. (1997). *African Muslims in Antebellum America*. New York, NY: Routledge.

Considine, Craig. (2017). *Islam, Race, and Pluralism in the Pakistani Diaspora*. London and New York, NY: Routledge.

Curtis, Edward E., IV. (2010). *Encyclopedia of Muslim-American History*. New York, NY: Facts on File.

Diouf, Sylviane A. (1998). *Servants of Allah: African Muslims Enslaved in the Americas*. New York, NY: New York University Press.

Dirks, Jerald F. (2006). *Muslims in American History: A Forgotten Legacy*. Beltsville, MD: Amana Publications.

Hussain, Amir. (2016). *Muslims and the Making of America*. Waco, TX: Baylor University Press.

Lawler, Andrew. (2017, February 7). "Muslims Were Banned from the Americas as Early as the 16th Century." *Smithsonian Magazine*.

Retrieved from https://www.smithsonianmag.com/history/muslims-were-banned-americas-early-16th-century-180962059/

Neal, Dale. (2015). "Melungeons Explore Mysterious Mixed-Race Origins." *USA Today*. Retrieved from https://www.usatoday.com/story/news/nation/2015/06/24/melungeon-mountaineers-mixed-race/29252839/

Neill, Edward D. (1886). *The Virginian Carolorum: The Colony under the Rule of Charles the First and Second, A.D. 1625–A.D. 1685*. Washington, DC: Library of Congress. Retrieved from https://www.loc.gov/item/rc01002794/

The Pluralism Project. (n.d.). "Omar Ibn Said, African Muslim." Harvard University. Retrieved from http://pluralism.org/document/omar-ibn-said-african-muslim/

Winkler, Wayne. (2005). *Walking toward the Sunset: The Melungeons of Appalachia*. Macon, GA: Mercer University Press.

Q2. DID THE U.S. FOUNDING FATHERS ENCOURAGE THE MIGRATION OF MUSLIMS TO AMERICAN SOIL?

Answer: Yes. Primary documents reveal that George Washington, Benjamin Franklin, and Thomas Jefferson all encouraged the migration of Muslims to American soil.

The Facts: In September 2015, Republican presidential hopeful Ben Carson stated in a *Meet the Press* (2015) interview that he would not advocate electing a Muslim to serve as the president of the United States. Although the U.S. Constitution expressly forbids a religious test in Article IV, Section III, for would-be presidents, Carson said he would oppose any Muslim White House aspirant who was "not willing to reject *sharia*," or Islamic law (Quraishi-Landes, 2016). Sharia is the Arabic word for "path" or "Islamic law" (Considine, 2017: 187). Carson's comment revived a conversation as old as the United States itself—how should U.S. citizens incorporate the Islamic faith into their nation?

The Founding Fathers deliberated this question in 1788 during the ratification of the U.S. Constitution in North Carolina. One speaker during the convention, William Lancaster, spoke about what would happen when, a few centuries down the road, a Muslim would be elected to the highest office in the land, the presidency of the United States (Hammer & Safi, 2013). Lancaster told his peers that they needed to remember to "form a government for millions not yet in existence." He stressed that in the centuries to come, a U.S. citizen of any religious background should be able to serve as president. Lancaster specifically mentions "Papists" (an 18th-century term used to identify Catholics) and "Mahometans," or Muslims, in his defense (Hammer & Safi, 2013). Lancaster's views on who could or could not occupy the highest political office in the United States prevailed. The U.S. Constitution today does not exclude Muslims or members of any other religious faith or background from serving as president. Indeed, the Founding Fathers were fully prepared to make a place for both the Islamic faith and Muslims in the new nation (Hutson, 2002).

The first U.S. president, George Washington, envisioned Muslims as part of U.S. society. Writing as president in March 1784, he stated in a letter that future U.S. citizens "may be of Asia, Africa, or Europe. They may be Mahometans (Muslims), Jews, or Christians of any Sect, or they may be Atheists" (Thompson, n.d.). In 1783, he echoed these sentiments in a letter to Irish Catholic immigrants living in New York City, which is clear evidence of his welcoming attitude toward Muslims. Catholics, at that time, had few legal protections in any state and had no right to hold political office in New York. In a show of solidarity, Washington insisted that the United States is "open to receive . . . the oppressed and persecuted of all Nations and Religions; whom we shall welcome to a participation of all our rights and privileges." Moreover, his personal correspondence in December 1789 with Muhammad Ibn Abdullah, the Sultan of Morocco, revealed a president assuring a foreign Muslim ruler that the U.S. government would "not cease to promote every measure that may conduce to the friendship and harmony which so happily subsist between [us]" (Washington, 1789).

Washington, however, owned Muslim slaves. His relationship with American Muslims can be further examined by turning to his private world and place of residence—Mount Vernon, Virginia. The Mount Vernon website, the official source of information for the National Historic Landmark, states that "elements of Islam" are found in the documentary and archaeological records of the plantation's enslaved population. According to Mary V. Thompson, a research historian of the Mount Vernon Estate and Gardens, "Washington expressed little preference as to the religion practiced by the Mount Vernon slaves" (Thompson, n.d.).

Thompson also noted that the "names of at least three female slaves indicate an Islamic influence" at Mount Vernon, "if not the actual practice of Islam" (Thompson, n.d.). Two women—thought to be a mother and her daughter—were listed as "Fatimer" and "Little Fatimer" in a 1774 tithe table. The two names closely resemble the popular Muslim name Fatima, or "Shining One" in Arabic. Fatima also is the name of one of Prophet Muhammad's daughters.

Another woman, named Letty, who lived at Muddy Hole Farm at Mount Vernon, gave birth in 1800 to a girl she called Nila. "Nila" is a variation of a Muslim woman's name "Naailah," which means "someone who acquires something" or "someone who gets what they want." Thompson concludes:

> Even if no one was actually practicing Islam at Mount Vernon by this time, this child's name provides evidence that some knowledge of Islamic tradition or a familiarity with Arabic could still be found in the larger African-American community in Fairfax County or Alexandria, if not at Mount Vernon itself, at the beginning of the nineteenth century. (Thompson, n.d.)

Historical documents also suggest that Sambo Anderson, an African-born slave, was a Muslim living at Mount Vernon. According to Thompson, the "name 'Sambou' is common throughout West Africa, and is used primarily for a second son among the Hausa people of what is now northwestern Nigeria and southern Niger" (Thompson, n.d.). The Hausa were impacted by their exposure to both Arabic and Islam, which reached them from Timbuktu, the capital of Mali, beginning in the late 14th century. Sambo was described as having a face "marked by both tribal cuts and tattooing" (Thompson, n.d.). He also is said to have worn gold rings in his ears.

Sambo stood out among the slaves at Mount Vernon. In an article entitled "Mount Vernon Reminiscence," which was published in the *Alexandria Gazette* in 1876, "an old citizen of Fairfax County" contends that Washington and Sambo had a close friendship. The "Reminiscence" stated that Sambo was a "great favorite" of Washington, "by whom [Sambo] was given a piece of land to build a house on," an unusual gift for a slave. The "old citizen" of Fairfax County also revealed that Washington allowed Sambo to keep a small boat or skiff to "cross over the creek in, and for other purposes," another "rare privilege for a slave. Washington would sometimes use Sambo's boat, but he never was the man to take it without asking [Sambo] if he could use it" (Thompson, n.d.).

George Washington may rightly be known as the Father of His Country. However, in the decades before the American Revolution, Benjamin Franklin was the world's most famous American (George Washington's Mount Vernon, n.d.). A celebrated scientist, inventor, diplomat, and philosopher of the U.S. Constitution, Franklin also welcomed Muslims to the United States. Writing in his *Autobiography* on the building of a non-denominational house of public worship in Philadelphia, Franklin called for the place of worship to be a space open to "any preacher of any religious persuasion who might desire to say something to the people at Philadelphia" (Franklin, n.d.). Franklin went as far as welcoming the *mufti*, of Constantinople (modern-day Istanbul, Turkey) to preach Islam to Americans (Franklin, n.d.). *Mufti* is an Arabic word referring to a specialist in Islamic law who is qualified to deliver a religious interpretation or legal brief (Considine, 2017: 186).

Like Franklin, Thomas Jefferson welcomed Muslims to the United States. In 1765, as a 22-year-old law student at the College of William and Mary in Williamsburg, Virginia, Jefferson purchased a copy of the Qur'an (Spellberg, 2017). According to Denise Spellberg (2013), author of *Thomas Jefferson's Qur'an: Islam and the Founders*, Jefferson's purchase is symbolic of a longer historical connection between the United States and Islam. This connection suggests that the Founding Fathers had a more robust view of religious pluralism (Spellberg, 2017).

A few months after writing the Declaration of Independence, Jefferson returned to draft legislation in Virginia. In his writings, he referred to "A Letter Concerning Toleration," a political treatise that John Locke wrote in 1689. Jefferson noted: "[Locke] says neither Pagan nor [Muslim] nor Jew ought to be excluded from the civil rights of the commonwealth because of his religion."

In his *Autobiography*, Jefferson recounted his satisfaction with the state of Virginia's landmark Bill for Establishing Religious Freedom, which passed in 1786. The passing of the bill meant that the Virginia legislature rejected, by a great majority, religious intolerance. Jefferson wrote a response to the bill, which noted how Muslims, alongside Jews, Gentiles, and Christian minority groups, would be "within the mantle of protection" in the state of Virginia as well as the United States (Hutson, 2002).

A year after drafting the Declaration, Jefferson also helped write the "Virginia Statute for Religious Freedom" in 1777. Part of the statute is inscribed on the northwest portico of the Jefferson Memorial in Washington, D.C. The statute states: "No man shall be compelled to frequent or support religious worship or ministry or shall otherwise suffer on account of his religious opinions or beliefs, but all men shall be free to profess and by argument to maintain, their opinions in matters of religion." Jefferson's words, as the Virginia Historical Society (n.d.) notes, represent a statement about freedom of conscience and the principle of separation of church and state, meaning that Muslims would not be subject to the rule of Christianity or Christians themselves. Indeed, the First Amendment of the Constitution prohibited federal acts "respecting an establishment of religion," a signal victory for Jefferson's views that government has no power to interfere with the religious beliefs of American Muslims, or coerce them in any respect regarding religious affairs (Walsh, Whittle, & Bauman, 2012).

In fact, scholars have asserted that Jefferson's fondness for the principle of freedom of religion and his study of the Arabic language, as well as his collection of books on the history of the Islamic faith and Muslim civilizations, suggest that he supported the academic study of Muslims in a way that could incorporate the Islamic faith into the American nation (Hammer & Safi, 2013).

John Quincy Adams—the son of John Adams and the last president to be born during the American Revolution—had firsthand encounters with Muslims. His interactions provide more evidence of early America's relations with Muslims. In February and March 1841, then representative John Quincy Adams of Massachusetts represented African slaves before the U.S. Supreme Court. (The case was later dramatized in the American historical film *Amistad*, directed by Steven Spielberg in 1997.) Preceding the trial, on July 1, 1839, 53 Africans who had been taken from their homes in West Africa and sold into slavery in Cuba staged a revolt while on board the schooner *Amistad*. During the revolt, the enslaved Africans killed both captain and crew and then demanded that their Spanish "owners" sail them home to Africa. Before that could happen, the ship was apprehended off the coast of Long Island, New York, on August 24, 1839, eventually docking land in New London, Connecticut. One of the Africans aboard the *Amistad*, Ba-u, reported that his father was a Marabout, a West African term for a Muslim teacher, religious leader, and "holy man" (Dirks, 2006). Additional confirmation of a Muslim presence on the *Amistad* is provided by Richard Robert Madden, a British government official who testified in Connecticut on behalf of the *Amistad* Africans on November 11, 1839. Madden reported that the Africans were familiar with such Arabic greetings and statements as *Salam Alaikum* ("peace be upon you") and *Allahu Akbar* ("God is greater") (Considine, 2017: 184).

In his diary, John Quincy Adams wrote that he and his co-counsel maintained [the Africans'] right of self-emancipation, but "spoke in cautious terms to avoid exciting southern passions and prejudices" (Adams, 1876: 430). In representing African Muslim slaves before the U.S. Supreme Court, John Quincy Adams stood for the rule of law and maintained that all people on American soil—regardless of race or religious background—should be entitled to liberty and justice.

The large number of primary sources from the 18th and 19th centuries shows that the Founding Fathers subscribed to national values which promoted religious pluralism as well as civil rights and liberties (Ahmed, 2010). The pluralist approach of these early American leaders marked a distinct difference to previous generations of Americans. Early American Christians from Western Europe had argued that the land of the modern-day United States was given to them by God and they were to occupy it regardless of who was living there. This aggressive approach led to the oppression of Natives, Africans, and non-Christian minority communities, as well as an arrogance that made it easy to demonize and destroy the "latest enemy" (Ahmed, 2010). The Founding Fathers opened a new phase by welcoming Muslims to the United States and granting them full citizenship rights as guaranteed by the U.S. Constitution. President Barack Obama reminded Americans of this history in February 2016, during his first and only visit to a U.S. mosque during his presidency. He stated at this appearance that "Islam has always been a part of America" (Obama, 2016).

Without taking the Founding Fathers to be paradigms of universalist pluralism, one can situate them in a broad Enlightenment tradition that actually looked to Islam as a more "rational" religion and offered fairly positive evaluations of the Islamic tradition (Hammer & Safi, 2013).

FURTHER READING

Adams, John Quincy. (1876). *Memoirs of John Quincy Adams: His Diary from 1795 to 1848.* Philadelphia, PA: J.B. Lippincott & Co.

Ahmed, Akbar. (2010, June 2). "Journey into America, Past and Present." *The Guardian.* Retrieved from https://www.theguardian.com/commentisfree/cifamerica/2010/may/31/islam-america-religion

Associated Press. (1997, December 20). "'Amistad' Sheds Light on John Quincy Adams." *Deseret News.* Retrieved from http://www.deseretnews.com/article/601655/Amistad-Sheds-light-on-John-Quincy-Adams.html

Boorstein, Michelle. (2016, February 3). "At Baltimore Mosque, President Obama Encourages U.S. Muslims: 'You Fit in Here.'" *The Washington Post.* Retrieved from https://www.washingtonpost.com/news/acts-of-faith/wp/2016/02/03/president-obamas-mosque-visit-will-spotlight-a-new-generation-of-muslim-americans/?hpid=hp_

local-news_no-name%3Ahomepage%2Fstory&tid=a_inl&utm_term=
.9685d33dc93f

Considine, Craig. (2017). *Islam, Race, and Pluralism in the Pakistani Diaspora*. London and New York, NY: Routledge.

Dirks, Jerald F. (2006). *Muslims in American History: A Forgotten Legacy*.
Beltsville, MD: Amana Publications.

Franklin, Benjamin. (n.d.). "In His Own Words." Ushistory.org. Retrieved
from http://www.ushistory.org/franklin/autobiography/page49.htm

George Washington's Mount Vernon. (n.d.). "Benjamin Franklin. Digital
Encyclopedia of George Washington." Mountvernon.org. Retrieved
from   http://www.mountvernon.org/digital-encyclopedia/article/benja
min-franklin/

Gilder Lehrman Institute of American History. (n.d.). *John Quincy
Adams and the Amistad Case, 1841*. New York, NY: The Gilder Lehrman Institute of American History. Retrieved from https://www
.gilderlehrman.org/history-by-era/slavery-and-anti-slavery/resources/
john-quincy-adams-and-amistad-case-1841

Hammer, Juliane, & Safi, Omid. (2013). *The Cambridge Companion to
American Islam*. Cambridge, UK: Cambridge University Press.

Hutson, James A. (2002). "The Founding Fathers and Islam: Library Papers
Show Early Tolerance for Muslim Faith." Washington, DC: Library of
Congress. Retrieved from https://www.loc.gov/loc/lcib/0205/tolerance
.html

Meet the Press. (2015, September 20). "Ben Carson Does Not Believe a
Muslim Should Be President." *NBC News*. Retrieved from http://
www.nbcnews.com/meet-the-press/ben-carson-does-not-believe-
muslim-should-be-president-n430431

Obama, Barack. (2016, February 3). "Remarks by the President at Islamic
Society of Baltimore." Washington, DC: The White House. Retrieved
from   https://obamawhitehouse.archives.gov/the-press-office/2016/02/
03/remarks-president-islamic-society-baltimore

Quraishi-Landes, Asifa. (2016, July). "5 Myths about Sharia Law
Debunked by a Law Professor." *Dallas News*. Retrieved from https://
www.dallasnews.com/opinion/commentary/2016/07/19/asifa-
quraishi-landes-5-myths-shariah-law

Spellberg, Denise A. (2013). *Thomas Jefferson's Qur'an: Islam and the
Founders*. New York, NY: Knopf.

Spellberg, Denise A. (2013, October 5). "Our Founding Fathers Included
Islam." Salon.com. Retrieved from http://www.salon.com/2013/10/05/
our_founding_fathers_included_islam/

Spellberg, Denise A. (2017). "Why Jefferson's Vision of American
Islam Matters Today." Theconversation. Retrieved from https://

theconversation.com/why-jeffersons-vision-of-american-islam-mat
ters-today-78155?utm_content=buffer132c0&utm_medium=social&
utm_source=facebook.com&utm_campaign=buffer

Thompson, Mary V. (n.d.). "Islam at Mount Vernon." *Mount Vernon.*
Retrieved from http://www.mountvernon.org/digital-encyclopedia/
article/islam-at-mount-vernon/

Virginia Historical Society. (n.d.). "Thomas Jefferson and the Virginia
Statue for Religious Freedom." Richmond, VA: Virginia Historical
Society. Retrieved from http://www.vahistorical.org/collections-and-
resources/virginia-history-explorer/thomas-jefferson

Walsh, Brian, Whittle, T. J., & Bauman, Garrett. (2012, December 17).
"Jefferson's Robust Views of Religious Freedom." Princeton, NJ: The
Witherspoon Institute. Retrieved from http://www.thepublicdiscourse
.com/2012/12/7382/

Washington, George. (1789, December 1). "Letter from George Washington to Muhammed Ibn Abdullah-Sultan of Morocco." R.V. Bey
Publications. Retrieved from http://rvbeypublications.com/sitebuilder
content/sitebuilderfiles/sultan1.pub.pdf

Q3. WAS A "MUSLIM NATION" THE FIRST NATION IN THE WORLD TO RECOGNIZE THE INDEPENDENCE OF THE UNITED STATES?

Answer: Yes. Several North African nations or what we today refer to as the country of Morocco is the first nation in the world to recognize the independence of the United States.

The Facts: During the American Revolution, a set of nations in North Africa, collectively called the Barbary States, agreed to the Treaty of Peace and Friendship with the United States. In doing so, the Barbary states became the first nation in the world to recognize the U.S. government. According to the Avalon Project at Yale University Law School, the treaty was sealed at Morocco with the seal of the Sultan of Morocco and delivered to Thomas Barclay, a U.S. diplomat, on June 28, 1786 (Avalon Project, n.d.a). The treaty was ratified by the U.S. government on July 18, 1787. The Treaty of Peace and Friendship officially established commercial and maritime rights for the United States on the coast of North Africa, and defined the amount of tribute to be paid by the United States to the "Governor" of Tripoli (Essel, 2016).

The Treaty of Peace and Friendship of 1796, also referred to as the Treaty of Tripoli, reaffirmed many of the agreements laid out in the treaty of 1786. Article 11 of the Treaty of Tripoli is particularly important in light of U.S. government relations with Muslims. The article reads:

> As the government of the United States of America is not in any sense founded on the Christian religion, as it has in itself no character or enmity against the laws, religion or tranquility of Musselmen, and as the said States never have entered into any war or act of hostility against any Muslim nation, it is declared by the parties that no pretext arising from religious opinions shall ever produce an interruption of the harmony existing between the two countries. (Avalon Project, n.d.b)

The Treaty of Tripoli was broken in 1801 when Barbary pirates attacked U.S. shipping vessels after the United States refused to pay more tribute (Essel, 2016). This led to the First Barbary War—immortalized in the Marine Corps hymn lyric "to the shores of Tripoli"—which ended with the signing of a second Treaty of Tripoli (1805). Article 14 of the treaty of 1805 reaffirmed that "the Government of the United States of America, has in itself no character or enmity against the laws, religion, or tranquility of [Muslims]."

According to Frank Lambert (2007), author of *The Barbary Wars: American Independence in the Atlantic World*, the imperative of free trade drove the Founding Fathers of the United States much more than any quarrel or misgivings about Islam: The Barbary Wars, he argues, were primarily about trade, not theology. Rather than being holy wars, they were an extension of the U.S.'s War of Independence.

FURTHER READING

Avalon Project. (n.d.a). "The Barbary Treaties (1786–1816)—Treaty with Morocco June 28 and July 15, 1786." Yale Law School. Retrieved from http://avalon.law.yale.edu/18th_century/bar1786t.asp.

Avalon Project. (n.d.b). "The Barbary Treaties (1786–1816)—Treaty of Peace and Friendship, Signed at Tripoli (November 4, 1796)." Yale Law School. Retrieved from http://avalon.law.yale.edu/18th_century/bar1796t.asp

Essel, Thomas. (2016, May 9). "Secularists, Please Stop Quoting the Treaty of Tripoli." Patheos.com. Retrieved from http://www.patheos.com/blogs/danthropology/2016/05/secularists-please-stop-quoting-the-treaty-of-tripoli/

Hammer, Juliane, & Safi, Omid. (2013). *The Cambridge Companion to American Islam*. Cambridge, UK: Cambridge University Press.

Lambert, Frank. (2007). *The Barbary Wars: American Independence in the Atlantic World*. New York, NY: Hill & Wang.

Q4. DOES THE UNITED STATES HAVE A HISTORY OF PASSING LEGISLATION TO PREVENT MUSLIMS FROM MIGRATING TO AMERICAN SOIL OR GAINING U.S. CITIZENSHIP?

Answer: Yes. The U.S. government has implemented immigration policies throughout history that have blocked or restricted the immigration of Muslims to American soil.

The Facts: In December 2015, Republican presidential front-runner Donald Trump called for banning all Muslims from entering the United States. The specifics of Trump's immigration proposal were outlined in a campaign press release in which he called for "a total and complete shutdown of Muslims entering the United States until our country's representatives can figure out what is going on" (Diamond, 2015). In an additional statement that explained his controversial decision, Trump commented: "We want to be very fair, but too many bad things are happening and the percentage of true hatred [among Muslims] is too great. People that are looking to destroy our country must be reported and turned in by the good people who love our country and want America to be great again" (Diamond, 2015).

Trump justified the "Muslim ban," or Executive Order 13769 at a February 2017 rally in Florida by citing a nonexistent "event" in Sweden as evidence of the dangers of Muslim immigration. The "event" stemmed from Tucker Carlson's Fox News show in which the host interviewed Ami Horowitz, a filmmaker who had previously tied Sweden's taking in of asylum seekers to increased violent crimes in the Scandinavian country (Bradner, 2017). Although the story was a complete fabrication, it supported the idea that banning Muslims from the United States would make the country safer.

This kind of anti-Muslim immigration policy did not begin with the 2016 presidential election, or even with 9/11. According to the Tanenbaum Center for Interreligious Understanding (n.d.), a secular nonprofit organization based in New York City, the U.S. government has a long history when it comes to bias against Muslim immigrants. The United

States' first immigration law, the Naturalization Act of 1790, excluded nonwhite people from eligibility to naturalize (Pew Research Center, 2015). The act specified that only "free white" people could apply for citizenship. Muslim "immigrants seeking lawful residence and citizenship were thus compelled to convince [immigration] authorities that they fit within the statutory definition of whiteness. Arabs, along with Italians, Jews, and others [minority populations], were forced to litigate their identities in line with prevailing conceptions of whiteness—which fluctuated according to geographic origin, physical appearance, and religion" (Beydoun, 2016). Ultimately, the Naturalization Act of 1790 set the precedent that would have made it virtually impossible for millions and millions of "nonwhite" Muslims worldwide to become U.S. citizens. In the following century, scores of Muslim immigrants were turned away at U.S. ports, and even some Christians were denied entry into the United States on the suspicion of being Muslims.

In the 1880s, Muslim immigrants from territories of the Ottoman Empire began to arrive at the United States. Prior to their being admitted, immigrants had to sign an oath confirming that they were no longer loyal to the Sultan, or leader of the Ottoman Empire (Burke, 2017). Even after the oath was signed, very few were allowed citizenship. In a notable 1891 case—*Ross v. McIntyre*, 140 U.S. 453—the U.S. Supreme Court claimed there is an "intense hostility of the people of Moslem faith to all other sects, and particularly to Christians." Decades later, in 1913, a South Carolina court rejected the citizenship petition of a Lebanese Christian. The court stated that his skin complexion, "about [the color] of walnut, or somewhat darker than is the usual mulatto of one-half mixed blood between the White and the Negro races," provided disqualifying evidence of miscegenation with Muslims (Beydoun, 2013).

The U.S. Congress enacted another widely restrictive immigration law, the Asiatic Barred Zone Act, in 1917. Also known as the Immigration Act of 1917, the legislation defined the "barred zone" as including India, Indo-China, Afghanistan, and parts of Arabia, among other countries and islands in the Pacific Ocean (Agarwal, 2017). The 1917 law was a response to demographic shifts at home and the general panic that "nonwhite foreigners" were taking over the United States. In years prior to the act, newspapers reported in sensationalist fashion that "dusky Asiatics" and "Hindu hordes" posed a bigger threat to job security and the cultural fabric than Japanese or Chinese laborers (Manseau, 2015).

In addition to prohibiting immigrants from almost the entire Asian continent from entering the United States, the Asiatic Barred Zone Act of 1917 imposed a native language literacy test—an English language test—and head taxes on immigrants (Agarwal, 2017). The act barred immigrants with disabilities, diseases, or any characteristics that the state determined to interfere with their ability "to earn a living." Not satisfied with the scope of the law, the commissioner general of immigration for the U.S. government at the time suggested that the zone be extended to Africa, "so as to exclude inhabitants who are of unassimilable classes or whose admission in any considerable number would tend to produce an economic menace to our population" (Agarwal, 2017). Oddly enough the barred zone included huge swaths of Central Asia but did not include the area today referred to as North Africa. This meant that the North African countries of modern-day Egypt, Libya, Algeria, Tunisia, and Morocco were not part of the 1917 ban.

The first U.S. law to create numerical quotas for immigration based on nationality was the 1921 Emergency Quota Act. This emergency bill limited the number of immigrants to 3 percent of the foreign-born population of a given nationality resident in the United States based on the 1910 census. The 1921 act severely limited the ability of the Muslim population in the United States to grow by means of new immigration. South and East Asian Muslims were excluded from the right to naturalize, and their co-nationals were denied entry to the country altogether (Howell, 2014). Syrians and Turks, in particular, found themselves defending their right to naturalize in U.S. courtrooms by arguing that they were "free white persons," a prerequisite for any naturalization or citizenship application stemming from the Naturalization Act of 1790 (Beydoun, 2013; Howell, 2014).

The National Origins Act of 1924 also limited the number of Muslim immigrants allowed entry into the United States through a national origins quota. The Origins Act addressed the perceived deficiencies of the Emergency Quota Act of 1921. Using the 1890 census rather than the 1910 census, the 1924 bill restricted the number of immigrants to 2 percent of "the U.S. native-born White population as determined by their national origins" (Douglas, 2008). The 1924 quota completely excluded immigrants from Asia.

According to a 2015 report by the Pew Research Center on 20th-century U.S. immigration, the Emergency Quota Act of 1921 and the Immigration Act of 1924 were intended to "try to restore earlier immigration patterns by capping total annual immigration and imposing numerical quotas based on immigration nationality that favored northern and western European countries" (Cohn, 2015). While both of these acts differentiated Europeans according to nationality and then ranked them along a hierarchy of desirability, the very act of their inclusion for immigration conferred upon them a designation of assimilability and the right to U.S. citizenship (Douglas, 2008: 938). Given that the U.S. Supreme Court had already legally codified citizenship along two racial lines (white and black), all Europeans—whether from northern, western, southern, or eastern Europe—were thus categorized as white (Douglas, 2008: 938). In both acts, Muslim immigrants "were placed into the non-White category and their immigration severely restricted" (Douglas, 2008: 938).

Until as late as 1942, Muslims were disqualified from U.S. citizenship because of their perceived nonwhite race, a point that highlights the racialization of the Islamic faith (Considine, 2017). In 1942, for example, Ahmed Hassan, a native of Yemen and the first Arab Muslim to apply for U.S. citizenship, was denied naturalization because a court said: "It cannot be expected that as a class they [meaning "Arabs," a term used synonymously with Muslims at the time] would readily intermarry with our population and be assimilated into our civilization" (Beydoun, 2016). The legalization of this racial bias began to shift toward the end of World War II. The United States' functional "ban" on Muslim immigration was lifted in 1944, due primarily to U.S. geopolitical interests. The naturalization of Arab Muslim immigrants promoted the broader project of enhancing the United States' influence in the Middle East, most notably in oil-rich Saudi Arabia (Beydoun, 2016). As Beydoun notes, "Indeed, the first court ruling to grant naturalization to an Arab-born Muslim was for a Saudi man," in the *Ex Parte Mohriez* case—of 1944—"and, even then, based only on the finding that Arabs should be considered part of 'the White race' " (Beydoun, 2016).

Racially restrictive naturalization and immigration legislation stifled the migration of Muslim immigrants until 1965 (Beydoun, 2013). Only after the dissolution of the Immigration Act of 1924 and the abolition of the nationality quota regime in 1965 were the barriers to Muslim immigration effectively lifted (Beydoun, 2013). In 1965, the U.S. Congress enacted a sweeping immigration law, the Immigration and Nationality Act (or the Hart-Celler Act), which replaced long-standing laws that favored white northern European immigrants. The new immigration system of 1965 allocated more visas to people from the Middle East and Asia—prior to the passage of the Immigration and Nationality Act, residents of Ireland, Germany, and the United Kingdom were entitled to nearly 70 percent of the quota visas available to enter the United States (Pew Research Center, 2015). The Act of 1965 declared in certain terms that "no person shall receive any preference or priority or be discriminated against in the issuance of an immigrant visa because of the person's race, sex, nationality, place of birth or place of residence."

Following 1965, when the United States opened its doors to various parts of the world, including the Middle East, South Asia, and Africa, the American Muslim population increased significantly, from 200,000 in 1951 to more than 1 million by 1971 (Beydoun, 2016). Not only did the number of Muslims in the United States increase, but so too did the diversity of the American Muslim population. The interaction of the new arrivals, and their American-born children with indigenous Muslims as well as converts, created many new challenges, as well as new opportunities to facilitate Islamic traditions in the United States (Curtis, 2010).

The Immigration and Nationality Act of 1965 is the foundation of the United States' current legal immigration system. This system, however, came under pressure during the 2016 presidential election. In 2015, Republican candidate Donald Trump stated in a Republican Party debate in Las Vegas that "[Muslims] aren't coming to this country if I'm president." Trump later called for the special immigration registration of all American Muslims and the warrantless surveillance of all Muslim places of worship.

The Center for American Progress, a progressive public policy research and advocacy organization based in Washington, D.C., responded to Trump's proposals by issuing a report titled "Anti-Muslim Sentiment Is a Serious Threat to American Security" (Khan, 2015). The report asserted that the "many knee-jerk policy proposals directed at all Muslims" serve only "to advance ISIS's goals. . . . This is dangerous and deadly serious. And it must stop" (Gude, 2015). Question 23 of this book provides further analysis on why anti-Muslim immigration policies help ISIS and other "radical Islamic" groups to legitimate its agenda.

Speaking on Executive Order 13769, the Council on American-Islamic Relations, the nation's largest Muslim civil rights and advocacy organization, said in a September 2017 press release that the order "is just one part of the administration's 'ugly white supremacist agenda' " (Council on American-Islamic Relations, 2017). The American Civil Liberties Union (ACLU) also challenged the order, which banned indefinitely people from Muslim-majority countries, including Iran, Libya, Syria, Yemen, and Somalia, and emphasized that these countries are banned because they had not cooperated in providing information for visa vetting (Wofsy, 2017). According to the ACLU, the Muslim ban is unconstitutional because, as the Court of Appeals for the Fourth Circuit recognized in May 2017, the ban violates the establishment cause of the U.S. Constitution by disfavoring a specific religion. "When the government chooses sides on religious issues," the court explained, "the inevitable result is hatred, disrespect and even contempt towards those who fall on the wrong side of the line" (United States Court of Appeals for the Fourth Circuit, n.d.).

Federal judges have ruled against the legality of President Trump's travel ban targeting people from Muslim-majority countries. However, the Supreme Court, in December 2017, signaled that it was likely to uphold the policy after the justices voted 7–2 to let the ban go into full effect while legal challenges by the state of Hawaii and others continue.

FURTHER READING

Agarwal, Kritika. (2017, February 5). "Shadows of the Past. South Asian American Digital Archive." Philadelphia, PA: South Asian American Digital Archive. Retrieved from https://www.saada.org/tides/article/shadows-of-the-past

Beydoun, Khaled A. (2013). "Between Muslim and White: The Legal Construction of Arab American Identity." *New York University Annual Survey of American Law*, 69(1), 29–76.

Beydoun, Khaled A. (2016). "America Banned Muslims Long before Donald Trump." *The Washington Post*. Retrieved from https://www.washingtonpost.com/opinions/trumps-anti-muslim-stance-echoes-a-us-law-from-the-1700s/2016/08/18/6da7b486-6585-11e6-8b27-bb8ba39497a2_story.html?utm_term=.7d6cdd8f8400

Bradner, Eric. (2017, February 20). "Trump's Sweden Comment Raises Questions." CNN.com. Retrieved from http://www.cnn.com/2017/02/19/politics/trump-rally-sweden/

Burke, Daniel. (2017, January 31). "America's Long History of 'Vetting' Muslims." CNN.com. Retrieved from http://www.cnn.com/2017/01/31/us/islamerica-excerpt-history/index.html

Cohn, D'vera. (2015, September 30). "How U.S. Immigration Laws and Rules Have Changed through History." Washington, DC: Pew Research Center. Retrieved from http://www.pewresearch.org/fact-tank/2015/09/30/how-u-s-immigration-laws-and-rules-have-changed-through-history/

Considine, Craig. (2017). "The Racialization of Islam in the United States: Islamophobia, Hate Crimes, and 'Flying while Brown.'" *Religions*, 8(9): 1–19.

Cornell Law School. (n.d.). "8 U.S. Code 1152—Numerical Limitations on Individual Foreign States." Ithaca, NY: Cornell University. Retrieved from https://www.law.cornell.edu/uscode/text/8/1152

Council on American-Islamic Relations. (2017, September 25). "CAIR Says Trump's New Muslim Ban Order Is Part of 'Ugly White

Supremacist Agenda.'" Washington, DC: Council on American-Is lamic Relations. Retrieved from https://www.cair.com/press-center/ press-releases/14647-cair-says-trump-s-new-muslim-ban-order-is-part- of-ugly-white-supremacist-agenda.html

Curtis, Edward E., IV. (2010). *Encyclopedia of Muslim-American History*. New York, NY: Facts on File.

Diamond, Jeremy. (2015, December 8). "Donald Trump: Ban All Mus lim Travel to U.S." CNN.com. Retrieved from http://www.cnn .com/2015/12/07/politics/donald-trump-muslim-ban-immigration/ index.html

Douglas, Karen M. (2008). "National Origins System." In Richard Schae fer (ed.). *Encyclopedia of Race, Ethnicity, and Society*. Thousand Oaks, CA: Sage Publications.

Enzerink, Suzanne. (2017, April 12). "The 1917 Immigration Act That Presaged Trump's Muslim Ban." *JSTOR Daily*. Retrieved from https:// daily.jstor.org/1917-immigration-law-presaged-trumps-muslim-ban/

Gude, Ken. (2015, November). *Anti-Muslim Sentiment Is a Serious Threat to American Security*. Washington, DC: Center for American Prog ress. Retrieved from https://cdn.americanprogress.org/wp-content/ uploads/2015/11/25074358/ISISTrap.pdf

Howell, Sally. (2014). *Old Islam in Detroit: Rediscovering the Muslim Amer ican Past*. New York, NY: Oxford University Press.

Khan, Suhail A. (2015, December 18). "Islam Is All-American." *For eign Policy*. Retrieved from http://foreignpolicy.com/2015/12/18/one- nation-under-allah-american-muslim-obama-trump/

Manseau, Peter. (2015, February 13). "A Forgotten History of Anti-Sikh Violence in the Early-20th-Century Pacific Northwest." Slate.com. Retrieved from http://www.slate.com/blogs/the_vault/2015/02/13/his tory_of_sikhs_in_america_violence_against_sikh_workers_in_bell ingham.html

Pew Research Center. (2015, September 28). *Chapter 1: The Nation's Immigration Laws, 1920 to Today*. Washington, DC: Pew Research Center. Retrieved from http://www.pewhispanic.org/2015/09/28/ chapter-1-the-nations-immigration-laws-1920-to-today/

Tanenbaum Center for Interreligious Understanding. (n.d.). *Islamopho bia: Challenges and Opportunities in the Workplace*. New York, NY: Tanenbaum Center. Retrieved from http://www.diversitybestpractices .com/sites/diversitybestpractices.com/files/attachments/2017/02/islam ophobia_paper_final.pdf

United States Court of Appeals for the Fourth Circuit. (n.d.). "No. 17–1351." Richmond, VA: 4th Cir. Retrieved from http://coop .ca4.uscourts.gov/171351.P.pdf

U.S. Department of State (USDOS). (n.d.). "The Immigration Act of 1924 (The Johnson-Reed Act)." Washington, DC: USDOS. Retrieved from https://history.state.gov/milestones/1921-1936/immigration-act

Wofsy, Cody. (2017, October 3). *We're Challenging Muslim Ban 3.0, Which Is Just More of the Same.* New York, NY: ACLU. Retrieved from https://www.aclu.org/blog/immigrants-rights/were-challenging-muslim-ban-30-which-just-more-same

Q5. DID AFRICAN AMERICAN MUSLIMS PLAY A VITAL ROLE IN THE EMERGENCE AND SUCCESS OF THE CIVIL RIGHTS MOVEMENT IN THE 20TH CENTURY?

Answer: Yes. The civil rights movement is generally perceived as a movement focused on the liberation of a racial group (African Americans), but it was also a liberation movement for Muslims and their own struggle for freedom.

The Facts: The civil rights movement was, to a considerable degree, a religious revolution, one whose social and spiritual impact inspired numerous other movements in the United States (Harvey, 2016). This movement of the mid-20th century was heavily influenced by "black Christian thought," which "helped to undermine the white supremacist racial system that had governed America for centuries" (Harvey, 2016). While the efforts of Martin Luther King Jr. and other black Christian thought leaders undoubtedly shaped the movement in a significant manner, there is a tendency to overlook non-Christian leaders who also led the march toward freedom and equality—including African American Muslims (Saahir, 2017). In fact, African American Muslims paid a serious price in the pursuit of human and civil rights, sacrifices that included surveillance, loss of jobs, murders, and unjust time in jail (Saahir, 2017).

The roots of the civil rights movement have been located in the Universal Negro Improvement Association (UNIA), which Marcus Garvey started organizing in Jamaica in 1914 (Hussain, 2016). The UNIA was an organization among blacks that sought "to improve the condition of the race, with the view of establishing a nation in Africa where Negroes will be given the opportunity to develop themselves" (Garvey, 1924). Garvey's goal in creating a new African nation for blacks was to avoid "the hatred and animosity that now exist in countries of the white race," where blacks and whites fought each other for positions in industry, government, politics, and society at large (Garvey, 1924). To achieve his goals, Garvey founded the UNIA as a better alternative for black people than inter-racial organizations such as the National Association for the Advance-ment of Colored People (NAACP) and the National Urban League. The UNIA represents the largest mass movement in African American history, proclaiming a black nationalist "Back to Africa" message (Van Leeuwen, n.d.).

A second African American liberation movement that gained steam in the early 20th century was rooted in the work of the Moorish Sci-ence Temple of America (MSTA) in Newark, New Jersey. The MSTA was founded by Noble Drew Ali (1886–1929). The MSTA is mostly known as an alternative black religious movement in the United States that combined black nationalism and the teachings of Prophet Muhammad. Scholar Susan Nance described the movement as "a Black Spiritualist-style religion steeped in the philosophies of mystical Free-masonry" (Nance, 2002: 125). The MSTA movement spread across the United States during the 1920s as Ali and his followers pioneered attempts to instill racial pride in black Americans.

Noble Drew Ali taught people that "Negroes" are "Asiatic" and "spe-cifically that they are Moorish whose forefathers inhabited Northwest and Southwest Africa before they were enslaved in North America" (Nance, 2002). Drawing on the Islamic tradition, Ali wrote the *Holy Koran of the Moorish Science Temple of America*, although scholars rightly note that this text has little to no connection with the Qur'an, the Islamic holy book, or *Hadith*, an Arabic word that refers to a narrative report of Prophet Muhammad's sayings and actions (Considine, 2017: 185). Instead, Ali's *Holy Koran* combined his own philosophical writings with principles pulled from Islamic holy texts.

The influence of the MSTA can be seen in more recently established movements, such as the Nation of Gods and Earths, also called the Five Percenters (Moorish Science Temple of America, n.d.a). This movement is an offshoot of the Nation of Islam (NOI) founded by a former member of the NOI named Clarence 13X (Moorish Science Temple of America, n.d.a). The Five Percenters, like the NOI, is concerned with African American identity and teaches that black people are actually "gods on Earth" (Moorish Science Temple of America, n.d.a).

The Ahmadiyya movement, an international revivalist movement of Islam founded on the Indian subcontinent in 1889, also emerged as an historical factor in the introduction of Islam to black Americans. Ahmadi missionaries were sent to the United States by the Ahmadiyya movement of South Asia to propagate Islam, the first being Mufti Muhammad Sadiq, who arrived on American soil in 1920. Muhammad Sadiq became close to the UNIA and preached Islam to the Garveyites (Murtaza, 1993). Once he settled, Sadiq founded the *Moslem Sunrise*, a monthly magazine with contemporary articles on Islam, including "issues of conscience" and "the names of new converts," most notably in Detroit and Chicago. The Ahmadiyya Muslim community is the only Islamic organization in the United States to believe that the long-awaited Messiah has come in the person of Mirza Ghulam Ahmad (1835–1908) of Qadian, Pakistan (Al Islam, n.d.).

In a similar spirit to the MSTA, the NOI, an indigenous African American Muslim movement and organization, drew many members and philosophies from Marcus Garvey's UNIA. The NOI was founded during the Great Depression of the 1930s in the ghettos of Detroit, Michigan, and other Midwestern cities, such as Chicago, Illinois. After migrating north in the hopes of finding employment prospects and protection from racial oppression in the South, thousands of Blacks found themselves in a crisis situation. As it turned out "the North was no promised land [but, in many ways,] was the South all over again":

> The starving, overcrowded Blacks living in the slums of Detroit (as in other Northern cities) became increasingly bitter towards the whites who seemed to control their lives. Police officers, who are the ever-present reminder of white power; white workers, who displaced blacks as jobs became more scarce or who retained their jobs as thousands of blacks were being laid off; even the welfare workers, who insulted the blacks and made them wait long hours before passing out the pitiful supplies of flour and lard—all these became the symbolic targets of a virulent hatred of whites. (Lincoln, 1994: 13)

The new northerners found themselves unable to establish the public institutions and social systems that buoyed them, despite the overt racism, in the South. The black migrants were in need of support. Their assistance arrived with the appearance of Wallace Fard Muhammad in the summer of 1930. Muhammad, founder of the NOI, came to Detroit claiming to be the messenger that God sent to liberate blacks in the United States. He called his movement "The Lost Found Nation of Islam in America" (Hussain, 2016). Recognized by the NOI as the Great Mahdi, or savior, Fard preached a message of black liberation. Referring to texts such as the Qur'an and the Bible, he claimed that blacks were not Americans and therefore owed no loyalty to the United States. He also told them that Christianity was the religion of the white slave master and that the true religion of Africans—Islam—would liberate them. Fard rejected Christianity and the domination of white "blue-eyed devils," and instead spoke of the "religion of the Black Man," or the Islamic faith (Esposito, 1998). Fard wrote two manuals on his movement: *The Secret Ritual of the Nation of Islam* and *Teaching for the Lost-Found Nation of Islam in a Mathematical Way*, both of which helped set the stage for the civil rights movement.

Fard mysteriously disappeared in 1934, but not before he saw a young African American Christian, Elijah Poole (1897–1975), convert to the NOI. Poole, who later became Elijah Muhammad, is recognized as one of the most important and controversial African Americans of the 20th century. His followers called him the Messenger of Allah, a contentious claim considering that most Muslims around the world consider Muhammad, the seventh-century prophet, to be the final messenger of Islam. While his followers referred to him as a prophet, his critics labeled him a teacher of hate (Clegg III, 2014). An FBI report on the NOI in 1955 charged that black Muslims demonstrate "fearless and outspoken anti-white, anti-Christian attitudes. . . . As long as racial inequity continues, the militant and arrogant manner of [NOI] cult members remains a potential threat of violent action" (Federal Bureau of Investigation, 1955).

In 1942, Elijah Muhammad, who encouraged African Americans not to register for the military draft, was himself sentenced to prison for draft evasion. The largest group of U.S. Muslims to resist the World War II draft was indeed African American Muslims, who opposed the draft on religious grounds. In September 1942, FBI agents arrested 80 black Muslims and charged them with encouraging sympathy for Japan (Murray, 1971: 665). When the U.S. government was unable to find any link between the NOI and Japanese agents, the Muslims were charged with failure to register for the draft (Murray, 1971). Their refusal to register was in keeping with the Islamic belief that "Allah forbids [Muslims] to bear arms or do violence to anyone whom [God] has not ordered to be killed" (Essien-Udom, 1962: 80).

Though the NOI was not formally a pacifist organization, its antiwar tradition is strong. During the Vietnam War, *Muhammad Speaks*, the NOI newspaper, became one of the most popular sources among all African Americans opposed to the Vietnam War and the United States' interference in Vietnam and the developing world more generally (Curtis, 2010). During the 1960s, the paper, which had a weekly circulation of 60,000, regularly featured articles, interviews, and political cartoons opposing the Vietnam War. The newspaper presented the war as part of America's ongoing racial struggles, highlighting racial inequalities in the armed forces, especially in the disproportionate casualty rates among blacks and other minorities (Curtis, 2010).

Despite receiving a cold shoulder from many mainstream Muslims, the NOI became an important part of African Americans' march toward civil rights, providing many in the black community with a sense of purpose and dignity (Ahmed, 2002). Muhammad's "message of self-transformation and self-reliance encompassed the physical and spiritual"—psychic, political, economic, and dietary—"needs of Black Americans" as addressed in his essay, "Message to the Blackman in America and How to Eat to Live" (Esposito, 1998). Muhammad denounced the political and economic oppression of blacks by the white majority, past and present, and the ways in which such oppression contributed to black self-hatred, poverty, and dependency. Under Elijah Muhammad's leadership, the number of NOI temples grew in number, and African Americans were encouraged to support black businesses (grocery stores, restaurants, bakeries). The NOI's message of black pride, self-respect, and militancy proved particularly attractive to back youth, many of whom were recruited into the NOI from ghetto streets and prisons. By the 1970s, the NOI would claim more than 100,000 members (Esposito, 1998).

In 1948, six years after Elijah Muhammad was sentenced to prison, the NOI received a significant boost when Malcolm Little, better known as Malcolm X, converted to Islam while in prison. Malcolm X is well known as a pioneer of the intellectual and liberation movement known as Black Power. In the early 1960s, he gained national prominence as the most outspoken critic of the nonviolent strategy of Martin Luther King Jr., a Christian civil rights leader. For several years, Malcolm X attempted to establish a black united front that transcended religious lines, but he was repeatedly rebuffed by other prominent African American civil rights leaders. He also opposed the idea of racial integration into American society and fought against police brutality.

Early in the 1960s, Malcolm started to diverge from the teachings of Elijah Muhammad and the NOI. While Elijah advocated a separation and self-sufficiency that excluded involvement in "white man's politics," Malcolm came to believe that the NOI "could be even a greater force in the American black man's overall struggle if [it] engaged in more action" (Esposito, 1998). He started to speak out passionately and forcefully on a variety of issues including the civil rights movement, the Vietnam War, and solidarity and liberation struggles in colonial Africa. After leaving the NOI in March 1964, Malcolm X "established the Organization of Afro-American Unity (OAAU), with the objective of building a broad coalition of Black groups to work jointly to empower the most oppressed [sections] of the [African American] community" (Esposito, 1998). Also, in 1964, Malcolm became a mainstream Sunni Muslim. In that year, he made his *hajj*, an Arabic word referring to the annual pilgrimage to Mecca required of all Muslims at least once in their lifetime (Considine, 2017: 185).

While in Mecca, Malcolm X wrote a letter which discussed the impact that the pilgrimage had on his views on race and equality (Malcolm X's Letter from Mecca, n.d.). "Never have I witnessed such sincere hospitality and overwhelming spirit of true brotherhood as is practiced by people of all colors and races here in this ancient Holy Land," he wrote. Malcolm X added: "There were tens of thousands of pilgrims. . . . They were of all colors. . . . But we were all participating in the same ritual, displaying a spirit of unity and brotherhood that my experiences in America had led me to believe never could exist between the white and non-white." Upon his return to the United States, Malcolm X abandoned the racial teachings of NOI and changed his name to El-Hajj Malik El-Shabazz (Hussain, 2016). El-Shabazz modified his antiwhite views and explored the possibility of working with whites on issues pertaining to civil rights. He was later assassinated by members of the NOI on February 21, 1965, as he spoke to an audience in New York City.

Muhammad Ali, the professional boxer and civil rights activist, also had a distinctively positive and remarkably broad-based influence as an African American Muslim organizer during the civil rights movement. Ali's public conversion to Islam, in 1964, was among the most defining moments of his remarkable life. The decision enraged his critics—his hometown newspaper continued to refer to Ali by his birth name, Cassius Clay, for years to come—and led him to refuse to serve in Vietnam, a stand that cost him his boxing title, his livelihood, and, ultimately, cemented his status as an American iconoclast. In a letter Ali wrote to his second wife, Khalilah Camacho-Ali, he recalled seeing a cartoon in the NOI newspaper *Muhammad Speaks*, outside a skating rink in his hometown of Louisville, Kentucky. The cartoon illustrated how white slave owners brutally beat their slaves, while insisting that they pray to Jesus. The message of the cartoon was that Christianity is the religion of the oppressive white establishment. "I like that cartoon," Ali wrote. "It did something to me. And it made sense" (Eig, 2017).

In 1966, at the height of the Vietnam War, Ali's draft status was revised to make him eligible to fight in Vietnam. He responded by saying that as an African American Muslim he was a conscientious objector, and he would refuse to enter the U.S Armed Forces. "My conscience won't let me go shoot my brother, or some darker people, or some hungry people in the mud for big powerful America," he said. "And shoot them for what?

They never called me n*****, they never lynched me, they didn't put no dogs on me, they didn't rob me of my nationality, rape and kill my mother and father. . . . How can I shoot them poor people? Just take me to jail."

Almost every major civil rights organization at one time or another praised Ali and defended his decision to resist serving in the U.S. Armed Forces during the Vietnam War, a decision that eventually led to an imprisonment sentence of five years in 1967. At the time of his imprisonment, Ali adhered to the teachings of Elijah Muhammad—that white people are "devils" (Hauser, n.d.). Like Malcolm X, Ali eventually denounced the NOI and embraced mainstream Sunni Islam. In 1984, he spoke out publicly against the separatist doctrine of Louis Farrakhan, the head of the modern-day NOI, declaring, "What [Farrakhan] teaches is not at all what [Muslims] believe in. He represents the time of our struggle in the dark and a time of confusion in us, and we don't want to be associated with that at all" (Hauser, n.d.). By the end of his life, Ali spoke passionately about freedom and equality and racial reconciliation.

Wallace Deen Mohammed (1933–2008), the son of Elijah Muhammad, followed in the footsteps of Malcolm X and Muhammad Ali. Like his predecessors, W. Deen Mohammed was sent to prison for refusing to serve in the Korean War (1950–1953). After his father passed away in 1975, W. Deen Mohammad took over the NOI and brought the majority of its members into the fold of the Sunnah, an Arabic word referring to the normative practice of racial tolerance as exhibited by Prophet Muhammad (Considine, 2017: 187). Following Malcolm X, who was drifting away from black separatism toward traditional Islam when he was assassinated in 1965, W. Deen Mohammad increasingly favored a nonracial approach to Islam that rejected categorizing white people as "devils," as his father had done. In fact, his father excommunicated him several times for this dissidence.

W. Deen Mohammad worked for the establishment of Muslim life in America and for freedom, justice, and equality for Muslims, African Americans, and all U.S. citizens (Masjid Muhammad, 2013). He pushed his followers toward a more orthodox faith, emphasizing study of the Qur'an and the Five Pillars of Islam: faith, charity, prayer five times per day, fasting during Ramadan, and pilgrimage to Mecca (Martin, 2008). He also taught that the Islamic faith is not only compatible with democracy but that Islam in fact gave birth to democratic principles during the time of Prophet Muhammad in the seventh century. In 1978, he created the Committee to Remove All Racism Images of Divine, which energized significant dialogue among Christians and Muslims around the effects of racial images in religious worship (Masjid Muhammad, 2013). Under Mohammed's vision, which was shared by a spectrum of U.S. citizens, the African American Muslim community became "increasingly active outside its mosques, launching and supporting new businesses, becoming more politically involved, and reaching out to Christians and Jews for interfaith dialogue" (Terry, 2002).

Today, many American Muslims view Islam as a religion that commands them to stand up for the oppressed and to fight oppression of all kinds (Hassan, 2011). To this end, American Muslims across the United States have been sympathetic to the Black Lives Matter movement and its activism to advance racial justice and equality. Linda Sarsour, a Palestinian American Muslim woman and racial justice advocate, is a case in point. Sarsour was the cofounder of Muslims for Ferguson in the aftermath of the August 2014 killing of Michael Brown, a young African American, by a police officer in Ferguson, Missouri. According to the Islamic Circle of North America (2016), an Islamic North American grassroots umbrella organization, Sarsour brought together Muslim organizers, activists, chaplains, and religious leaders to discuss American Muslims' commitment and action toward protecting the lives of African Americans. Leaders of the Black Lives Matter movement returned the support when the Black Lives Matter Global Network (BLMGN) issued a statement on President Trump's Executive Order named "Protecting the Nation from Foreign Terrorist Entry into the United States"—concerning immigration restrictions, or what has been commonly referred to as the "Muslim ban." The BLMGN statement read:

> The war against Muslims and refugees, the separation of families, immigrants deported and detained, the turning away of those seeking asylum and the denial of basic human dignity must stop. . . . Hate has no borders. Because of the Trump administration's actions, Muslims everywhere are at risk, and we must rise in solidarity whenever and wherever necessary. (Morrison, 2017)

FURTHER READING

Ahmed, Akbar. (2002). *Islam Today: A Short Introduction to the Muslim World*. London and New York, NY: I.B. Tauris.

Al Islam. (n.d.). "Ahmadiyya Muslim Community." London, UK: The official website of the Ahmadiyya Muslim Community. Retrieved from https://www.alislam.org/contactus/

Amistad Digital Resource. (n.d.). "Malcolm X." Amistadresource.org. New York, NY: Columbia University. Retrieved from http://www.amistadresource.org/civil_rights_era/malcolm_x.html

Calamur, Krishnadev. (2016, June 4). "Muhammad Ali and Vietnam." *The Atlantic*. Retrieved from https://www.theatlantic.com/news/archive/2016/06/muhammad-ali-vietnam/485717/

Clegg, Claude A., III (2014). *The Life & Times of Elijah Muhammad*. Chapel Hill, NC: University of North Carolina Press.

Considine, Craig. (2017). *Islam, Race, and Pluralism in the Pakistani Diaspora*. London and New York, NY: Routledge.

Curtis, Edward E., IV. (2010). *Encyclopedia of Muslim-American History*. New York, NY: Facts on File.

Eig, Jonathan. (2017). *Ali: A Life*. Boston, MA: Houghton Mifflin Harcourt.

Esposito, John. (1998). *Islam: The Straight Path*. New York, NY: Oxford University Press.

Essien-Udom, Essien Udom. (1962). *Black Nationalism: The Search for an Identity*. Chicago, IL: University of Chicago Press.

Ezra, Michael. (2016, June 5). "How Muhammad Ali Influenced the Civil Rights Movement." AlJazeera.com. Retrieved from http://www.aljazeera.com/indepth/features/2016/06/muhammad-ali-influenced-civil-rights-movement-160605055700822.html

Federal Bureau of Investigation. (1955). Federal Bureau of Investigation—Freedom of Information/Privacy Acts Section: Subject: Nation of Islam. Washington, DC: FBI. Retrieved from https://vault.fbi.gov/Nation%20of%20Islam/Nation%20of%20Islam%20Part%201%20of%203

Garvey, Marcus. (1924). *Aims and Objects of Movement for Solution of Negro Problem*. Durham, NC: National Humanities Center.

Gregory, Sean. (2017, June 2). "Exclusive: The Real Reason Muhammad Ali Converted to Islam." *TIME*. Retrieved from http://time.com/4798179/muhammad-ali-islam-conversion/

Harvey, Paul. (2016, August). "Civil Rights Movements and Religion in America." Oxford Research Encyclopedias. Retrieved from http://religion.oxfordre.com/view/10.1093/acrefore/9780199340378.001.0001/acrefore-9780199340378-e-492

Hassan, Nabeed. (2011, March 3). "What Does the Civil Rights Movement Mean for Muslims?" *Muslim Matters*. Retrieved from http://muslimmatters.org/2011/03/03/what-does-the-civil-rights-movement-mean-for-muslims/

Hauser, Thomas. (n.d.). *The Importance of Muhammad Ali*. Washington, DC: The Gilder Lehrman Institute of American History. Retrieved from https://www.gilderlehrman.org/history-by-era/civil-rights-movement/essays/importance-muhammad-ali

Hussain, Amir. (2016). *Muslims and the Making of America.* Waco, TX: Baylor University Press.

Islamic Circle of North America. (2016, July 19). *American-Muslims on Black Lives Matter and Anti-Racism.* New York, NY: Islamic Circle of North America. Retrieved from http://www.icna.org/american-muslims-on-black-lives-matter-anti-racism/

Izadi, Elahe. (2016, April 19). "Black Lives Matter and America's Long History of Resisting Civil Rights Protestors." *The Washington Post.* Retrieved from https://www.washingtonpost.com/news/the-fix/wp/2016/04/19/black-lives-matters-and-americas-long-history-of-re sisting-civil-rights-protesters/?utm_term=.783389f25fbc

Lincoln, C. Eric. (1994). *The Black Muslims in America.* Lawrenceville, NJ: Red Sea Press.

Malcolm X's Letter from Mecca. (n.d.). "The Pilgrimage to Makkah." Athens, GA: University of Georgia. Retrieved from http://islam.uga.edu/malcomx.html

Martin, Douglas. (2008, September 9). W. Deen Mohammed, 74, Top U.S. Imam, Dies. *The New York Times.* Retrieved from http://www.nytimes.com/2008/09/10/us/10mohammed.html?mcubz=0

Masjid Muhammad. (2013, October 6). "The Late, Imam WD Mohammed." Washington, DC: The Nation's Mosque. Retrieved from http://thenationsmosque.org/about/the-late-imam-wd-mohammed/

Moorish Science Temple of America. (n.d.a). "What Effects and Influences Has the MSTA Had on African-American Islam?" Moorish Science Temple. Retrieved from http://moorishsciencetemple.weebly.com/

Moorish Science Temple of America. (n.d.b). "Moorish American History." Msta1913.org. Retrieved from http://msta1913.org/Moorish History.html

Morrison, Aaron. (2017, January 31). "Exclusive: Black Lives Matter Releases Statement on Trump's Muslim Ban." Mic.com. Retrieved from https://mic.com/articles/167242/exclusive-black-lives-matter-releases-statement-on-trump-s-muslim-ban#.nezIcHSZJ

Murray, Paul T. (1971). "Blacks and the Draft: A History of Institutional Racism." *Journal of Black Studies,* 2(1): 57–76.

Murtaza, Ali. (1993, May 22). "Islamic Movement Came to U.S. in 1920." *The New York Times.* Retrieved from http://www.nytimes.com/1993/05/22/opinion/l-islamic-movement-came-to-us-in-1920-424693.html?mcubz=0

Nance, Susan. (2002, Summer). "Mystery of the Moorish Science Temple: Southern Blacks and American Alternative Spirituality in 1920s Chicago." *Religion and American Culture,* 12(2): 123–166.

NBC News & *Wall Street Journal.* (2015, September). "NBC News/Wall Street Journal Survey." MSNBC.com. Retrieved from http://msnbcme dia.msn.com/i/MSNBC/Sections/A_Politics/15398%20NBCWSJ%20 September%20Poll%20(2).pdf

PBS News Hour & Marist. (2016). "How the Survey Was Conducted." Retrieved from http://maristpoll.marist.edu/wp-content/misc/usapolls/ us150910/PBS%20NewsHour_Marist%20Poll_National%20 Release%20and%20Tables_September%202015.pdf#page=2

Raza, Hamzah. (2016, December 31). "Why Muslims Must Support #BlackLivesMatter." *The Huffington Post.* Retrieved from https://www .huffingtonpost.com/hamzah-raza/muslims-must-support-blacklives matter_b_8899156.html

Saahir, Michael. (2017, May 11). "Islam's Contributions to American Civil Rights." *Indianapolis Recorder.* Retrieved from http://www.indi anapolisrecorder.com/religion/article_e66cd270-3659-11e7-a926- 039dfe6e1dd5.html

Terry, Don. (2002, October 20). "W. Deen Mohammed: A Leap of Faith." *The Chicago Tribune.* Retrieved from http://www.chicagotribune.com/ news/chi-021020-mohammedprofile-story.html

Van Leeuwen, David. (n.d.). "Marcus Garvey and the Universal Negro Improvement Association." Durham, NC: National Humanities Center Organization. Retrieved from http://nationalhumanitiescenter.org/ tserve/twenty/tkeyinfo/garvey.htm

2

❖

Demographics and Diversity

Q6. ARE MUSLIMS IN THE UNITED STATES A DIVERSE POPULATION IN TERMS OF ETHNICITY, CULTURE, AND RELIGIOUS IDENTITIES?

Answer: Yes. The U.S. Muslim population encompasses a wide range of racial, ethnic, cultural, and religious identities. The United States is home to one of the most diverse Muslim populations in the world, including people of almost every ethnicity, country, and school of Islamic thought.

The Facts: After World War II, Western governments such as the United States focused their attention on fighting communism. Today, as "terrorist" activity is increasingly linked to jihad and "radical Muslims," some Americans are under the impression that Islam is a totalitarian movement fueled by a monolithic religious ideology. For example, Sarah Palin, the former governor of Alaska and vice presidential candidate, told an audience at the Western Conservative Summit in Denver, Colorado, that "the most sinister threat is Islamic ideology. . . . Islam put the 'I' in 'ISIS.'" Other Americans have depicted Islam as an inherently violent religion as well. Notable anti-Muslim blog editor Robert Spencer of Jihad Watch, for example, has referred to jihad as "warfare against non-believers in order to institute 'Sharia'" and claimed that this understanding of Islam "is a constant element of mainstream Islamic theology" (Council on American-Islamic Relations, 2017). Both Palin and Spencer not only represented Islam as a totalitarian ideology rather than a religion, but they also conflated the views and actions of "radical" Muslim groups with the 1.8 billion Muslims around the world.

Such fears have no foundation in history or reality, according to many historians, lawmakers, political scientists, and religious scholars. Nonetheless, the representation of Islam as a monolithic and violent entity is one of the most challenging pedagogical problems faced by American Muslims today. If one, however, simply considers the racial, ethnic, and religious diversity of Muslims in the United States, the perception of Muslims as a monolithic entity becomes much more difficult to sustain.

The Pew Research Center, a nonpartisan think tank based in Washington, D.C., serves as a window into the diversity of American Muslims. In the first-ever nationally representative study of a randomly selected sample of American Muslims, the Gallup Center revealed that American Muslims are one of the most racially diverse religious group in the United States (Younis, 2009). Another Pew Research Center (2011) report, "A Demographic Portrait of American Muslims," revealed that no single racial or ethnic group of the U.S. Muslim population makes up more than 30 percent of the national population. In total, approximately 30 percent of Muslims in the United States described themselves as white, 23 percent as black, 21 percent as Asian, 6 percent as Hispanic, and 19 percent as other or mixed race. Those figured changed slightly in Pew's 2014 Religious Landscape Study, which reported that blacks, whites (including some people of North African or Middle Eastern descent), and Asians each make up a quarter of the American Muslim population.

Racial breakdowns of the American Muslim population vary considerably in terms of the foreign-born and native-born populations in the United States. More than 8 in 10 American Muslims from the Middle East and North Africa describe themselves as either white (60 percent) or other/mixed race (22 percent) (Pew Research Center, 2011). By contrast, the native-born Muslim population contains a higher proportion of blacks, and lower proportions of whites and Asians, than the foreign-born population (Pew Research Center, 2011) Among native-born American Muslims, 40 percent describe themselves as black, 18 percent as white, 10 percent as Asian, and 10 percent as Hispanic; 21 percent say they are of some other race or are mixed race (Pew Research Center, 2011). As impressively diverse as these numbers are, they minimize the diversity of American Muslims, who can trace their ancestry back to more than 80 nations (Strum, 2005). The Pew Research Center's "Religious Landscape Study" of 2014 found that Muslims are the second most racially and culturally diverse religious group in the United States. The only religious group in the United States with greater diversity than American Muslims is Seventh Day Adventists (Lipka, 2017).

There is no way of knowing exactly how many Muslims live in the United States, as the separation of religion and state mandated by the U.S. Constitution prevents the federal government from asking U.S. residents about their religion. What is known about American Muslims is that they represent a relatively small but rapidly growing portion of the U.S. religious landscape. The Pew Research Center (2017) estimates that there are 3.35 million Muslims of all ages living in the United States—up from about 2.75 million in 2011 and 2.35 million in 2007. Other organizations suggest that the American Muslim population might be as high as 6 million (Interfaith Alliance & First Amendment Center, n.d.). In terms of demographic projection, the Pew Research Center estimates that Muslims will make up 2.1 percent of the U.S. population by the year 2050, surpassing people who identify as Jewish on the basis of religion as the second-largest religious group in the United States as early as 2040 (Mohamed, 2018). Research also shows that U.S. Muslims are a young group in terms of age. Most Muslim adults (60 percent) are under the age of 40, whereas just 38 percent of the U.S. adult population as a whole is younger than 40 years old (Pew Research Center, 2017).

American Muslims are quite varied in their religious allegiances and observances. According to Pew's 2017 survey, slightly more than half of American Muslims are Sunnis (55 percent), but significant minorities identify as Shiite (16 percent) or as "just Muslim" (14 percent). Most Muslims in the United States say religion is very important in their lives (65 percent), and about 4 in 10 (42 percent) say they pray five times a day. According to the 2017 Pew survey, however, many other U.S. Muslims (58 percent) say they do not pray all five daily prayers.

While nearly all American Muslims say they are proud to be Muslim, they are not of one mind about what is essential to being Muslim. The majority of U.S. Muslims (64 percent) say there is more than one true way to interpret Islam. They also are more likely to say that traditional understandings of Islam need to be reinterpreted in light of modern contexts (52 percent) than to say that traditional understandings are all that is needed (38 percent) (Pew Research Center, 2017).

The diversity among American Muslims is not just racial or religious. According to Ahmed Younis of the Gallup Center for Muslim Studies, the diversity of Muslims in the United States can also be viewed through income, levels of education, geography, and generations (National Public Radio, 2009). There are American Muslims among the Asian Muslim community making more than $5,000 a month in household income, whereas only 17 percent of black Muslim families report the same level of income. American Muslims are fairly distributed across the United States, living in small towns, suburbs, and cities. According to the Pew Research Center (2015), 31 percent of American Muslims reside in the Northeast, 23 percent in the Midwest, 26 percent in the South, and 20 percent in the West. Though many Muslim immigrants in the early 20th century did indeed settle in large, cosmopolitan cities like New York, Chicago, and Los Angeles, a significant number also made their way to small towns in rural America (Sadar, 2015).

In terms of generational differences, 63 percent of American Muslims are first-generation migrants to the United States, with 45 percent having arrived in the country after 1990 (Pew Research Center, 2011). The first-generation Muslim migrants in the United States come from a wide range of countries. About 4 in 10 (41 percent) are immigrants from the Middle East or North Africa, while about a quarter (26 percent) come from South Asian countries including Pakistan (14 percent), Bangladesh (5 percent), and India (3 percent) (Pew Research Center, 2011). Other Muslim migrants moved to the United States from sub-Saharan Africa (11 percent), countries in the European Union (7 percent), Iran (5 percent), or other countries (9 percent) (Pew Research Center, 2011). More than a third of American Muslims (37 percent) were born in the United States and 81 percent of all American Muslims are citizens of the country (Pew Research Center, 2011).

American Muslims themselves regularly highlight the diversity of the Islamic faith in the United States. After watching an upsurge in anti-Muslim rhetoric and hate crimes during the 2016 presidential campaigns, Carlos Khalil Guzman, a 28-year-old Brooklyn-based photographer, created "Muslims of America," an ongoing photo series that shows Muslims from all 50 states, from New York to Hawaii. The purpose of Guzman's "Muslims of America" is to showcase the diversity of the Muslim population— in ethnicity, gender, geography, and life experience—with special focus on women, whom he believes are more often the targets of Islamophobia. The photo series includes Muslims of Palestinian, Filipino, Ecuadorian, Somali, Bangladeshi, Pakistani, Moroccan, Lebanese, and African American descent living in the United States (Kandil, 2017).

The diversity of the American Muslim community presents both unique challenges and tremendous opportunities, as people of different races, ethnicities, cultures, and interpretations of Islam come into contact with one another (The Pluralism Project, n.d.). Amina Wadud (n.d.), an American academic and scholar of Arabic and Islamic Studies, notes that Muslim immigrants—rather than native-born American Muslims—hold hegemony over leadership roles in Islamic organizations and mosques, which she attributes to their financial resources and socioeconomic status. According to her, first-generation American Muslim immigrants use their international contacts as a source of funding to start and maintain some of their Islamic organizations and to build mosques and community centers (Wadud, n.d.). While American Muslims are freed from the control of a supreme religious cleric, their freedom also means that they are less equipped to counter criticisms and generalizations, since no one Islamic organization or mosque speaks for all American Muslims (Hasan, 2004).

Although Islam emphasizes balance (*adl* in Arabic) and order, the American Muslim community—like all societies worldwide—shows signs of internal disagreements over a wide array of topics and issues. Akbar Ahmed (2002), an Islamic scholar who carried out a year-long ethnographic book study called *Journey into America: The Challenge of Islam*, claims that the internal differences among Muslim communities are typically not Islamic differences, but often tribal, cultural, or ethnic. In terms of intra-Muslim differences of experience, race is one of the primary driving factors (National Public Radio, 2009). The racial diversity of the American Muslim population provides certain challenges for Islamic institutions and leaders who are working to project a unified "Islamic" voice (National Public Radio, 2009). While all mosques of some affluence are inclusive of members from lower socioeconomic groups, affluent immigrant Muslims will not always participate with the same fervor in grassroots mosques established by economically struggling African Americans (Wadud, n.d.).

In recognition of these divisions within the American Muslim population, many mosques in the United States work to bring together disparate peoples for the purpose of dissolving racial and cultural barriers, as well as Sunni/Shi'a divisions. American Muslim organizations also work to move beyond racial and cultural boundaries by embracing the overall Muslim population regardless of racial, ethnic, cultural, or sectarian differences. Three national groups—the Islamic Society of North America, the Council on American-Islamic Relations, and the Muslim Public Affairs Council—are bodies hoping to project a more unified "Muslim voice" in the United States (The Pluralism Project, n.d.).

It is also worth highlighting how the diversity of the American Muslim population reflects the heterogeneity of the *ummah*, or global Muslim population. Current figures estimate that there are approximately 1.8 billion Muslims in the world, making Islam the world's second-largest religious tradition after Christianity (DeSilver & Masci, 2017). Although many people, especially in the United States, associate Islam with Arabs or the Middle East, nearly two thirds (62 percent) of Muslims live in the Asia-Pacific region (DeSilver & Masci, 2017). In fact, more Muslims live in India and Pakistan (344 million combined) than in the entire Middle East-North African region (317 million) (DeSilver & Masci, 2017).

Islamic holy texts encourage Muslims to embrace the diversification of their communities, societies, and homeland. The Qur'an readily supports an ethic of racial diversity and cultural tolerance. According to Khaled Abou El Fadl (2002), a prominent critic of Islamic puritanism and advocate of religious pluralism, the *"Qur'an* not only expects, but it even accepts the reality of difference and diversity within human society." El Fadl points to the following Qur'anic verse (49:13): "O humankind, God has created you from male and female and made you into diverse nations from tribes so that you may come to know each other. Verily, the most honored of you in the sight of God is he who is the most righteous." This passage reveals that every human being is honored solely by virtue of being human, without any further considerations of race, origin, or creed (Hathout, 1995).

Elsewhere, as El Fadl continues, "the *Qur'an* asserts that diversity is part of the divine intent and purpose in creation: 'If thy Lord had willed, He would have made humankind into a single nation, but they will not cease to be diverse. . . . And for this God created them [humankind].' " The Islamic spirit of humanity and pluralism is embodied in the demographic makeup of the U.S. Muslim population.

FURTHER READING

Ahmed, Akbar. (2002). *Islam Today: A Short Introduction to the Muslim World.* London and New York, NY: I.B. Tauris.

Council on American-Islamic Relations. (2017, October 5). "U.S. Islamophobia Network: Robert Spencer." Islamophobia.org. Retrieved from http://www.islamophobia.org/islamophobic-individuals/robert-spen cer/78-robert-spencer.html

DeSilver, Drew, & Masci, David. (2017, January 31). *World's Muslim Population More Widespread Than You Might Think.* Washington, DC: Pew Research Center. Retrieved from http://www.pewresearch.org/ fact-tank/2017/01/31/worlds-muslim-population-more-widespread-than-you-might-think/

El Fadl, Khaled A. (2002). *The Place of Tolerance in Islam.* Boston, MA: Beacon Press.

Gregorian, Vartan. (2004). *Islam: A Mosaic, Not a Monolith.* Washington, DC: Brookings Institution Press.

Hasan, Asma G. (2004). *Why I Am a Muslim: An American Odyssey.* London: Element.

Hathout, Hassan. (1995). *Reading the Muslim Mind.* American Trust Publications. Retrieved from http://hhlf.org/Reading%20Muslim%20Mind.pdf

Interfaith Alliance & The First Amendment Center. (n.d.). *What Is the Truth about American Muslims?* Washington, DC: Interfaith Alliance. Retrieved from http://interfaithalliance.org/americanmuslimfaq/

Kandil, Caitlin Y. (2017, June 19). "'Muslims in America' Portraits Showcase Community's Diverse Roots." NBC News. Retrieved from http://www.nbcnews.com/news/asian-america/muslims-america-por traits-showcase-community-s-diverse-roots-n770521

Lipka, Michael. (2015, July 27). "The Most and Least Racially Diverse U.S. Religious Groups." Washington, DC: Pew Research Center. Retrieved from http://www.pewresearch.org/fact-tank/2015/07/27/the-most-and-least-racially-diverse-u-s-religious-groups/

Mohamed, B. (2018, January 3). "New Estimates Shows U.S. Muslim Population Continues to Grow." Washington, DC: Pew Research Center. Retrieved from http://www.pewresearch.org/fact-tank/2018/01/03/new-estimates-show-u-s-muslim-population-continues-to-grow/

National Public Radio. (2009, March 3). "Study: Diversity, Disparity within American-Muslims." Washington, DC: NPR.com. Retrieved from http://www.npr.org/templates/story/story.php?storyId=101368728

Pew Research Center. (2011, August 30). *Section 1: A Demographic Portrait of Muslim Americans.* Washington, DC: Pew Research Center. Retrieved from http://www.people-press.org/2011/08/30/section-1-a-demographic-portrait-of-muslim-americans/

Pew Research Center. (2015, May 12). *Chapter 3: Demographic Profiles of Religious Groups.* Washington, DC: Pew Research Center. Retrieved from http://www.pewforum.org/2015/05/12/chapter-3-demographic-profiles-of-religious-groups/

Pew Research Center. (2017, July 26). *U.S. Muslims Concerned about Their Place in Society, But Continue to Believe in the American Dream.* Washington, DC: Pew Research Center. Retrieved from http://www.pewforum.org/2017/07/26/findings-from-pew-research-centers-2017-survey-of-us-muslims/

The Pluralism Project. (n.d.). "Unity and Diversity." Boston, MA: Harvard University. Retrieved from http://pluralism.org/religions/islam/issues-for-muslims-in-america/unity-and-diversity/

Sadar, Claire. (2015, December 20). "Countering Myths about American Muslims: Demographics." Muftah.org. Retrieved from https://muftah.org/countering-myths-about-american-muslims-demographics/#.WUKk1xPyuT-

Strum, Philippa (ed.). (2005, May 11). *Muslims in the United States: Identity, Influence, Innovation*. Washington, DC: Woodrow Wilson International Center for Scholars.

Wadud, Amina. (n.d.). *American Muslim Identity—Race and Ethnicity in Progressive Islam*. Waltham, MA: Brandeis University. Retrieved from http://www.brandeis.edu/diversity/events/diversitypdfs/American_Muslim_Identity.pdf

Wangnsness, Lisa. (2013, January 31). "Roman Catholic Diocese of Worcester Cancels Speech by Critic of Islam." *Boston Globe*. Retrieved from http://www.bostonglobe.com/metro/2013/01/31/roman-catholic-diocese-worcester-cancels-speech-critic-islam/I7NCZ8XFtPB8PXXQuAct1J/story.html

Woods, John, & Barna, Alexander. (n.d.). "Examining Stereotypes: 'Islam Represents a Monolithic Religion and Culture.' " Retrieved from http://teachmiddleeast.lib.uchicago.edu/historical-perspectives/rulership-and-justice/islamic-period/examining-stereotypes/stereotype-01.html

Younis, Mohamed. (2009, March 2). "Muslim Americans Exemplify Diversity, Potential." Gallup.com. Retrieved from http://www.gallup.com/poll/116260/muslim-americans-exemplify-diversity-potential.aspx

Q7. ARE AMERICAN MUSLIMS WELL EDUCATED, AND HAVE THEY CONTRIBUTED TO SCIENTIFIC PROGRESS IN THE UNITED STATES?

Answer: Yes. American Muslims are one of the most educated religious groups in the United States, above par in comparison to the "average American," and they are also making significant contributions to the scientific fields in institutions across the country. In terms of their housing, income, and career choices, American Muslims are similar to "mainstream Americans."

The Facts: American Muslims are one of the most highly educated religious groups in the United States. On average, they have about 14 years of total education, making them the third most educated religious group in the country behind Hindus and Jews (Kauffman, 2016). According to research carried out by the Pew Research Center, approximately 39 percent of all American Muslims hold a bachelor's degree from a four-year college in the United States (Murphy, 2016). Another 25 percent have had "some college" experiences (Murphy, 2016). Muslims (26 percent) in the United States are as likely as the American public (28 percent) to have graduated from college (Pew Research Center, 2011a). In 2011, the Pew Research Center found that a high percentage (26 percent) of American Muslims said that they were currently enrolled in college or university campuses in the United States, compared with only 13 percent of the total U.S. population (Pew Research Center, 2011b). The percentage of American Muslims who graduated from four-year colleges or universities also compares favorably to Christians (36 percent overall) and Christian minority communities such as Mormons (33 percent), Methodists (37 percent), Lutherans (36 percent), and Catholics (26 percent) (Pew Research Center, 2011b). These Pew Research Center findings reveal that religious minorities in the United States are far more likely to have attended college or vocational school than members of the Christian majority (Stack, 2016).

The high level of educational attainment among American Muslims does not, however, correlate with the educational levels of Muslims around the world. Muslims rank as one of the least educated major religious groups on the planet, with an average of just 5.6 years of schooling (Kauffman, 2016). Muslims worldwide, however, have registered some of the greatest gains in educational achievement in recent decades. The share of Muslim adults (ages 25 and older) with at least some formal schooling has risen by 25 percent in the past three generations, from fewer than half (46 percent) among the oldest group to 72 percent among the youngest (Pew Research Center, 2016).

Due to their high levels of educational attainment, American Muslims qualify for higher-paying occupations in the United States. According to the Pew Research Center, 45 percent of American Muslims report making at least $30,000 per year, a higher share than the 36 percent of Americans as a whole (Pew Research Center, 2011b). The Pew Research Center's data also revealed that American Muslims report owning a business or being self-employed at a higher rate than the general population. Forty percent of American Muslims hold a college degree—compared with 29 percent of the population as a whole—and one in three have a professional job. Muslim women are among the most educated in the country—second only to Jewish women—and work outside the home at the same rate as Muslim men. The gender gap in pay among American Muslims is smaller than that of any other religious group (Pew Research Center, 2011b).

American Muslims are about as likely as other Americans to report household incomes of $100,000 or more (14 percent of Muslims, compared with 16 percent of all U.S. adults), and they express similar levels of satisfaction with their personal financial situation (Pew Research Center, 2011a). Notwithstanding their comparable educational attainment to that of the U.S. general public, Muslims (35 percent) are significantly more likely than any other faith group (18 percent) to report low household income (less than $30,000) (Mogahed & Chouhoud, 2017). This data suggests that economic inequality is a significant issue within the American Muslim population.

Considering the American Muslim population's focus on education, it will come as no surprise that Muslims in the United States are significant contributors to the educational and scientific development of the nation. The contributions of American Muslim scientists came to public light following President Donald Trump's sweeping Executive Order 13769 of January 27, 2017 (titled "Protecting the Nation from Foreign Terrorist Entry into the United States"), which made traveling in and out of the United States more difficult for Muslims in academia and scientific fields (Morello & Reardon, 2017). Following the announcement of the ban (which was promptly struck down as unconstitutional), Muslim scientists living in the United States expressed fear and shock about Trump's stance. These Muslims joined more than 12,000 other research scientists—including 40 Nobel Prize winners—in signing a petition denouncing Trump's actions as both "anti-science" and "anti-Muslim" (Academics against Immigration Executive Order, 2016). The American Civil Liberties Union (ACLU) and other civil rights organizations also supported Muslim scientists impacted by Executive Order 13769 by filing lawsuit against the U.S. government to overturn the order.

Madrassas, an Arabic word referring to a religious college, university, or seminary (Considine, 2017: 186), are also starting to appear on U.S. soil. In 2009, Zaytuna College was established in Berkeley, California, and shortly thereafter had its inaugural freshman class for the fall 2010 semester. Zaytuna's aims include educating and preparing "morally committed professional, intellectual, and spiritual leaders who are grounded in the Islamic scholarly tradition and conversant with the cultural currents and critical ideas shaping modern society" (Zaytuna College, n.d.). The president of Zaytuna College, Sheikh Hamza Yusuf, is a prominent American Muslim convert who also serves as the vice president of the Forum for Promoting Peace in Muslim Societies (n.d.), a transnational organization that emphasizes the peaceful and just teachings of Islam.

Muslim women serve in many prominent educational and scientific positions throughout the country. The Women's Islamic Initiative in Spirituality and Equality (n.d.), a faith-based global program, social network, and grassroots social justice movement, has an online database that documents America Muslim women, scholars, scientists, and writers, among other notable professions, who are pioneers in their respective fields. In terms of the relationship between Islam and science, roughly 60 percent of American Muslims said there was no conflict between science and religion in a 2013 survey.

According to Nobel Prize–winning theoretical physicist Steven Weinberg, the idea that Muslims and Islam are "anti-science" ignores considerable historical evidence to the contrary. Weinberg stated that during the *golden age* of Islamic science, which ended somewhere between 1100 and 1200, "Muslim scientists were way ahead of their contemporaries in Christian Europe" (Worrall, 2015). Muslims were the first to establish astronomical observatories, which led to advances not only in astronomy but also in oceanic navigation, and individuals such as Ibn Khaldun and Ibn Batuta also contributed significantly to geography. Khaldun and Batuta are still well respected for their written accounts of exploration.

Prophet Muhammad, too, emphasized the importance of seeking knowledge in different ways. Muhammad told people to "seek knowledge from the cradle to the grave" and to "seek knowledge even if it is far as China" (Rizvi, 1993).

FURTHER READING

Academics against Immigration Executive Order. (2016). "The Petition." Retrieved from https://notoimmigrationban.com/

American Civil Liberties Union. (n.d.). "Lawsuits Related to Trump's Muslim Ban." New York, NY: ACLU. Retrieved from https://www.aclu.org/other/lawsuits-related-trumps-muslim-ban

Center for Peace & Spirituality. (n.d.). "Importance of Learning in the Quran." Retrieved from http://www.cpsglobal.org/contact

Considine, Craig. (2017). *Islam, Race, and Pluralism in the Pakistani Diaspora*. London and New York, NY: Routledge.

Forum for Promoting Peace in Muslim Societies. (n.d.). "Forum's Idea." Abu Dhabi, UAE: Promoting Peace in Muslim Societies. Retrieved from http://peacems.com/?page_id=1769&lang=en

Jacobson, Louise. (2016, June 18). "Donald Trump Wrong That 'There's No Real Assimilation' by U.S. Muslims." *Politifact*. Retrieved from http://www.politifact.com/nbc/statements/2016/jun/18/donald-trump/donald-trump-wrong-theres-no-real-assimilation-us-/

Kauffman, Gretel. (2016, December 14). "Hindus, Muslims among America's Best Educated Groups, Report Finds." *Christian Science*

Monitor. Retrieved from http://www.csmonitor.com/USA/2016/1214/Hindus-Muslims-among-America-s-best-educated-groups-report-finds

Meng Lai Yew, Ahmad, Abdul R., & Wan, Chang D. (eds.). (2016). *Higher Education in the Middle East and North Africa: Exploring Regional and Country Specific Potentials.* New York, NY: Springer.

Mogahed, Dalia, & Chouhoud, Youssef. (2017). *American Muslim Poll 2017: Muslims at the Crossroads.* Washington, DC: Institute for Social Policy and Understanding. Retrieved from http://www.ispu.org/wp-content/uploads/2017/05/AMP-2017_Full-Report.pdf

Morello, Lauren, & Reardon, Sara. (2017, January 30). "Meet the Scientists Hit by Trump's Immigration Ban." *Scientific American.* Retrieved from https://www.scientificamerican.com/article/meet-the-scientists-hit-by-trump-rsquo-s-immigration-ban/

Murphy, Caryle. (2016, November 4). "The Most and Least Educated U.S. Religious Groups." Washington, DC: Pew Research Center. Retrieved from http://www.pewresearch.org/fact-tank/2016/11/04/the-most-and-least-educated-u-s-religious-groups/

Pew Research Center. (2011a, August 30). *Muslim Americans: No Signs of Growth in Alienation or Support for Extremism.* Washington, DC: Pew Research Center. Retrieved from http://www.people-press.org/2011/08/30/muslim-americans-no-signs-of-growth-in-alienation-or-support-for-extremism/

Pew Research Center. (2011b, August 30). Section 1: A Demographic Portrait of Muslim Americans. Washington, DC: Pew Research Center. Retrieved from http://www.people-press.org/2011/08/30/section-1-a-demographic-portrait-of-muslim-americans/

Pew Research Center. (2013, April 30). Appendix A: U.S. Muslims—Views on Religion and Society in a Global Context. Washington, DC: Pew Research Center. Retrieved from http://www.pewforum.org/2013/04/30/the-worlds-muslims-religion-politics-society-app-a/

Pew Research Center. (2016, December 13). *Religion and Education around the World. Pew Research Center.* Washington, DC: Pew Research Center. Retrieved from http://www.pewforum.org/2016/12/13/muslim-educational-attainment/

Rizvi, Sayyid M. (1993, October 12–13). "Education in Islam." Ahlul Bayt. Retrieved from https://www.al-islam.org/articles/education-in-islam-sayyid-muhammad-rizvi

Southern Poverty Law Center. (n.d.). "Act For America." Montgomery, AL: Southern Poverty Law Center. Retrieved from https://www.splcenter.org/fighting-hate/extremist-files/group/act-america

Stack, Liam. (2016, December 13). "Christians in U.S. Are Less Educated Than Religious Minorities, Report Says." *The New York Times.*

Retrieved from https://www.nytimes.com/2016/12/13/world/christians-educated-religious-minorities-pew.html

Women's Islamic Initiative in Spirituality and Equality. (n.d.). "Muslim Women: Past and Present. Women's Islamic Initiative in Spirituality and Equality." New York, NY: Women's Islamic Initiative in Spirituality and Equality. Retrieved from http://www.wisemuslimwomen.org/muslimwomen/summary/C67/category-search/academic_leaders

Worrall, Simon. (2015, February 27). "Is Islam Hostile to Science?" *National Geographic*. Retrieved from http://news.nationalgeographic.com/news/2015/03/150301-aristotle-archimedes-einstein-darwin-ptolemy-razi-ngbooktalk/

YouTube. (2016, November 28). "Brigitte Gabriel on Reason Why Muslims Won't Assimilate into Western Culture. Now the End Begins." Retrieved from https://www.youtube.com/watch?v=hE1ZBtE1x8E

Zaytuna College. (n.d.). "Mission." Berkeley, CA: Zaytuna. Retrieved from https://www.zaytuna.edu/mission

Q8. DO SOME ORGANIZATIONS APPEAR TO REAP FINANCIAL BENEFITS FROM ANTI-MUSLIM RHETORIC AND MESSAGING?

Answer: Yes. The United States is home to an extensive and lucrative network of activists and organizations that are sometimes collectively known as the "Islamophobia industry." Major Islamic organizations and experts on Islamophobia have documented both their operations and their steady rise in influence, particularly during and after the 2016 presidential election and have identified what they describe as clear evidence that these groups accrue financial benefits—in the form of donor contributions, for example—for their anti-Islamic activities and statements.

The Facts: *Islamophobia* is a word that is now part of the American lexicon, having come into use as a tool to describe the American public's fear and hatred of Muslims and Islam.

The Council on American-Islamic Relations (CAIR), a civil rights organization that documents Islamophobic incidents and hate crimes against Muslims in the United States, provides the following definition of Islamophobia: "[It is] is closed-minded prejudice against or hatred of Islam and Muslims" (Council on American-Islamic Relations, n.d.). A more detailed definition of Islamophobia provided by Gallup reads as follows: "the exaggerated fear, hatred and hostility towards Islam and Muslims that is perpetuated by negative stereotypes resulting in bias, discrimination and the marginalization and exclusion of Muslims from America's social, political, and civic life" (Ali, 2011).

The *Islamophobia industry*, on the other hand, is a term used to describe a right-wing network of bloggers, pundits, religious leaders, and politicians who work to convince U.S. citizens that Muslims are the enemy of the nation (Lean, 2012). According to a joint report by CAIR and the Center for Race and Gender at the University of California–Berkeley, 33 Islamophobic groups had access to at least US$205 million in total revenue between 2008 and 2013 (Council on American-Islamic Relations, 2016). Further, in 2011, the Center for American Progress [CAP], a public policy research and advocacy organization based in Washington, D.C., [asserted] that seven charitable foundations spent $42.6 million between 2001 and 2009 to support the spread of anti-Muslim and anti-Islam rhetoric in the United States (Ali et al., 2011). CAP's report, titled "Fear, Inc.: The Roots of the Islamophobia Network in America," identified several key foundations that help to fuel Islamophobia (Ali et al., 2011). CAIR categorizes these and other groups of the Islamophobia industry by using one of two key terms: *inner core groups* and *outer core groups*. Inner core groups are groups "whose primary purpose is to promote prejudice against or hatred of Islam and Muslims, and whose work regularly demonstrates Islamophobic themes" (Council on American-Islamic Relations, 2017a). Outer core groups are groups that help the inner core by sharing the latter's propaganda.

Corey Saylor's study found that inner core groups enjoyed access to at least US$119,662,719 in total revenue between 2008 and 2011, and he also found that these groups are tightly linked. For example, the Middle East Forum, which the Southern Poverty Law Center calls "a major funder of Muslim-bashers," granted US$1,242,000 over three years to the Investigative Project on Terrorism (Saylor, 2014). These organizations are what scholars of Islamophobia sometimes refer to as "misinformation experts" or "pseudo-scholars" who generate false facts and material that end up being used by Islamophobia grassroots groups, media outlets, religious leaders, and U.S. politicians.

The Center for American Progress (n.d.) identified several more individuals as the "central nervous system" of anti-Muslim propaganda in the United States. In addition to the inner core groups of the Islamophobia industry, CAIR in 2017 identified 32 outer core groups whose primary purpose does not appear to include promoting prejudice against or hatred of Islam and Muslims but appears to include regularly demonstrating or supporting Islamophobia themes. These groups range from organizations that tout themselves as public policy "think tanks" to powerful voices in national media (Council on American-Islamic Relations, 2017a).

American Muslims often take to social media and other forums of self-expression to decry the Islamophobia industry because it is giving oxygen to "radical Muslims." The Islamic Networks Group, a nonprofit organization with affiliates and partners around the country, counters forms of anti-Muslim bigotry through education and interfaith engagement while working within the framework of the First Amendment's protection of religious freedom and pluralism. Founded in 1983, "ING reaches millions of individuals and hundreds of groups a year at the grassroots level by building relationships, understanding and peaceful communities of all types and backgrounds" (Islamic Networks Group, n.d.).

FURTHER READING

Ali, Wajahat. (2011, August 29). "Exposing the Islamophobia Network in America." *The Huffington Post*. Retrieved from http://www.huffing tonpost.com/wajahat-ali/exposing-the-islamophobia_b_938777.html

Ali, Wajahat, Clifton, Eli, Duss, Matthew, Fang, Lee, Keyes, Scott, & Shakir, Faiz. (2011, August). *Fear, Inc.: The Roots of the Islamophobia Network in America.* Washington, DC: Center for American Progress. Retrieved from https://cdn.americanprogress.org/wp-content/uploads/issues/2011/08/pdf/islamophobia_intro.pdf

Center for American Progress. (n.d.). "Steve Emerson." Washington, DC: Center for American Progress. Retrieved from https://islamopho bianetwork.com/misinformation-expert/steven-emerson

Council on American-Islamic Relations. (2016, June 20). "New CAIR, UC Berkeley Report Reveals Funding, Negative Impact of Islamophobic Groups in America." Washington, DC: Council on American-Islamic Relations. Retrieved from http://www.cair.com/press-center/press-releases/13618-new-cair-uc-berkeley-report-reveals-funding-negative-impact-of-islamophobic-groups-in-america.html

Council on American-Islamic Relations. (2017a, April 24). "Islamophobic Organizations." Washington, DC: Council on American-Islamic Relations. Retrieved from http://www.islamophobia.org/islamophobic-or ganizations.html

Council on American-Islamic Relations. (2017b, April 6). "David Yerushalmi." Washington, DC: Council on American-Islamic Relations. Retrieved from http://www.islamophobia.org/22-islamophobic-individuals/102-david-yerushalmi.html

Council on American-Islamic Relations. (n.d.). "Islamophobia." Washington, DC: Council on American-Islamic Relations. Retrieved from http://www.cair-dfw.org/islamophobia

Elliot, Andrea. (2011, July 30). "The Man behind the Anti-Shariah Movement." *The New York Times*. Retrieved from http://www.nytimes.com/2011/07/31/us/31shariah.html

Institute for Social Policy and Understanding. (2015, February 11). "Muslims React Swiftly to Chapel Hill, NC, Killings." Washington, DC: Institute for Social Policy and Understanding. Retrieved from https://www.ispu.org/muslims-react-swiftly-to-chapel-hill-nc-killings/

Islamic Networks Group. (n.d.). "Welcome Overview." San Jose, CA: Islamic Networks Group. Retrieved from https://ing.org/welcome-overview/

Lean, Nathan. (2012). *The Islamophobia Industry: How the Right Manufactures Fear of Muslims*. London: Pluto Press.

Saylor, Cory. (2014, Spring). "The U.S. Islamophobia Network: Its Funding and Impact." *Islamophobia Studies Journal*, 2(1), 99–118 Retrieved from http://crg.berkeley.edu/sites/default/files/Network-CSaylor.pdf

Southern Poverty Law Center. (2016, October 25). "A Journalist's Manual: Field Guide to Anti-Muslim Extremists." Montgomery, AL: Southern Poverty Law Center. Retrieved from https://www.splcenter.org/20161025/journalists-manual-field-guide-anti-muslim-extremists

Q9. ARE MUSLIM WOMEN OPPRESSED IN THE UNITED STATES?

Answer: Yes and no. Muslim women in the United States hold many positions of power, but they also face barriers and challenges inside and outside of their communities.

The Facts: While Muslim women are confined to second-class citizenship status in many parts of the "Muslim world," that is not the case among American Muslims. In terms of levels of educational achievement, American Muslim women are one of the most highly educated female religious groups in the United States, second only to Jewish American women (Younis, 2009). U.S. Muslim women hold more college or postgraduate degrees than Muslim men, and they are more likely to work in professional fields than women from most other major U.S. religious groups (Yan, 2015). These levels of educational achievement, as The Pluralism Project (n.d.) of Harvard University notes, contribute to Muslim women occupying a wide variety of important positions in American life, ranging from medical doctors, engineers, lawyers, chemists, professors, broadcast journalists, clerical workers, businesswomen, and school teachers.

According to a Pew Research Center (2009) report, roughly 62 percent of American Muslims say that the quality of life for Muslim women in the United States is better than the quality of life for women in Muslim-majority countries. Another Pew Research Center (2011) report, "Muslim Americans: No Signs of Growth in Alienation or Support for Extremism," found that virtually all American Muslim women (90 percent) agree that women should be able to work outside of the home. Most (68 percent) also think that there is no difference between men and women political leaders (Pew Research Center, 2011).

Muslim women in the United States use their agency and decision-making power to challenge stereotypes of Muslims. *Agency* refers to an individual making their own choices by transcending barriers over class, religion, gender, and ethnicity, all of which might limit them and determine their decisions. Indeed, Muslim women in the United States are actively engaged in the most important social and political issues of our time. Daisy Khan, an Indian-born American Muslim, is the cofounder and executive director of the American Society for Muslim Advancement and the founder of Women's Islamic Initiative in Spirituality and Equality. Rana Abdelhamid, founder of the Women's Initiative for Self-Empowerment, devotes her energy to helping Muslim women find strength within themselves to combat Islamophobia. Abdelhamid created the photography series "Hijabis of New York," a photo blog that features street portraits and interviews mirroring the "Humans Of New York" series started by photographer Brandon Stanton; she also teaches self-defense workshops for Muslim women, who are overwhelmingly targeted in acts of Islamophobic violence (Blumberg, 2016).

While American Muslim women continue to face rising Islamophobia, they do not remain silent in the face of challenging stereotypes and fighting for the rights of minority groups in the United States. Ilhan Omar, a Somali refugee who arrived to the United States at the age of 12 after spending four years in a refugee camp in Kenya, became the first Somali American Muslim women elected to a state legislature in 2016. Omar campaigned on a progressive platform, advocating for affordable college, criminal justice reform, economic equality, and clean energy (Blumberg, 2016).

Although Muslim women in the United States are countering anti-Muslim bigotry in the public sphere, they are also increasingly challenging gender imbalances inside of their own communities. According to the 2013 "Women and the American Mosque" report by the Islamic Society of North America, a small percentage (4 percent) of U.S. mosques said women's activities or programs were a "top priority" in their community. Most mosques (63 percent) scored "fair" or "poor" on a scale for a women-friendly mosque (Sayeed, Al-Adawiya, & Bagby, 2013). One common complaint of second-class treatment, for example, is that in some mosques, women are relegated to crowded basements or balconies during worship services, leaving only men in the main prayer halls. The acceptance of female leadership in mosques across the United States is a significant challenge as well, since women are only empowered to lead prayer services if the congregation is composed entirely of other women.

American Muslim women today are working toward the mainstream acceptance of some form of female Islamic authority (Bano & Kalmbach, 2012). In addition, they are pushing for reforms in how space is allocated by gender inside mosques across the United States. In 2015, meanwhile, the first female-only mosque opened in the United States. The Women's Mosque of America was formed by a group of Muslim women and men in California dedicated to creating a space for women and girls to feel welcome, respected, and actively engaged in the local Muslim community. The Women's Mosque of America empowers Muslim women and girls through direct access to Islamic scholarship and leadership opportunities in the United States (Women's Mosque of America, n.d.). M. Hasna Maznavi, the president and founder of the Women's Mosque of America, said that her project was inspired by Prophet Muhammad, whom she called "arguably the greatest feminist that ever lived" (Maznavi, 2016). Maznavi claimed that Muhammad "liberated women, fought for them to have the right to divorce and manage their own finances, and ended the practice of female infanticide" in seventh-century Arabia (Maznavi, 2016).

Through writing both fiction and nonfiction, U.S. Muslim women aim "to express their own experiences, which are separate from both the religious leaders of their own communities and from the mainstream portrayal of them" in American society; these books are as diverse as the women who wrote them, and all provide readers with a piece of the Muslim experience both in the United States and around the "Muslim world" (Jarema, 2017).

Female scholars and academics also write about the experiences of being an American Muslim woman living in the United States. Some important scholarly voices include Dalia Mogahed, an American scholar of Egyptian origin and director of research at the Institute for Social Policy and Understanding (ISPU) in Washington, D.C. In 2009, she served on President Barack Obama's Advisory Council on Faith-Based and Neighborhood Partnerships by advising the president on how faith-based organizations can help government solve persistent social problems. Ingrid Mattson, a Canadian-born convert to Islam, is the first woman ever to have been elected and to serve as vice president and president of the ISNA. Mattson founded the Islamic Chaplaincy Program at Hartford Seminary, and she currently serves as Chair in Islamic Studies at Huron University College at Western University in Canada. Amina Wadud, a black American convert to Islam and an Islamic studies scholar, led Friday prayers at an Islamic congregation of Muslim men and women in New York in 2005, breaking an Islamic tradition that reserves that role exclusively for men.

Despite the diversity of lived experiences among Muslim women in the United States, they tend to share the experience of being uniquely vulnerable to both Islamophobia and sexism. According to a 2017 Pew Research Center survey, Muslim women have a higher level of concern than Muslim men about the place of Muslims in American society. More Muslim women than men, for example, say that there is "a lot" of discrimination against Muslims in the United States today, that they have personally experienced discrimination, and that it has become more difficult to be Muslim in the United States in recent years. Overall, 83 percent of Muslim women said that there is a lot of discrimination against Muslims in the country, and 55 percent said that they had personally experienced at least one specific incident of discrimination in the past year.

American Muslim women are currently visible targets for harassment and discrimination, especially for women who wear headscarves denoting their Islamic faith (Foran, 2016). The American Civil Liberties Union, a leading civil rights organization that documents hate crimes in the United States, notes that Muslim women have been discriminated against because they wear *hijab* (American Civil Liberties Union, n.d.). Hijab is the Arabic word for the head-covering veil worn by Muslim women in public (Considine, 2017: 185). Muslim women have filed complaints on being denied the right to wear a headscarf while at work, at school, and in law enforcement contexts (American Civil Liberties Union, n.d.). In some schools, Muslim girls who wore headscarves have been harassed, assaulted, and even, in several cases, denied the right to wear *hijab*. Muslim girls and women have also been denied the right to enter public buildings, shopping malls, swimming pools, and amusement parks unless they submit to being searched by male officers or agree to remove their head coverings that they wear for religious reasons.

Civil rights complaints filed by the Council on American-Islamic Relations (CAIR), a Muslim advocacy group, rose from 366 in 2000 to 2,467 in 2006, an increase of 674 percent (Council on American-Islamic Relations, 2007). In January 2017, CAIR filed civil rights complaints with the U.S. Customs and Border Protection (CPB), the U.S. Department of Homeland Security, and the U.S. Department of Justice over reports of systematic questioning of American Muslim citizens by CPB about their religious and political views. The complaints outlined increased scrutiny of American Muslims' social media accounts and the contents of mobile phones, along with interrogations about constitutionally protected beliefs (Council on American-Islamic Relations, 2017).

Domestic violence is a less visible, but equally important, challenge that some U.S. Muslim women face. While there are no solid statistics on the rate of domestic violence within the American Muslim population, advocacy groups say that it is a significant problem. A survey carried out by Peaceful Families Project (PFP), an initiative with international reach that works toward ending all types of abuse, including emotional, spiritual, physical, and sexual abuse, in Muslim families, is a case in point. A PFP poll of 801 Muslim women found that 31 percent experienced abuse within an intimate partner relationship, and 53 percent reported experiencing some form of domestic violence during their lifetime (Peaceful Families Project and Project Sakinah, 2011). Another survey carried out by the ISPU, a solution-seeking research organization that seeks to empower American Muslims, found that among American Muslims, 13 percent said that they knew someone in their faith community who was a victim of domestic violence in 2016 (Mogahed & Chouhoud, 2017). The ISPU poll also revealed that Muslim women were equally likely to report domestic violence as Jews, Catholics, Protestants, and non-affiliated Americans.

Speaking on domestic violence, Dalia Mogahed, the director of research of ISPU, stated that Muslims stood out "not in the frequency of domestic violence, but in the way victims looked to community and religious leaders for supports, where the majority of Muslims said the victim reported the incident to a faith or community leader. . . . This suggests that Muslim victims believed that behavior was reprehensible in their faith tradition and therefore expected to find support from an *imam*" (Mogahed, 2017). Imam is an Arabic word meaning "leader" or "prayer leader" (Considine, 2017: 184).

In light of the challenge of combatting domestic violence, American Muslim women joined together to form Daya, a South Asian immigrant organization that documents domestic and sexual violence (Daya, n.d.). Daya saw a dramatic increase in 2008 of distress calls to its domestic violence hotline. Its records revealed 3,308 calls in 2007 compared to 189 calls in 2003 (Fox News, 2008). Another women's rights organization, the Asian Pacific Institute on Gender-Based Violence, created an online "directory of domestic violence programs serving Muslim communities for Muslim victims/survivors of domestic violence [and] service providers and advocates who assist abused Muslim women." The directory included a breakdown of "organizations serving Muslim women, immigrant and refugee women from the Middle East and Central, East, South, Southeast and West Asia" (Asian Pacific Institute, n.d.). The rate of domestic violence against Muslim women in the United States might even be higher considering that only half say that the crime was reported to law enforcement (Asian Pacific Institute, n.d.).

Speaking on the legacy of Prophet Muhammad, Akbar Ahmed, author of the award-winning book *Islam Today: A Short Introduction to the Muslim World*, claims that the women in Muhammad's household provide ideal models for Muslim women: "They are caring, committed and, most important, involved in life around them. Above all, they have immense dignity. These are not the shy, retiring, ineffectual creatures of the [Islamophobic] stereotypes. They participate in the lives of their family, contributing to and enriching it" (Ahmed, 2002).

The unfortunate stories of prominent ex-Muslim women, like Ayaan Hirsi Ali, are often held up as "proof" of the inherent misogyny of Islam and the barbarity of Islamic law (sharia) as it concerns the treatment of women in Muslim communities. Hirsi's global best-selling book *Infidel: My Life* (Ali, 2008) transported readers to Somalia, where she endured genital mutilation as a young girl, and to Kenya, where she willingly wore a full *hijab* and supported the *fatwa* calling for the death of those who insult Islam. Years later, when she moved to the Netherlands, she denounced Islam and worked with Director Theo Van Gogh on a film critical of the faith's treatment of women (Dominus, 2015).

In another book, *Heretic: Why Islam Needs a Reformation Now* (Ali, 2015), Hirsi Ali argues that "Islamic violence is rooted not in social, economic or political conditions—or even in theological error—but rather in the foundational texts of Islam itself." Such narratives are then extrapolated to make widespread claims about Islam being an outdated patriarchal faith that calls for the oppression of women (Muhammad, 2016). Such stories and declarations have had a significant impact on assumptions within the U.S. general public that the lives of American Muslim women are severely circumscribed by sexist if not outright misogynistic attitudes about gender roles. Many American Muslims, however—both men and women—argue that these assumptions are erroneous, outdated, or incomplete.

FURTHER READING

Ahmed, Akbar. (2002). *Islam Today: A Short Introduction to the Muslim World.* New York, NY: I.B. Tauris.

Ali, Ayaan H. (2008). *Infidel: My Life.* New York, NY: Atria Books.

Ali, Ayaan H. (2015). *Heretic: Why Islam Needs a Reformation Now.* New York, NY: Harper.

American Civil Liberties Union. (n.d.). "Discrimination against Muslim Women—Fact Sheet." New York, NY: ACLU. Retrieved from https://www.aclu.org/other/discrimination-against-muslim-women-fact-sheet

Asian Pacific Institute. (n.d.). *Directory of Domestic Violence Programs Serving Muslims.* Oakland, CA: Asian Pacific Institute. Retrieved from http://www.api-gbv.org/resources/programs-serving-muslims.php

Bano, Masooda, & Kalmbach, Hilary E. (2012). *Women, Leadership, and Mosques: Changes in Contemporary Islamic Authority.* Leiden, The Netherlands: Brill.

Blumberg, Antonia. (2016, December 12). "17 Muslim American Women Who Made America Great in 2016." *The Huffington Post.* Retrieved from http://www.huffingtonpost.com/entry/17-muslim-american-women-who-made-america-great-in-2016_us_584204b7e4b09e21702ec3b1

Considine, Craig. (2017). *Islam, Race, and Pluralism in the Pakistani Diaspora.* London and New York, NY: Routledge.

Council on American-Islamic Relations. (2007). *The Status of Muslim Civil Rights in the United States 2007.* Washington, DC: Council on American-Islamic Relations. Retrieved from https://www.cair.com/images/pdf/CAIR-2007-Civil-Rights-Report.pdf

Council on American-Islamic Relations. (2017, January 18). "CAIR Files Complaints with CPB, DHS and DOJ Over Questioning of American Muslims about Religious and Political Views." Washington, DC: Council on American-Islamic Relations. Retrieved from https://www.cair.com/press-center/press-releases/14021-cair-files-complaints-with-cbp-dhs-and-doj-over-questioning-of-american-muslims-about-religious-and-political-viewswww.html

Daya Houston. (n.d.). "Our Mission." Dayahouston.org. Retrieved from https://www.dayahouston.org/mission-history

Dominus, Susan. (2015, April 1). "Ayaan Hirsi Ali's 'Heretic.'" *The New York Times.* Retrieved from https://www.nytimes.com/2015/04/05/books/review/ayaan-hirsi-alis-heretic.html

Eltantawy, Nahed M. (2007). "U.S. Newspaper Representation of Muslim and Arab Women Post 9/11." scholarworks.gsu.edu. Retrieved from https://scholarworks.gsu.edu/cgi/viewcontent.cgi?referer=https://www.google.com/&httpsredir=1&article=1017&context=communication_diss

Faith Trust Institute. (n.d.a.). "About Us." Faithtrustinstitute.org. Seattle, WA: Faith Trust Institute. Retrieved from http://www.faithtrustinstitute.org/about-us

Faith Trust Institute. (n.d.b.). "Domestic Violence and Muslim Women FAQs." Seattle, WA: Faith Trust Institute. Retrieved from http://www.faithtrustinstitute.org/resources/learn-the-basics/dv-muslim-women-faqs#Are Muslim women abused more?

Foran, Clare. (2016, August 24). "How American Muslim Women Are Taking on Trump." *The Atlantic.* https://www.theatlantic.com/politics/archive/2016/08/muslim-women-trump-islamophobia-ghazala-khan/496925/

Fox News. (2008, January 31). "Abuse of U.S. Muslim Women Is Greater Than Reported, Advocacy Group Says." FoxNews.com. Retrieved from http://www.foxnews.com/story/2008/01/31/abuse-us-muslim-women-is-greater-than-reported-advocacy-groups-say.html

Hasan, Asma G. (2004). *Why I Am a Muslim: An American Odyssey.* London: Element.

Hussein, Asmaa. (2015). *A Temporary Gift: Reflections on Love, Loss, and Healing.* Ruqaya's Bookshelf.

Iovine, Anna. (2017, February 1). "Woman Has Explosive Reaction after Being Told 'Muslim Women Are Oppressed.'" AOL.com. Retrieved from https://www.aol.com/article/news/2017/02/01/woman-has-explosive-reaction-after-being-told-muslim-women-are/21704978/

Islam Web. (n.d.). "Are Muslim Women Oppressed." IslamWeb.net. Retrieved from http://www.islamweb.net/en/article/109366/are-muslim-women-oppressed

Jarema, Kerri. (2017, March 27). "11 Books by Muslim Women Writers to Add to Your TBR Right Now." *Bustle.* Retrieved from https://www.bustle.com/p/11-books-by-muslim-women-writers-to-add-to-your-tbr-right-now-47140

Lamrabet, Asma. (2016). *Women in the Qu'ran: An Emancipatory Reading.* Markfield, UK: Kube Publishing.

Ma'ruf, Sakdiyah. (2016, November 16). "Want to Talk about Oppressed Muslim Women? Let's Talk about Kendall Jenner First." *The Sunday Morning Herald.* Retrieved from http://www.smh.com.au/lifestyle/news-and-views/opinion/sakdiyah-maruf-how-to-spot-a-muslim-20161115-gspoh0.html

Maznavi, M. Hasna. (2016, May 20). "9 Things You Should Know about the Women's Mosque of America—and Muslim Women in General." *The Huffington Post*. Retrieved from http://www.huffingtonpost.com/ m-hasna-maznavi/9-things-you-should-know-about-the-womens_ b_7339582.html

Messina-Dysert, Gina, Zobair, Jennifer, & Levin, Amy. (2015). *Faithfully Feminist: Jewish, Christian, and Muslim Feminists on Why We Stay*. Ashland, OR: White Cloud Press.

Mogahed, Dalia. (2017, May 22). "Foreword." YaqeenInstitute.org. Retrieved from https://yaqeeninstitute.org/en/tesneem-alkiek/islam-and-violence-against-women/#Foreword

Mogahed, Dalia, & Chouhoud, Youssef. (2017). *American Muslim Poll 2017: Muslims at the Crossroads*. Washington, DC: The Institute for Social Policy and Understanding. Retrieved from http://www.ispu.org/ wp-content/uploads/2017/05/AMP-2017_Full-Report.pdf

Mogahed, Yasmin. (2015). *Reclaim Your Heart: Personal Insights on Breaking Free from Life's Shackles*. FB Publishing.

Muhammad, Hakeem. (2016, July 14). "The Oppression of Muslim Women by White Supremacy." Patheos.com. Retrieved from http://www .patheos.com/blogs/truthtopower/2016/07/theoppressionofmuslim womenbywhitesupremacy/

Peaceful Families Project. (n.d.). "Mission." Great Falls, VA: Peaceful Families Project. Retrieved from http://www.peacefulfamilies.org/mission-and-objectives/

Peaceful Families Project and Project Sakinah. (2011). *The Attitudes of Muslim Men and Women towards Domestic Violence*. Great Falls, VA and Abiqui, NM: Peaceful Families Project and Project Sakinah. Retrieved from http://projectsakinah.org/2011-Survey

Pew Research Center. (2009, December 17). *Little Support for Terrorism among Muslim Americans*. Washington, DC: Pew Research Center. Retrieved from http://www.pewforum.org/2009/12/17/little-support-for-terrorism-among-muslim-americans/

Pew Research Center. (2011, August 30). *Muslim Americans: No Signs of Growth in Alienation or Support for Extremism*. Washington, DC: Pew Research Center. Retrieved from http://www.people-press.org/ 2011/08/30/muslim-americans-no-signs-of-growth-in-alienation-or-support-for-extremism/?beta=true&utm_expid=53098246-2.Lly 4CFSVQG2lphsg-KopIg.1&utm_referrer=https%3A%2F%2Fwww .google.com%2F

Pew Research Center. (2017, July 26). *U.S. Muslims Concerned about Their Place in Society, but Continue to Believe in the American*

Dream. Washington, DC: Pew Research Center. Retrieved from http:// www.pewforum.org/2017/07/26/findings-from-pew-research-centers-2017-survey-of-us-muslims/

The Pluralism Project. (n.d.). "Women in Islam." Retrieved from http://pluralism.org/religions/islam/issues-for-muslims-in-america/ women-in-islam/

Sayeed, Sarah, Al-Adawiya, Aisha, & Bagby, Ihsan. (2013, March). *Women and the American Mosque.* Plainfield, IN: Islamic Society of North America. Retrieved from http://www.hartfordinstitute.org/The-American-Mosque-Report-3.pdf

TED Speaker. (n.d.). "Dalia Mogahed." TED.com. Retrieved from https:// www.ted.com/speakers/dalia_mogahed

Women's Mosque of America. (n.d.). "About." WomensMosque.com. Retrieved from http://womensmosque.com/about-2/

Yan, Holly. (2015, December 9). "The Truth about Muslims in America." CNN.com. Retrieved from http://www.cnn.com/2015/12/08/us/muslims-in-america-shattering-misperception/index.html

Yiannopoulos, Milo. (2017, January 28). "MILO Thrashes Heckling Muslim Women at New Mexico." *Breitbart.* Retrieved from https://www .youtube.com/watch?v=SHZBGidQcEs

Younis, Mohamed. (2009, March 2). "Muslim Americans Exemplify Diversity, Potential." Washington, DC: Gallup.com. Retrieved from http://www.gallup.com/poll/116260/muslim-americans-exemplify-diversity-potential.aspx

Q10. DO AMERICAN MUSLIM VOTERS ADHERE TO ONE POLITICAL IDEOLOGY IN TERMS OF PARTIES AND SOCIAL VALUES IN THE UNITED STATES?

Answer: No. All American Muslim citizens do not vote for the same political party in the United States. Their primary political allegiances, however, have shifted markedly since the late 1990s, when they were more likely to vote Republican. The overwhelming majority of American Muslims today vote in support of Democratic candidates in U.S. elections.

The Facts: Data and expert opinion reveal that American Muslims have assimilated into the U.S. political culture by adopting mainstream ideologies, political party identifications, and policy positions held by longer-settled U.S. citizens (Wilson & Nowrasteh, 2015). When it comes to social, cultural, and political views, U.S. Muslims are more likely to identify with or lean toward the Democratic Party than the Republican Party. Two thirds of American Muslims today either identify as Democrats or prefer the Democratic Party; far fewer (13 percent) identify as Republican or lean toward the GOP (Pew Research Center, 2017).

When asked by Pew how they voted in the 2016 presidential election, over three quarters of Muslim voters (78 percent) said they backed Hillary Clinton, 8 percent said they voted for Donald Trump, and 14 percent said they voted for another candidate or declined to say how they voted (Pew Research Center, 2017). In terms of their views of the Republican Party, just 15 percent of American Muslim respondents to a 2016 survey said Republicans are friendly toward Muslims.

In the 2008 presidential election, one poll found that an overwhelming 92 percent of American Muslims voted for Senator Barack Obama, a Democrat. The American Muslim Task Force on Civil Rights and Elections, a research outlet of the Council on American-Islamic Relations (CAIR), found that 89 percent of 600 Muslims from more than 10 states, including swing states like Florida and Pennsylvania, voted for Senator Obama in 2008 (*Newsweek*, 2008). The Gallup Center found that American Muslims favored Obama in greater numbers than did Hispanics (67 percent of whom voted for Obama) and nearly matched that of African Americans, 93 percent of whom voted for Obama (*Newsweek*, 2008). Many American Muslims voted for Obama because, among other reasons, he rejected the politics of fear, and challenged Americans to embrace the collective identity of the United States, where each American has a stake in the success and well-being of every American. He considered Muslims "a valued part of the American family" (Obama, 2016).

Research carried out by the Council on American-Islamic Relations (2012) reveals other reasons why American Muslims tend to vote for Democratic candidates. With respect to perception of political party commitment and to core American principles, 61 percent of Muslims in the United States felt that Democrats are more concerned with protecting religious freedom, a 7 percent hike since a similar 2008 CAIR survey. The 2012 CAIR survey also revealed that 68 percent of American Muslims think that Democrats are more likely to treat all Americans equally (Council on American-Islamic Relations, 2012). Both the Democratic and Republican parties were also evaluated by perceptions of "friendliness to Muslims." Forty-nine percent of the respondents said the Democratic Party was friendly toward Muslims, while only 12 percent said that the Republican Party was friendly (Council on American-Islamic Relations, 2012).

U.S. Muslim citizens have not always looked so unfavorably upon the Republican Party. In the 2000 presidential election, more than 70 percent of American Muslims voted for George W. Bush and the Republican Party (Khan, 2015a). During his campaign, Bush met regularly with American Muslims across the country and visited a prominent Islamic center in Michigan—the first major presidential candidate from either the Republican or Democratic party to do so (Khan, 2015b).

President Dwight D. Eisenhower, a Republican, is believed to hold the distinction of being the first president to visit a U.S. mosque (Begley, 2016). In 1957, President Eisenhower visited the Islamic Center of Washington, DC, where he gave a speech emphasizing the importance of religious freedom. He noted, "under the American Constitution . . . this place of worship, is just as welcome as could be a similar edifice of any other religion." Eisenhower even went as far as stating that the United States "would fight with her whole strength for your right to have here your own church and worship according to your own conscience" (Eisenhower, 1957).

President George W. Bush followed Eisenhower's lead six days after the 9/11 attacks when he visited the same Washington, D.C., mosque. President Bush gave an address in which he famously said "Islam is peace" (Bush, 2001). "The face of terror is not the true faith of Islam. . . . These terrorists don't represent peace."

The Republican Party National Convention of 2000 in Philadelphia was the first in either national party's history to feature an Islamic prayer. Bush's inclusive efforts during that year's presidential campaign ultimately earned him the endorsement of major American Muslim organizations. Weeks before the 2000 presidential election, the American Muslim Political Coordinating Council Political Action Committee (AMPCC-PAC), an umbrella organization that includes the four major American Muslim organizations, endorsed George W. Bush over Al Gore, the Democratic candidate. The AMPCC-PAC is made up of the American Muslim Alliance, American Muslim Council, Council on American-Islamic Relations, and Muslim Public Affairs Council (Beliefnet, 2000). In its endorsement, the AMPCC-PAC cited Bush's outreach to the Muslim community and his stand in opposition to the use of "secret evidence" against American Muslims in U.S. courts (Beliefnet, 2000). At that time, U.S. Islamic organizations believed "secret evidence," as it had been used in Immigration and Naturalization Service deportation hearings, was unconstitutional; they also believed that American Muslims had been disproportionately targeted (Beliefnet, 2000).

In the hotly contested state of Florida during the 2000 presidential election, most of the state's 50,000 Muslim voters voted for Bush, who won the state by a mere 537 votes after a dispute that was eventually decided by the U.S. Supreme Court (Farivar, 2016a). Once in the White House, President Bush appointed a record number of American Muslims to senior positions within his administration. According to Suhail Khan, a prominent American Muslim Republican and former board member of the American Conservative Union, Muslims in the United States are by and large both socially and economically conservative and therefore a natural Republican constituency (Farivar, 2016a). Many American Muslims also share conservative Republican positions on traditional marriage and abortion (Farivar, 2016a).

Despite the tremendous support for George W. Bush during the 2000 presidential election, the American Muslim voting bloc shifted its political allegiance to the Democratic Party in 2004. The most obvious reason for the shift was the adoption of anti-Muslim rhetoric by some Republican politicians and the perception among many Muslims that the Republican Party was transforming into a "hotbed of Islamophobia" (Farivar, 2016a). Robert McCaw of the CAIR described the Republican Party as the epicenter of Islamophobia due to their introducing anti-Muslim policy proposals or anti-foreigner laws in at least 10 state legislatures since 2000 (Farivar, 2016a). Reports have also suggested that American Muslims turned away from the Republican Party during the Bush administration because of their unhappiness with GOP stances on civil liberties, from wiretapping U.S. Muslim citizens to detaining Muslims in the United States and Guantanamo Bay, Cuba, without due process and trial (*Newsweek*, 2008). Moreover, the 2003 invasion of Iraq to overthrow Saddam Hussein was initially popular with the American public. But the troubled subsequent occupation of the country, which included heavy U.S. troop casualties, brought heavy public criticism of the administration. All of these factors have been cited as contributors to the shift of American Muslims toward the Democratic Party in the 2004, 2008, and 2016 presidential elections.

In the 2016 presidential election, comments made by Republican Party candidate Donald Trump were decried by many American Muslims—and indeed many other U.S. citizens—as both racist and Islamophobic.

In an interview with *Yahoo News!* in November 2015, for example, Trump did not rule out the idea of establishing a government database specifically to track Muslims. Asked if the database would include "registering Muslims in a database or giving them a form of special identification that noted their religion," Trump did not say "yes" or "no"; instead, he stated, "We're going to have to look at a lot of things very closely. We're going to have to look at the mosques. We're going to have to look very, very carefully" (Walker, 2015). One month later, he called for "a total and complete shutdown of Muslims" entering the country.

Trump also fought publicly with Khizr and Ghazala Khan, a Gold Star family whose son, Humayun, died fighting for the U.S. Armed Forces in Iraq. After Khizr Khan criticized Trump in a speech at the Democratic National Convention, Trump suggested that Ghazala was an "oppressed Muslim woman" who had not been allowed to speak at the Democratic National Convention because Islam prevents women from speaking openly. This remark was roundly condemned by American Muslims, Democrats, and the Khans themselves.

An Institute for Social Policy and Understanding poll revealed that only 15 percent of Muslims favored a Trump presidency, while a slim majority (54 percent) supported a Hillary Clinton presidency (Mogahed & Chouhoud, 2017). A substantial portion of the American Muslim population (30 percent) also did not favor either of the two major party presidential candidates in 2016 (Mogahed & Chouhoud, 2017). In another poll carried out in October 2016 by CAIR, only 3 percent of Muslim voters said they would vote for Donald Trump in the upcoming election, while 72 percent of Muslims said that they intended to cast their vote for Hillary Clinton (Council on American-Islamic Relations, 2016). The percentage of those who said their politics aligned more closely with the Democratic Party remained constant, from 66 percent in a similar poll taken in 2012 to 67 percent in October 2016, after having increased from 49 percent in a similar poll taken in 2008 (Council on American-Islamic Relations, 2016).

In December 2016, American Muslim leaders sent an open letter to President-elect Donald Trump, calling on him to "reconsider and reject" some of the individuals recently named to his administration who had "a well-documented history of outright bigotry directed at Muslims or advocating that Muslims should not have the same rights as their fellow Americans" (Muslim Letter to Trump, 2016). The letter read, in part, "[American Muslims] are deeply troubled by reports that your team is actively considering proposals that would target Muslims based on religion and violate their Constitutional rights" (Muslim Letter to Trump, 2016).

Notwithstanding these concerns, some American Muslims did vote for Trump in 2016. According to a survey carried out by Zogby Analytics, a research outlet that produces data on American Muslims, a total of 12 percent of Arab Americans, some of them Muslims, said they voted for Trump (Guadiano, 2016). More American Muslims also voted for Trump than for Republican presidential nominee Mitt Romney during the 2008 presidential election. According to a CAIR exit poll, a total of 13 percent of Muslims voted for Trump and 74 percent voted for Hillary Clinton

(Council on American-Islamic Relations, 2016). In 2012, President Barack Obama received 85.7 percent of the Muslim vote and Romney received 4.4 percent (Council on American-Islamic Relations, 2016).

Saba Ahmed, an attorney and president of the Republican Muslim Coalition, voted for Trump despite Trump's rhetoric. In a 2016 Al Jazeera interview, Ahmed stated that the Republican Party appeals to her because of shared values such as being pro-life, in favor of traditional marriage, and supportive of business- and trade-friendly policies. She differentiated herself from the Democratic Party, which she described as too liberal in terms of its pro-choice, pro-LGBTQ, pro-tax positions (Younes, 2016).

Political party preferences aside, American Muslims are increasingly involved in U.S. politics at the local, state, and national levels. In terms of voter registration, CAIR found in a survey that 86 percent of registered American Muslim voters intended to vote in the 2016 elections (Council on American-Islamic Relations, 2016). The U.S. Council of Muslim Organizations, an umbrella group of two dozen Muslim advocacy organizations, claimed that more than one million American Muslims were registered to vote in the 2016 U.S. elections, a record number that put the community in a position to tip the race in swing states (Farivar, 2016b). The U.S. Council of Muslim Organizations also initiated a yearlong campaign called "One Million Voters," which more than doubled the number of registered Muslim voters in the United States since the 2012 presidential election (Farivar, 2016b). To get more Muslims to vote, Islamic advocacy organizations set up registration booths at more than 2,500 mosques, 500 schools, and a multitude of community centers throughout the year (Farivar, 2016b).

Jetpac, a nonprofit organization that "exists to empower minority communities through targeted training and civic education programs," is one of several voter movements to increase the level of political participation and engagement among U.S. Muslims (Jetpac, n.d.). Founded by Nadeem Mazen, the first Muslim city councilor in Massachusetts, Jetpac was started to provide training and resources for American Muslim candidates and allies "so that they too can represent and serve their communities" (Jetpac, n.d.).

U.S. Muslims are increasingly involved in running for—and serving in—political offices. In 2006, Keith Ellison (D-MN) became the first ever Muslim to serve in Congress, having been elected to represent Minnesota's fifth congressional district. Ellison, an African American convert, was reelected to Congress in 2010 and 2014.

Ellison is known for swearing his oath of allegiance on a Qur'an that had belonged to Thomas Jefferson, a coauthor of *The Declaration of*

Independence and the third president of the United States. Jefferson wrote in 1821 about freedom of religion extending to "the Jew and the Gentile, the Christian and Mahometan [Muslim], the Hindoo [Hindu] and infidel of every denomination" (Library of Congress, n.d.). There was, however, controversy over the ceremony. Conservative commentators insisted that Ellison be sworn in on the Bible, even though legal scholars agreed that such a requirement would amount to an unconstitutional "religious test" (Hussain, 2016).

André Carson (D-IN), the U.S. representative of Indiana's seventh congressional district, is the second ever Muslim elected to Congress. In 2015, he became the first Muslim lawmaker to serve on the House Intelligence Committee, which is charged with oversight of the United States' most sensitive national intelligence capabilities and operations. Carson also is the ranking member on its Emerging Threats Subcommittee and a member of the U.S. Department of Defense Intelligence and Overhead Architecture Subcommittee.

Several other American Muslims have emerged as the next line of U.S. politicians. Abdul El-Sayed, a U.S. physician and a Democratic candidate for governor of Michigan in the 2018 Democratic Party primary, was inspired to run for governor following the water crisis in Flint (Rifai, 2017). He has received support from many notable U.S. public figures, including author Reza Aslan, Women's March Organizer Linda Sarsour, and civil rights activist Shaun King. If El-Sayed wins, he will be the first Muslim governor in the history of the United States (Philip, 2017).

At the state level, American Muslims serve in political leadership positions across the country. Faisal Gill, a Pakistani-born lawyer and one-time Democratic candidate for the Vermont State senate in Chittenden county, served as the chair of the Vermont Democratic Party as of 2018. He is believed to be the country's first Muslim chairperson of a state political party.

Several Islamic organizations and Muslim advocacy groups also involve themselves in U.S. politics. The Muslim Political Affairs Council, founded in 1988, represents a broad range of national Islamic organizations whose aim is to expose discrimination of Muslims, organize Muslims as a mainstream political force, and lobby Congress and other administration bodies on issues of concern to American Muslims. The American Muslim Democratic Caucus, a political organization, has been working with the Democratic Party to help provide better political representation for American Muslims across the country (Voice of America, 2016). While these institutions are influenced by the ideas of "political Islam," their goals are not the same. None have worked to establish an "Islamic state" in the United States (Khan, 2015a).

Despite the recent strides that American Muslims have made in becoming politically assimilated, they still enter the U.S. political realm with an inherent disadvantage. Anti-Muslim bias is reflected in the way the American public views Muslims as potential political leaders. A Muslim candidate for president today would face a significant amount of prejudice in seeking the presidency, the highest political office in the United States (Keeter & Kohut, 2005). Polls indicate that a Muslim candidate would face significant resistance in a presidential election. According to Gallup, 40 percent of Americans in 2015 said they would not support a "qualified" Muslim for president (Saad, 2015). Sixty-six percent of Protestants said they would not vote for a qualified Muslim in a presidential election (Saad, 2015). A 2003 Pew Research Center poll found similar data—38 percent of Americans said that they would not vote for a well-qualified Muslim for president (Keeter & Kohut, 2005). In contrast, only 10 percent said this about a Jewish candidate and 8 percent said it about a Catholic candidate (Keeter & Kohut, 2005).

Another disadvantage facing American Muslims in terms of entering the American political system is that they lack experience—although this will of course fade as the years progress, which has been the case with other religious and ethnic communities over the course of U.S. history (Nimer, 2005). In terms of their voting power, the American Muslim vote remains relatively small, but with larger Muslim communities in Florida, Ohio, Virginia, Michigan, and Pennsylvania, experts say their vote is likely to prove critical in tipping tight races in key swing states in the future (Farivar, 2016a).

FURTHER READING

Begley, Sarah. (2016, February 3). "Here's the First Time a U.S. President Visited an American Mosque." *TIME*. Retrieved from http://time.com/4205979/obama-mosque-visit-history/

Beliefnet. (2000, October 23). "American Muslim Group Endorses Bush." Beliefnet.com. Retrieved from http://www.beliefnet.com/faiths/2000/11/american-muslim-group-endorses-bush.aspx

Bush, George W. (2001, September 17). " 'Islam Is Peace' Says President." Washington, DC: The White House Archives. Retrieved from https://georgewbush-whitehouse.archives.gov/news/releases/2001/09/20010917-11.html

Center for Security Policy. (2015, February 24). *Center Releases Dossier Documenting a House Intelligence Committee Member's Extensive Ties* to the *Muslim Brotherhood*. Washington, DC: Center for Security Policy. Retrieved from https://www.centerforsecuritypolicy.org/2015/02/24/center-releases-dossier-documenting-a-house-intelligence-committee-members-extensive-ties-to-the-muslim-brotherhood/

Council on American-Islamic Relations. (2012, October 24). *American Muslim Voters and the 2012 Election: A Demographic Profile and Survey of Attitudes.* Washington, DC: Council on American-Islamic Relations. Retrieved from https://www.cair.com/images/pdf/American_Muslim_Voter_Survey_2012.pdf

Council on American-Islamic Relations. (2016, October 13). *American Muslim Voters and the 2016 Election: A Demographic Profile and Survey of Attitudes.* Washington, DC: Council on American-Islamic Relations. Retrieved from https://www.cair.com/images/pdf/CAIR_2016_Election_Report.pdf

Cowen, Tyler. (2017, February 23). "The Real Assimilation Dilemma." marginalrevolution.com. Retrieved from http://marginalrevolution.com/marginalrevolution/2017/02/real-assimilation-dilemma.html

Eisenhower, Dwight D. (1957, June 28). "U.S. Presidential Visits to Domestic Mosques." Washington, DC: The White House Historical Association. Retrieved from https://www.whitehousehistory.org/press-room/press-fact-sheets/u-s-presidential-visits-to-domestic-mosques

Ellison, Keith. (2016, September 10). "I'm the First Muslim in Congress. I Believe American Can Beat Islamophobia." *The Washington Post.* Retrieved from https://www.washingtonpost.com/posteverything/wp/2016/09/10/im-the-first-muslim-in-congress-i-believe-america-can-beat-islamophobia/?utm_term=.3cad9a61ed6b

Farivar, Masood. (2016a, September 7). "How Muslim-Americans Drifted to the Democratic Party." Voice of America News. Retrieved from http://www.voanews.com/a/muslim-americans-drifted-democratic-party/3496782.html

Farivar, Masood. (2016b, November 2). "More Than 1 Million US Muslims Now Registered to Vote." Voice of America News. Retrieved from https://www.voanews.com/a/us-election-muslim-voters/3576727.html

Garsd, Jasmine. (2015, January 13). "Rep. André Carson to Become First Muslim on House Committee on Intelligence." NPR.org. Retrieved from http://www.npr.org/sections/thetwo-way/2015/01/13/376998473/congressman-andr-carson-to-become-first-muslim-on-house-committee-on-intelligenc

Goldfarb, Zachary A. (2006, December 21). "Va. Lawmaker's Remarks on Muslims Criticized." *The Washington Post*. Retrieved from http://www.washingtonpost.com/wp-dyn/content/article/2006/12/20/AR2006122001318.html?tid=a_inl

Groppe, Maureen. (2015, December 8). "Muslim Congressman Reports Death Threat." *USA Today*. Retrieved from https://www.usatoday.com/story/news/politics/2015/12/08/muslim-rep-andre-carson-says-he-received-death-threat/76999142/

Guadiano, Nicole. (2016, October 25). "Despite Rhetoric, Trump Backed by Some Arab-American Muslims." Zogby Analytics. Retrieved from https://zogbyanalytics.com/news/758-despite-rhetoric-trump-backed-by-some-arab-american-muslims

Huda, Qamar-ul. (2006, February). *The Diversity of Muslims in the United States—Special Report*. Washington, DC: United States Institute of Peace. Retrieved from https://www.usip.org/sites/default/files/sr159.pdf

Hussain, Amir. (2016). *Muslims and the Making of America*. Waco, TX: Baylor University Press.

Ismail, Aymann. (2017, March 7). "What Assimilation Problem, Donald." Slate.com. Retrieved from http://www.slate.com/articles/news_and_politics/politics/2017/03/the_white_house_s_beliefs_about_muslim_assimilation_are_completely_bogus.html

Jetpac. (n.d.). "Our Mission." Cambridge, MA: Jetpac, Inc. Retrieved from http://www.jet-pac.com/about/#mission

Keeter, Scott, & Kohut, Andrew. (2005, May 11). "American Public Opinion about Muslims in the U.S. and Abroad." In: *Muslims in the United States: Identity, Influence, Innovation*. Washington, DC: Woodrow Wilson International Center for Scholars.

Khan, M. A. Muqtedar. (2015a). "Political Muslims in America: From Islamism to Exceptionalism." *Middle East Policy*, 22(1): 32–40.

Khan, Suhail A. (2015b, December 18.). "Islam Is All-American." *Foreign Policy*. Retrieved from http://foreignpolicy.com/2015/12/18/one-nation-under-allah-american-muslim-obama-trump/

Library of Congress. (n.d.). "The Thomas Jefferson Papers at the Library of Congress." Washington, DC: Library of Congress. Retrieved from https://www.loc.gov/teachers/classroommaterials/connections/thomas-jefferson/history3.html

Malone, Scott. (2017, October 1). "Muslim-American Massachusetts Activist Launches Run for Congress." *Reuters*. Retrieved from https://www.reuters.com/article/us-massachusetts-congress-mazen/muslim-american-massachusetts-activist-launches-run-for-congress-idUSKCN1C61A5

Mogahed, Dalia, & Chouhoud, Youssef. (2017). *American Muslim Poll 2017: Muslims at the Crossroads.* Washington, DC: The Institute For Social Policy and Understanding. Retrieved from http://www.ispu.org/wp-content/uploads/2017/05/AMP-2017_Full-Report.pdf

Muslim Letter to Trump. (2016, December 5). "Open Letter: From American Muslim Leaders to President-Elect Trump." Retrieved from http://www.muslimlettertotrump.com/

Neufeld, Jeremy L. (2017, April 3). "Do Muslim Immigrants Assimilate?" Washington, DC: Niskanen Center. Retrieved from https://niskanen center.org/blog/muslim-immigrants-assimilate/

Newsweek. (2008, November 6). "American Muslims Overwhelmingly Backed Obama." Retrieved from http://www.newsweek.com/american-muslims-overwhelmingly-backed-obama-85173

Nimer, Abu. (2005, May 11). *Muslims in the United States: Identity, Influence, Innovation.* Washington, DC: Woodrow Wilson International Center for Scholars.

Obama, Barack. (2016, July 21). President Obama to Muslim Americans: "You're a Valued Part of the American Family." Washington, DC: The White House. Retrieved from https://obamawhitehouse.archives.gov/blog/2016/07/25/president-obama-hosts-eid-reception

Pew Research Center. (2011, August 30). *Muslim Americans: No Signs of Growth in Alienation or Support for Extremism.* Washington, DC: Pew Research Center. Retrieved from http://www.people-press.org/2011/08/30/muslim-americans-no-signs-of-growth-in-alienation-or-support-for-extremism/

Pew Research Center. (2017, July 26). *U.S. Muslims Concerned about Their Place in Society, but Continue to Believe in the American Dream.* Washington, DC: Pew Research Center. Retrieved from http://www.pew forum.org/2017/07/26/findings-from-pew-research-centers-2017-survey-of-us-muslims/

Philip, Drew. (2017, August 24). " 'The New Obama': Will Abdul El-Sayed Be America's First Muslim Governor?" *The Guardian.* Retrieved from https://www.theguardian.com/us-news/2017/aug/24/next-obama-abdul-el-sayed-first-muslim-governor-michigan

The Pluralism Project. (n.d.). "Muslims and American Politics." Harvard University. Retrieved from http://pluralism.org/religions/islam/issues-for-muslims-in-america/muslims-and-american-politics/

Rifai, Ryan. (2017, March 27). "Q&A: The Man Running to Be US' First Muslim Governor." *The Guardian.* Retrieved from https://www.aljazeera.com/indepth/features/2017/03/abdul-el-sayed-running-muslim-governor-170314044707977.html.

Saad, Lydia. (2015, June 24). "Support for Nontraditional Candidates Varies by Religion." Gallup.com. Retrieved from http://www.gallup .com/poll/183791/support-nontraditional-candidates-varies-religion .aspx

Vermont Democratic Party. (n.d.). "Faisal Gill—Chair. Vermont Democratic Party." Retrieved from http://www.vtdemocrats.org/state-committee/ faisal-gill-chair

Voice of America. (2016, August 4). "Muslim-Americans Becoming More Involved in US." Retrieved from https://learningenglish.voan ews.com/a/some-muslim-americans-are-becoming-more-involved-in-us-politics/3445857.html

Walker, Hunter. (2015, November 19). "Donald Trump Has Big Plans for 'Radical Islamic' Terrorists, 2016 and 'That Communist' Bernie Sanders." *Yahoo! News.* Retrieved from https://www.yahoo.com/news/ donald-trump-has-big-plans-1303117537878070.html

Wilson, Sam, & Nowrasteh, Alex. (2015, February 24). "The Political Assimilation of Immigrants and Their Descendants." Washington, DC: CATO Institute. Retrieved from https://www.cato.org/publications/ economic-development-bulletin/political-assimilation-immigrants-their-descendants

Younes, Ali. (2016, February 24). "Saba Ahmed: Urging US Muslims to Vote Republican." AlJazeera.com. Retrieved from http://www .aljazeera.com/indepth/features/2016/02/saba-ahmed-urging-muslims-vote-republican-160223122816776.html

Younis, Mohamed. (2009, March 2). "Muslim Americans Exemplify Diversity, Potential." Gallup.com. Retrieved from http://www.gallup .com/poll/116260/muslim-americans-exemplify-diversity-potential .aspx

Q11. ARE THERE MANY "RADICAL" MOSQUES AROUND THE UNITED STATES?

Answer: No. While there are no precise statistics that measure the number of so-called radical mosques in the United States, several key studies indicate that the overwhelming majority of U.S. mosques are "mainstream" and "integrated" into their multiethnic and multicultural communities.

The Facts: In January 2011, Peter King, a Republican U.S. Representative of New York, appeared on *The Laura Ingraham Show* of Fox News to discuss his claim that mosques in the United States were "infected" by "radical jihad sentiment." Specifically, he told Ingraham that "over 80 percent of mosques in this country are controlled by radical imams" (Keyes, 2011). In previous statements appearing in the media, Representative King had referred to American Muslims as "an enemy living amongst us" and declared there are "too many mosques in this country" (Khanna, 2007). In December 2015, King appeared again on Fox News and stated that mosques in the United States should be under "24/7 surveillance" (Ahmed, 2015). He called on U.S. Department of Homeland Security Committee officials to step up their monitoring of American Muslims. King's demand was criticized by opponents, who charged that he was supporting the type of surveillance used against communists during the "McCarthy era" of the 1950s.

Mosques are not new to the country. According to The Pluralism Project of Harvard University, the first known American mosques were established in Biddeford, Maine, in 1915; in Ross, North Dakota, in 1920; in Highland Park, Michigan, in 1923, and in Michigan City, Indiana, in 1925 (The Pluralism Project, n.d.b.). Declining Muslim immigration and rising assimilation, The Pluralism Project argues, caused most of these mosques to close. In 1934, the building now known as the Mother Mosque of America was established by a Syrian-Lebanese Muslim community in Cedar Rapids, Iowa. The community dates to Muslims who settled in the area in the late 1800s—the Mother Mosque formally opened in 1934, during the Great Depression (Dias, 2016). The area also is home to the Muslim National Cemetery, whose land is in honor of military servicemen who fought in World War II (Dias, 2016).

Researchers from the Council on American-Islamic Relations (CAIR) estimated a total of 2,106 mosques in the United States as of 2012. The CAIR study indicated that the number of U.S. mosques increased 74 percent since 2000 and that Islamic houses of worship are ethnically diverse institutions (Bagby, 2012). According to the Hartford Institute for Religion Research (n.d.), which analyzed the CAIR study, the number of mosques in urban areas is decreasing, while the number of mosques in suburban areas is increasing. In 2011, 28 percent of mosques were located in suburbs, up from 16 percent in 2000 (Hartford Institute for Religion Research, n.d.). In a rough estimate by the Hartford Institute for Religion Research, there is one mosque for every 1,562 Muslims as compared to about one Christian church for every 524 Christians. New York and California have the largest number of mosques, with 257 and 246 mosques, respectively (Hartford Institute for Religion Research, n.d.).

While there are no precise statistics available on the number of so-called radical mosques, CAIR's "Mosque Study," which was conducted over the telephone in English with a sample of more than 500 mosques, asked about how imams or heads of operating boards approach their religion. The overwhelming majority of U.S. mosques were found to be "mainstream" (Bagby, Perl, & Froehle, 2001). On the more conservative end, 21 percent of mosque leaders said that they look toward more traditional interpretations of Islam, and only 6 percent said they are Salafi (Bagby, Perl, & Froehle, 2001). Salafi is a strain of Sunni Islam that derives its name from the Arabic term *salaf*, or "predecessors." Salafism has been described as "literalist," "strict," and "puritanical" and criticized for stifling religious innovation (*bida*) and enforcing Islamic law in Muslim communities (Considine, 2017: 193).

Another comprehensive 2012 survey of American mosque leaders, created by the CAIR, the Islamic Society of North America, and the Islamic Circle of America, "asked hundreds of mosque leaders about the demographics and theological and political leanings of their congregation. More than 98 percent of mosque leaders, which included imams or heads of operating boards, said in the survey that Muslims should be involved in American society, while 91 percent said that Muslims should be involved in politics. The survey also found that 87 percent of mosque leaders disagree that [radicalization] is increasing among young Muslims, whereas 6 percent agreed that it was increasing" (Kaleem, 2012).

While some critics have claimed that mosques try to spread sharia in the United States, in reality, "most mosques in America do not even teach Islamic law for a simple reason: It's too complicated for the average believer and even for some imams" (Curtis, 2010). American Muslims, like Muslims worldwide, do not even agree on what sharia says; there is no one sharia book of laws (Curtis, 2010). According to Asifa Quraishi-Landes, a law professor and expert on Islamic law, sharia is not a book of statutes or judicial precedent imposed by a government, and it is not a set of regulations adjudicated in court (Quraishi-Landes, 2016). Rather, it is a body of Qur'an-based guidance that points Muslims toward living an Islamic life (Quraishi-Landes, 2016).

Representative King's claim that 80 percent of all U.S. mosques are "radical" suggests that all mosques in the country are nearly identical in terms of beliefs, practices, and activities. In reality, the diversity of U.S. mosques around the country reflects the heterogeneity of both the American Muslim population and the *ummah*, or global Muslim population, itself (Considine, 2017: 187). U.S. mosques are diverse in terms of their sects of Islam, ethnic and racial groups, level of outreach, as well as their size and capacity to assist their community members. The Pluralism Project (n.d.a.) of Harvard University, an initiative that documents the religious diversity of American Muslims and U.S. citizens at large, notes that in some larger cities across the country, there appear to be as many different mosques as there are Muslims (The Pluralism Project, n.d.a.). The vast majority of mosques (87 percent) were founded after 1970–62 percent since 1980 (Bagby, 2005). Mosque leadership also reflects this beginning stage, with the current leadership being composed largely of first-generation Americans or first-generation Muslims (Bagby, 2005).

Critics of American Muslims claim that groups and governments unfriendly to the United States fund the construction of mosques on American soil. Yehudit Barsky, whom the *Jerusalem Post* referred to as "an expert on terrorism at the American Jewish Committee [AJC]," claimed that 80 percent of the mosques in the United States "have been radicalized by Saudi money and influence" (Rettig, 2005). Barsky, who also headed the AJC's Division on Middle East and International Terrorism, said this means that "the people now in control of teaching religion [to American Muslims] are extremists" (Rettig, 2005). Brigitte Gabriel, an anti-Islam activist, also baselessly claimed that "over 90 percent of mosques in America" are funded by the Saudi Arabia government in order to teach radical ideology aimed at overturning the U.S. government (Holt, 2017).

In 2007, questions were raised about a US$24 million mosque and cultural center built by the Islamic Society of Boston (ISB) of Boston, Massachusetts. A lawsuit charged against the ISB included claims that the organization "receives funds from Wahhabis and/or Muslim Brotherhood and/or other Saudi/Middle Eastern sources" and that "the ISB Project was supported financially by donors from Saudi Arabia and the Gulf States 'with known connections to radical Islamists' " (Jacoby, 2007). Critics claimed that Wahhabism was the form of "radical Islamism" practiced at the ISB. Wahhabism is a branch of Sunni Islam described as "ultraconservative," "fundamentalist," or "puritanical" (Considine, 2017: 194). The lawsuit charged that the "ISB receives funds from Wahhabis and/or Muslim Brotherhood and/or other Saudi/Middle Eastern sources" (Jacoby, 2007).

Research carried out by the *Boston Globe* found that the major funding of the ISB mosque had been provided by the Islamic Development Bank in Jeddah, Saudi Arabia. The ISB acknowledged receiving US$1 million in financing from the Saudi bank, but its website noted that "all donors are cross checked against the government's terrorist watch list, and that funding is accepted only with no strings attached" (Jacoby, 2007). It noted too that it "rejects any interpretation of Islam that is considered fundamentalist, oppressive, radical, anti-Western, or anti-Semitic" (Jacoby, 2007).

Allegations that America is rife with "radical mosques" and disloyal Muslims have contributed to a marked rise in nationwide anti-mosque activity. In August 2017, the CAIR compiled data on the escalation of anti-Islamic incidents at mosques. According to CAIR's figures, in the first half of 2017, there were 85 such incidents. That is more than the total number of incidents in any year between 2009 and 2015 (Coleman, 2017). CNN also mapped 63 publicly reported incidents from January to July 2017, where mosques "were targets of threats, vandalism or arson" (Coleman, 2017). On average, that comes down to nine attacks every month and at least two a week. According to a joint report tracking increasing Islamophobia issued by CAIR and the University of California–Berkeley Center for Race and Gender, there were 78 attacks on mosques in 2015, the highest number of attacks since CAIR began monitoring such incidents in 2009 (Rathod, 2016). The number of attacks in 2014 reported by organizations like CAIR was only 20, which means mosque attacks in the United States almost quadrupled in a single year (Rathod, 2016).

One attack in particular caught the attention of U.S. media. Just one month after Trump's victory, many mosques across the country reported receiving the same hate-filled Islamophobic letter from California. This letter demanded that American Muslims leave the United States or face genocide (Al Jazeera, 2016). The "letters appeared to be photocopies of a handwritten note referring to Muslims as 'vile and filthy people' and [stating] that Trump would do to Muslims what Hitler did to Jews" during World War II. The CAIR asked the FBI to investigate the Islamophobic letters, but the latter reportedly declined (Al Jazeera, 2016).

In January 2017, the Islamic Center of Victoria in Texas was destroyed in an arson attack (Malewitz, 2017). The Center was set on fire hours after President Trump signed Executive Order 13769 (titled "Protecting the Nation from Foreign Terrorist Entry into the United States"), which barred refugees from entering the United States and restricted travel from seven Muslim-majority countries (Malewitz, 2017). Following the news that its mosque was completely destroyed, the Islamic Center of Victoria set up an online donation drive through GoFundMe to rebuild their place of worship. The online campaign received more than US$600,000 of its US$850,000 goal in 24 hours (Newton, 2017). After the mosque was devastated, the leaders of a local Jewish congregation gave the Victoria Muslim community the keys to their synagogue so they could continue to worship (Criss, 2017).

Discussion on the most controversial "radical" mosque in the United States erupted over the proposed Park51, an Islamic cultural center popularly referred to as the "Ground Zero Mosque." A mosque would have been located inside the final Park51 building, but the structure itself would not serve as a traditional mosque. Alongside a prayer space for Muslims, Park51 would have also included a fitness facility, a 500-seat auditorium, a restaurant and culinary school, a library, an art studio, as well as a 9/11 memorial (Gore, 2010).

The proposed imam of Park51, Feisal Abdul Rauf, had a long history of cooperation with the U.S. government. During the presidential administration of George W. Bush, Abdul Rauf led cultural awareness training for FBI employers in the Bureau's New York field office (Gore, 2010). On three separate occasions between 2007 and 2010, Abdul Rauf "traveled to the Middle East to talk about religious tolerance and Islam in America as part of a speaker program" organized by the U.S. Department of State's Bureau of International Information Programs (Gore, 2010).

Despite the assurances that Park51 would serve as a cultural and inter-faith center, among other services, a stream of U.S. politicians, religious leaders, and anti-Muslim activists came out against the construction (Saletan, 2010). Representative Peter King (R-NY) called the project "particularly offensive" because "so many Muslim leaders have failed to speak out against radical Islam, against the attacks" (this claim is examined in Q27). Other noted conservatives opposed to Park51 included Rick Lazio (R-NY), who was then a candidate for governor. Lazio decried the project on "personal security and safety" grounds (Saletan, 2010). Debra Burlingame, the cofounder of 9/11 Families for a Safe and Strong America, a loose-fit organization of 9/11 family members who view national security as the country's top priority, accused Imam Abdul Rauf of hatching a plot "to bring people to Islam" and creating a "Muslim-dominant America" (Saletan, 2010).

The anti-Park51 efforts contributed to wider opposition to the construction. A poll carried out by Quinnipiac University showed that the majority of New York City voters (52 percent) opposed the idea of Park51. A *TIME* magazine poll found that public opinion was firmly against the construction—61 percent of respondents opposed the construction, compared with 26 percent who supported it (Altman, 2010).

Anti-Islam activists such as Robert Spencer of the Jihad Watch blog and Pamela Geller of the Atlas Shrugs website descended to Ground Zero to oppose Park51 with their organization, Stop the Islamization of America (SIOA). SIOA justified resistance to Park51 on the grounds that mosques insulted the victims of 9/11 and that Imam Abdul Rauf was trying to establish a center for "political Islam" and "Islamic supremacy" in New York City (CNN, 2010). These accusations were widely condemned as false by American Muslims and Islamic organizations across the country. The Southern Poverty Law Center currently classifies SIOA as a hate group and Spencer and Geller as hate-group leaders. While both anti-Muslim activists and American Muslims speak of Islamization, their meaning and use of the term differ. For organizations like SIOA, Islamization refers to the introduction of sharia, including the implementation of radical Islamic laws, the enforced veiling of women, separate facilities for men and women, and the "subordinated" status (*dhimmi* in Arabic) of non-Muslims. The majority of mainstream American Muslims, however, view Islamization as a process that is far more dynamic and creative than the aforementioned interpretation, relying on an historical and largely secular view toward incorporating Islamic values, beliefs, and practices into the fabric of their everyday life in the United States.

FURTHER READING

Ahmed, Beenish. (2015, December 28). "Congressman Calls for 24/7 Surveillance of Mosques." ThinkProgress.org. Retrieved from https://thinkprogress.org/congressman-calls-for-24-7-surveillance-of-mosques-d01488762695

Al Jazeera. (2016, December 1). "Letter Threatening Genocide Sent to Several US Mosques." AlJazeera.com. Retrieved from http://www.aljazeera.com/news/2016/12/letter-threatening-genocide-mosques-161201074007755.html

Altman, Alex. (2010, August 19). "TIME Poll: Majority Oppose Mosque, Many Distrust Muslims." *TIME*. Retrieved from http://content.time.com/time/nation/article/0,8599,2011799,00.html

Bagby, I. A. (2005, May 11). *Muslims in the United States: Identity, Influence, Innovation*. Washington, DC: Woodrow Wilson International Center for Scholars. Retrieved from https://www.wilsoncenter.org/publication/muslims-the-united-states-identity-influence-innovation

Bagby, Ihsan. (2012, January). *The American Mosque 2011: Report Number 1 from the US Mosque Study 2011*. Washington, DC: Council on American-Islamic Relations. Retrieved from https://www.cair.com/images/pdf/The-American-Mosque-2011-part-1.pdf

Bagby, Ihsan, Perl, Paul M., & Froehle, Bryan T. (2001, April 26). *A Report from the Mosque Study Project*. Washington, DC: CAIR. Retrieved from http://www.allied-media.com/muslim_americans/mosque_study.htm

CNN. (2010, June 7). "Protestors Descend on Ground Zero for Anti-Mosque Demonstration." CNN.com. Retrieved from http://www.cnn.com/2010/US/06/06/new.york.ground.zero.mosque/

Coleman, Nancy. (2017, August 7). "On Average, 9 Mosques Have Been Targeted Every Month This Year." CNN.com. Retrieved from http://www.cnn.com/2017/03/20/us/mosques-targeted-2017-trnd/index.html

Considine, Craig. (2017). *Islam, Race, and Pluralism in the Pakistani Diaspora*. London and New York, NY: Routledge.

Criss, Doug. (2017, February 2). "Jews Hand Muslims Keys to Synagogue after Texas Mosque Burns." CNN.com. Retrieved from http://www.cnn.com/2017/02/02/us/mosque-burns-synagogue-keys-trnd/index.html

Curtis, Edward E., IV. (2010, August 29). "Five Myths about Mosques in America." *The Washington Post*. Retrieved from http://www.washingtonpost.com/wp-dyn/content/article/2010/08/26/AR2010082605510.html

Dias, Elizabeth. (2016, January 5). "Oldest Mosque in America Invites Donald Trump to Visit." *Time*. Retrieved from http://time.com/4167859/donald-trump-mosque-visit-iowa/

Gore, D'Angelo. (2010, August 26). "Questions about the 'Ground Zero Mosque.'" FactCheck.org. Retrieved from http://www.factcheck.org/2010/08/questions-about-the-ground-zero-mosque/

Hartford Institute for Religion Research. (n.d.). "How Many Muslims Are There in the United States." Hartford, CT: Hartford Institute. Retrieved from http://hirr.hartsem.edu/research/fastfacts/fast_facts.html

Holt, Jared. (2017, September 12). "Brigitte Gabriel: 90 Percent of U.S. Mosques Teach Radical Ideology to Destroy America." Right Wing Watch. Retrieved from http://www.rightwingwatch.org/post/brigitte-gabriel-90-percent-of-u-s-mosques-teach-radical-ideology-to-destroy-america/

Jacoby, Jeff. (2007, January 10). "The Boston Mosque's Saudi Connection." *Boston Globe*. Retrieved from http://archive.boston.com/news/globe/editorial_opinion/oped/articles/2007/01/10/the_boston_mosques_saudi_connection/

Kaleem, Jaweed. (2012, February 29). "Islam in America: Mosques See Dramatic Increase in Just over a Decade, According to Muslim Survey." *The Huffington Post*. Retrieved from http://www.huffingtonpost.com/2012/02/29/mosques-in-united-states-study_n_1307851.html

Keyes, Scott. (2011, January 25). "Rep. Peter King: 80 Percent of Mosques in This Country Are Controlled by 'Radical Imams.'" ThinkProgress.com. Retrieved from https://thinkprogress.org/rep-peter-king-80-percent-of-mosques-in-this-country-are-controlled-by-radical-imams-b1c3b3c5ce76

Khanna, Satyam. (2007, September 19). "Rep. King: There Are 'Too Many Mosques in This Country,' We Should 'Infiltrate Them.'"

ThinkProgress.org. Retrieved from https://thinkprogress.org/rep-king-there-are-too-many-mosques-in-this-country-we-should-infiltrate-islam-475561900d7a

Malewitz, Jim. (2017, February 8). "Investigators: Fire That Ravaged Victoria Mosque Was Arson." *The Texas Tribune*. Retrieved from https://www.texastribune.org/2017/02/08/investigators-fire-ravaged-victoria-mosque-arson/

Newton, Creede. (2017, January 29). "Americans Raise $600,000 to Rebuild Burned Texas Mosque." AlJazeera.com. Retrieved from http://www.aljazeera.com/news/2017/01/americans-raise-600000-rebuild-burned-texas-mosque-170129205625913.html

The Pluralism Project. (n.d.a.). "Unity and Diversity." Harvard University. Retrieved from http://pluralism.org/religions/islam/issues-for-muslims-in-america/unity-and-diversity/

The Pluralism Project. (n.d.b.). "Early American Mosques." Harvard University. Retrieved from http://pluralism.org/religions/islam/islam-in-america/early-american-mosques/

Quraishi-Landes, Asifa. (2016, July). "5 Myths about Sharia Law Debunked by a Law Professor." *Dallas News*. Retrieved from https://www.dallasnews.com/opinion/commentary/2016/07/19/asifa-quraishi-landes-5-myths-shariah-law

Rathod, Sara. (2016, June 20). "2015 Saw a Record Number of Attacks on US Mosques." MotherJones.com. Retrieved from http://www.motherjones.com/politics/2016/06/islamophobia-rise-new-report-says

Rettig, Haviv. (2005, December 5). "Expert: Saudis Have Radicalized 80% of US Mosques." *The Jerusalem Post*. Retrieved from http://www.jpost.com/International/Expert-Saudis-have-radicalized-80-percent-of-US-mosques

Saletan, William. (2010, August 2). "Muslims, Keep Out: The Republican Campaign against a Ground Zero Mosque." Slate.com. Retrieved from http://www.slate.com/articles/news_and_politics/frame_game/2010/08/muslims_keep_out.html

Q12. DO AMERICAN MUSLIMS ENGAGE IN INTERFAITH AND INTERCULTURAL DIALOGUE WITH NON-ISLAMIC RELIGIOUS AND CULTURAL COMMUNITIES IN AMERICA?

Answer: Yes. American Muslims are at the forefront of interfaith efforts to improve relations between Muslims and non-Muslims in the United

States. Islamic organizations, Muslim leaders, and Muslim communities across the country are regularly involved in interfaith efforts to better educate Americans about Islam and to build interfaith bonds of solidarity in American society.

The Facts: The faith of American Muslims is often depicted and described by anti-Muslim activists and organizations as "intolerant," "fanatical," and "anti-American." This narrative of Muslims portrays them as living in isolation from other Americans and uninterested in finding common ground with people outside the Islamic faith.

While few studies have produced quantitative data on interfaith relations between Muslims and non-Muslims in the United States, there is ample evidence that American Muslims have long strived to build better relations with their non-Muslim neighbors. The Islamic Society of North America (ISNA), one of the largest Islamic organizations in the United States, regularly engages in interfaith dialogue programs in order to "connect Muslims and people of other faiths with one another in order to build mutual respect and understanding" (Islamic Society of North America, n.d.a.). Since 1996, the Midwest Dialogue of Catholics and Muslims has held an annual joint initiative of ISNA and the U.S. Conference of Catholic Bishops, whose mission is to engage Catholic and Muslim scholars and leaders in interreligious dialogue. In 2010, ISNA initiated the Shoulder-to-Shoulder Campaign. This interfaith movement of 28 national religious organizations unites in their dedication to ending anti-Muslim sentiment by strengthening the voice of freedom and peace (Shoulder-to-Shoulder, n.d.). Between 2009 and 2012, ISNA partnered with Andover Newton Theological Seminary and a coalition of national Baptist organizations for the first ever National Baptist-Muslim Dialogues.

Another ISNA-led program—"Children of Abraham: Jews and Muslims in Conversation"—is an interfaith dialogue program jointly organized and facilitated by ISNA and the Union for Reform Judaism (URJ). The ISNA and the URJ partnered in 2007 to promote a nationwide series of local interfaith dialogues focusing on Muslim and Jewish communities, to promote mutual respect, understanding, and communication and to strengthen their capacity to advance peace and social justice on a global scale" (Islamic Society of North America, n.d.b). ISNA also works regularly with numerous religious, faith-based, and interfaith organizations for interfaith dialogue and advocacy on a range of public policy issues. A sampling of these organizations, which are listed on ISNA's website, include the following: American Baptist Churches USA; Cooperative Baptist Fellowship; Church World Service; Episcopal Church; the Foundation for Ethnic Understanding; Jewish Council for Public Affairs; the Jewish Theological Seminary of America; and the National Peace Foundation (Islamic Society of North America, n.d.b).

The Council on American-Islamic Relations (CAIR), referred to by the Anti-Defamation League as the "go to" American-Muslim civil rights organization, also actively participates in interfaith matters and interfaith dialogue events (Anti-Defamation League, n.d.). In April 2008, CAIR representatives met with Pope Benedict XVI at an interfaith gathering in Washington, D.C. The meeting, with the theme "Peace: Our Hope," included leaders from a number of American faith communities (Council on American-Islamic Relations, 2015a). One year later, CAIR officials joined world religious leaders at a conference in Vienna, Austria, to agree to establish an International Center for Inter-Religious Dialogue to help promote world peace and reconciliation between Muslims and Catholics.

Chapters of CAIR, in fact, hold regular interfaith dialogue events to educate Americans on Islam and to condemn Islamophobic hate crimes. The CAIR-Cincinnati chapter, in cooperation with the Franciscan Christian network, completed a month-long interfaith dialogue series between Christians and Muslims in 2013. The entire series included four sessions on topics such as death and resurrection, creation and evolution, women and religion, and power and violence (Council on American-Islamic Relations, 2015a). In November 2015, in the wake of hate vandalism targeting the Islamic Center of Burlington in Burlington, Massachusetts, CAIR-Massachusetts held an interfaith "We Are Americans" event, where members of the mosque and local interfaith leaders re-tagged the vandalized walls of the mosque with more positive messages about Islam and religious diversity in the United States (Council on American-Islamic Relations, 2015b).

In terms of U.S. legislation, CAIR supported the state of Ohio in its court battle to use the motto "With God, all things are possible." CAIR's statement on the issue read in part: "The statement 'With God, all things are possible' is not, as the court stated, 'a uniquely Christian thought.' In fact, a similar phrase is used many times throughout the *Qur'an*" (Council on American-Islamic Relations, 2015a). Similarly, "CAIR was critical of a 2000 U.S. Supreme Court ruling that barred student-led prayers at high school sporting events," but it later "welcomed a Supreme Court ruling allowing after-hours meeting space for school religious groups" (Council on American-Islamic Relations, 2015a).

In addition to national efforts such as these, local and regional relationships have been crafted between Islamic and non-Islamic religious groups. The Christian-Muslim Consultative Group of Southern

California, for example, arranges regular lectures and tours of churches and mosques to encourage interactions and religious literacy between Christians and Muslims. In 2008, the Christian-Muslim Consultative Group started an initiative, "Standing Together," which aims to reveal the richness and vibrancy of Christian and Islamic teachings. The goals of Standing Together include breaking down dehumanizing stereotypes, creating opportunity for Muslims and Christians to engage with one another about beliefs and practices, and laying the foundation for possible future collaboration (Christian-Muslim Consultative Group, n.d.). According to Edward E. Curtis, author of *Encyclopedia of Muslim-American History*, Standing Together also enables member mosques and churches to support one another in the event of a hate crime at either location.

An emerging Catholic dialogue with Muslims aims to show public support for American Muslim communities throughout the country. The dialogue, underway since February 2016, stems from concerns expressed by U.S. bishops in the wake of rising Islamophobia. These dialogues have involved Muslim and Christian scholars and religious leaders and have focused largely on academic discussions and comparisons of their respective religious texts. The regional dialogues—mid-Atlantic, Midwest, and West Coast—have been effective in creating a better understanding among Muslim and Catholic leaders on a theological level, according to Anthony Cirelli, who is associate director of the Secretariat for Ecumenical and Interreligious Affairs at the U.S. Conference of Catholic Bishops (Martone, 2017).

Academic units also have taken up the call to improve relations between Muslims and Christians in the United States and beyond. The MacDonald Center for the Study of Islam and Christian-Muslim Relations, founded in 1973, is the country's oldest center for such study. The MacDonald Center challenges scholars, students, the media and the general public to move beyond stereotypes and develop an accurate awareness and appreciation of Islamic religion, law and culture" (Hartford Seminary, n.d.). The Prince Alwaleed bin Talal Center for Muslim-Christian Understanding at Georgetown University also works to build stronger bridges of understanding between the Muslim world and the West as well as between Islam and Christianity (Prince Alwaleed bin Talal Center for Muslim-Christian Understanding, n.d.). Founded in 1993, the Center's faculty includes prominent American Muslim scholars, including Jonathan Brown and Yvonne Haddad, as well as non-Muslim scholars such as John Esposito and John Voll.

In light of the rising level of Islamophobia nationwide in 2017, CAIR-National urged local mosques to host the "Fast Forward" interfaith *iftar*, or fast-breaking meals during the month of Ramadan (Council on American-Islamic Relations, 2017a). The purpose of Fast Forward reflects the need for Americans "to go forward united in support of traditional American values of inclusion and respect for diversity during a time of increasing political division and rising bigotry targeting minority groups."

CAIR's solidarity for the American Jewish community stems (among other issues) from the fact that Islamophobic and anti-Semitic incidents in the United States have both surged in recent years (Anti-Defamation League, 2017; Considine, 2017). Following the victory of Donald Trump in the 2016 presidential election, Muslims and Jews expressed grave concern that his campaign had stoked xenophobia and that his appointment of *Breitbart* executive Steve Bannon as chief strategist for his administration would exacerbate strains of Islamophobia, anti-Semitism, and white supremacy in American society. In response to Trump's victory, leading Muslims and Jews banded together to form a new alliance, the Muslim-Jewish Advisory Council, based in Washington, D.C. (Mangla, 2016). The Council, comprised of 31 initial members, includes politicians, religious clergy, academics, and business leaders.

Over the last several years, CAIR has condemned anti-Semitic incidents throughout the United States and beyond. The group denounced "an Iranian cartoon contest mocking the Holocaust, an anti-Semitic article published in a British Columbia Muslim Newsletter, and called on an Arab publication that printed excerpts of the protocols of the Elders of Zion to apologize" (Council on America-Islamic Relations, 2015b). In September 2017, the Maryland Outreach Department of CAIR condemned fliers distributed in that state promoting anti-Semitism and white supremacy (Council on American-Islamic Relations, 2017b). In their press release, CAIR Maryland Outreach manager Zainab Chaudry stated, "We stand in solidarity with the local Jewish community and condemn these attempts to incite fear and division" (Council on American-Islamic Relations, 2017b).

The interfaith and intercultural engagement of American Muslims, however, is not a new phenomenon. Back in the 19th century, Alexander Russell Webb, a U.S.-born American citizen born in the Hudson River valley in 1846, became a proponent of interfaith interactions between Muslims and non-Muslims in the United States and beyond (Curtis, 2010). In 1888, while serving as U.S. consul to the Philippines, Webb converted to Islam. He gave several lectures in India about Islam in 1892 and founded a monthly magazine, the *Moslem World*, in 1893 (Curtis, 2010). In 1893, Webb published a short book, *Islam in America*, and several years later he published two journals—the *Moslem World* and *Voice of Islam*—with the stated purpose "to spread the light of Islamic truth in the United States and to assist in uniting under a common brotherhood all who accept the Moslem faith, intelligently, honestly, unselfishly and sincerely" (Curtis, 2010).

The White House's annual *iftar* has been a staple of interfaith relations in the United States. The first "White House *iftar*" occurred on December 9, 1805, when Sidi Soliman Mellimelli, a Tunisian diplomat, visited Washington, D.C., during Ramadan. To accommodate his guest's religious obligation, President Thomas Jefferson invited Mellimelli to the White House and even changed the time of dinner from the usual "half after three" to "precisely at sunset" to accommodate Mellimelli's observance (Thomas Jefferson Encyclopedia, n.d.). The Ramadan tradition at the White House restarted in 1996 when First Lady Hillary Clinton hosted an interfaith celebration dinner. Presidents Bill Clinton, George W. Bush, and Barack Obama all continued the annual Ramadan gathering, but the Trump administration declined the request to hold the Ramadan event in 2017, breaking with a bipartisan tradition in place with few exceptions for nearly 20 years (Torbati, 2017). The Ramadan reception is historically attended by prominent members of the American Muslim community, including political and religious leaders and students, as well as many non-Muslims who join the celebration.

Interfaith events, councils, organizations, and campaigns have emerged as a significant new development in American society over the last two centuries (The Pluralism Project, n.d.). These entities have been born from the practical necessity of addressing serious community issues that impact interfaith and interethnic relations in the United States. Getting to know one another and developing relationships of trust is a process that takes time. Every public institution in the U.S. today faces the challenges of religious pluralism. Developing an interfaith infrastructure for increasingly multi-religious cities and suburbs is becoming a priority of U.S. faith leaders. American Muslims are thus building a vast network of interfaith leaders from a broad range of traditions around the country to promote and uphold core American and core Abrahamic values as they relate to their communities' relations with one another (Muslim Public Affairs Council, n.d.).

FURTHER READING

Ahmed, Akbar. (2002). *Islam Today: A Short Introduction to the Muslim World*. New York, NY: I.B. Tauris.

Anti-Defamation League. (2017, April 24). "U.S. Anti-Semitic Incidents Spike 86 Percent So Far in 2017 after Surging Last Year, ADL Finds."

Houston, TX: Anti-Defamation League. Retrieved from https://www.adl
.org/news/press-releases/us-anti-semitic-incidents-spike-86-percent-
so-far-in-2017

Anti-Defamation League. (n.d.). "The Council on American Islamic
Relations (CAIR)." Houston, TX: Anti-Defamation League. Retrieved
from https://www.adl.org/education/resources/profiles/the-council-on-
american-islamic-relations-cair

Bunzl, Matti. (2005, November). "Between Anti-Semitism and Islamophobia: Some Thoughts on the New Europe." *American Ethnologist*,
32(4): 499–508.

Christian-Muslim Consultative Group. (n.d.). "About Standing Together."
Los Angeles, CA: Christian-Muslim Consultative Group. Retrieved
from http://www.thecmcg.org/contact_us

Considine, Craig. (2016). "Religious Pluralism and Civic Rights in a
'Muslim Nation': An Analysis of Prophet Muhammad's Covenants
with Christians." *Religions*, 7(15): 1–21.

Considine, Craig. (2017). "The Racialization of Islam in the United
States: Islamophobia, Hate Crimes, and 'Flying while Brown.'" *Religions*, 8(9): 165–184.

Council on American-Islamic Relations. (2015a, March 11). "CAIR:
Who We Are." Washington, DC: Council on American-Islamic
Relations. Retrieved from https://www.cair.com/about-us/cair-who-we-
are.html#Interfaith

Council on American-Islamic Relations. (2015b, November 4). "CAIR-
MA: Vandalized Mass. Mosque to Hold Interfaith 'We Are Americans'
Event." Washington, DC: Council on American-Islamic Relations.
Retrieved from https://www.cair.com/press-center/press-releases/13219-
cair-ma-vandalized-mass-mosque-to-hold-interfaith-we-are-ameri
cans-event.html

Council on American-Islamic Relations. (2017a, May 22). "CAIR: U.S.
Muslims Urged to Hold 'Fast Forward' Interfaith Iftars During Ramadan."
Washington, DC: Council on American-Islamic Relations. Retrieved
from https://www.cair.com/press-center/press-releases/14342-cair-u-s-
muslims-urged-to-hold-fast-forward-interfaith-iftars-during-ramadan
.html

Council on American-Islamic Relations. (2017b, September 13). "CAIR
Condemns Fliers Promoting White Supremacy, Anti-Semitism Distributed in Maryland." Washington, DC: Council on American-
Islamic Relations. Retrieved from https://www.cair.com/press-center/
press-releases/14608-cair-condemns-fliers-promoting-white-supremacy-
anti-semitism-distributed-in-maryland.html

Curtis, Edward E., IV. (2010). *Encyclopedia of Muslim-American History.* New York, NY: Facts on File.

Gold, Matea. (2017, February 3). "Bannon Film Outline Warned U.S. Could Turn into 'Islamic States of America.'" *The Washington Post.* Retrieved from https://www.washingtonpost.com/politics/bannon-film-outline-warned-us-could-turn-into-islamic-states-of-america/2017/02/03/f73832f4-e8be-11e6-b82f-687d6e6a3e7c_story.html?utm_term=.f9b1ec9a90de

Hartford Seminary. (n.d.). "Macdonald Center." Hartford, CT: Hartford Seminary. Retrieved from http://www.hartsem.edu/macdonald-center/

Hasan, Asma G. (2004). *Why I Am a Muslim: An American Odyssey.* London: Element.

Hathout, Hassan. (1995). *Reading the Muslim Mind.* American Trust Publications. Retrieved from http://hhlf.org/Reading%20Muslim%20Mind.pdf

Hoare, Marko A. (2017). "Islamophobia and Anti-Semitism in the Balkans." In James Renton and Ben Gidley (eds.). *Antisemitism and Islamophobia in Europe: A Shared Story*, pp. 165–185. London: Palgrave Macmillan.

Islamic Society of North America. (n.d.a.). "Interfaith Dialogue." Plainfield, IL: Islamic Society of North America. Retrieved from http://www.isna.net/interfaith-relations/

Islamic Society of North America. (n.d.b.). "ISNA's Interfaith Partners." Plainfield, IL: Islamic Society of North America. Retrieved from http://www.isna.net/interfaith-partners/

Mangla, Ismat S. (2016, November 15). "A New Council Will Unite Jewish and Muslim-American Groups in a US Alliance after the Election." Qz.com. Retrieved from https://qz.com/837794/a-new-council-will-unite-jewish-and-muslim-american-groups-in-a-us-alliance-after-the-election/

Martone, James. (2017, January 10). "Catholic-Muslim Dialogue Opens to Support American Muslims." Crux.com. Retrieved from https://cruxnow.com/cns/2017/01/10/catholic-muslim-dialogue-opens-support-american-muslims/

Musaji, Sheila. (2004, December 20). "Qur'an 9:29 Commentary." TheAmericanMuslim.com. Retrieved from http://theamericanmuslim.org/tam.php/features/articles/quran_929_commentary

Muslim Public Affairs Council. (n.d.). "Interfaith Relations." Los Angeles, CA: Muslim Public Affairs Council. Retrieved from https://www.mpac.org/programs/interfaith.php

The Pluralism Project. (n.d.). "America's Growing Interfaith Infrastructure." Harvard University. Retrieved from http://pluralism.org/encounter/ todays-challenges/americas-growing-interfaith-infrastructure/

Prince Alwaleed bin Talal Center for Muslim-Christian Understanding. (n.d.). "About ACMCU." Washington, DC: Georgetown. Retrieved from https://acmcu.georgetown.edu/

Rosa Menocal, Maria. (2003). *Ornament of the World: How Muslims, Jews, and Christians Created a Culture of Tolerance in Medieval Spain*. Boston, MA: Back Bay Books.

Schiffer, Sabine, & Wagner, Constantin. (2011). "Anti-Semitism and Islamophobia—New Enemies, Old Patterns." *Race & Class*, 52(3): 77–84.

Shoulder-to-Shoulder. (n.d.). "About." shouldertoshouldercampaign.org. Retrieved from http://www.shouldertoshouldercampaign.org/about/

Thomas Jefferson Encyclopedia. (n.d.). "Tunisian Envoy." Monticello, VA: Thomas Jefferson Foundation. Retrieved from https://www.mon ticello.org/site/research-and-collections/tunisian-envoy

Torbati, Yeganeh. (2017, May 29). "Exclusive: Tillerson Declines to Host Ramadan Event at State Department." *Reuters*. Retrieved from http://www.reuters.com/article/us-religion-ramadan-usa-tillerson-exclsu-idUSKBN18M2IE

3

❖

Politics

Q13. ARE MUSLIMS IN THE UNITED STATES RESPONSIBLE FOR THE MAJORITY OF TERRORIST ATTACKS ON AMERICAN SOIL?

Answer: No. In the years since 9/11, far-right-wing extremists have committed more—and more deadly—acts of terrorism on American soil, such as the 2015 murder of nine African Americans at a church in Charleston, South Carolina, by Dylann Roof, a white supremacist. Most mass shooting events on American soil since 9/11 have also been perpetrated by non-Muslims. The deadliest mass shootings of 2017—the October attack in Las Vegas, Nevada, that killed 58 and injured 500 more, and the November attack at a church in Sutherland Springs, Texas, that killed 26 parishioners and injured 20 more—were both carried out by non-Muslim white male Americans.

The Facts: The idea that far-right-wing terrorists do not pose the same level of danger to Americans as so-called "radical Muslims" or "jihadists" was raised in a February 2017 CNN interview between anchor Alysyn Camerota and Representative Sean Duffy, a Republican from Wisconsin (Hasan, 2017). Representative Duffy set off a firestorm after claiming that a recent terrorist attack committed by a "white extremist" was a rare event. When asked about a shooting at a mosque in Quebec, Canada, which left six Muslims dead and 17 others injured, Duffy told CNN,

"That was a one-off" (Hertel & Anderson, 2017). When Camerota asked Duffy why, he stated, "I don't know, but I would just tell you there's a difference" (Scott, 2017). Duffy added: "You don't have a group like ISIS or Al-Qaeda that's inspiring people around the world to take up arms and [killing] innocents," Duffy added.

Duffy's claims are sharply different to a report prepared by the Government Accountability Office (GAO), a legislative branch of government that provides fact-based, nonpartisan information to Congress (Government Accountability Office, 2017). The GAO report noted that "fatalities resulting from attacks by far-right wing violent extremists have exceeded those caused by radical Islamist violent extremists in 10 of the 15 years [since 9/11]" (Government Accountability Office, 2017). Of the 85 violent extremist incidents that resulted in death since 9/11, "far-right wing violent extremist groups were responsible for 62 (73 percent) while radical Islamist violent extremists were responsible for 23" (27 percent). The total number of violent attacks carried out on American soil by far-right white supremacists has spiked since the beginning of the 21st century, rising from a yearly average of 70 attacks in the 1990s to a yearly average of more than 300 since 2001 (Government Accountability Office, 2017).

According to a 2015 survey of 283 law enforcement groups carried out by the Triangle Center on Terrorism and Homeland Security, law enforcement agencies in the United States consider antigovernment violent extremists, not "radical Muslims," to be the most severe threat of political violence that they face (Kurzman & Schanzer, 2015b). One year later, another expert reported that the problem of antigovernment and white supremacist extremists is actually getting worse, citing evidence that extremists are conducting surveillance of Muslim schools, community centers, and mosques in at least nine states (Eichenwald, 2016). These incidents have grown even more common since Donald Trump's election victory; the Trump administration has cut spending for programs crafted to identify and stop terrorist threats from non-Muslim domestic groups and individuals (Perliger, 2017).

Other studies concur that far-right-wing extremists pose the most serious threat to U.S. national security.

- Charles Kurzman of the University of North Carolina and David Schanzer of Duke University carried out a joint study that found that Islam-inspired terror attacks accounted for 50 deaths since 9/11, while right-wing extremists have averaged 337 attacks per year since 9/11, causing a total of 254 fatalities (Kurzman & Schanzer, 2015a).

- The Global Terrorism Database (2017) maintained by the National Consortium for the Study of Terrorism and Responses to Terrorism (START) at the University of Maryland, College Park, a research and education center, includes 65 attacks in the United States associated with "far-right-wing ideologies" and only 24 by "radical Muslims" since 9/11 (Kurzman & Schanzer, 2015a).
- The International Security Program at the New America Foundation identifies 39 fatalities from "non-jihadist" homegrown extremists and 26 fatalities from "jihadist," or "radical Muslim," extremists (New America Foundation, 2017). These three studies conclude that Muslims are far less likely than non-Muslims to carry out violent acts of terrorism on American soil.
- A joint project by the Investigative Fund at The Nation Institute (a nonprofit media center) and the Reveal news outlet from the Center for Investigative Reporting looked at the 201 designated terrorism incidents within the United States from 2008 to 2016 (Sampathkumar, 2017). This analysis found that "right wing extremists were behind nearly twice as many incidents" as terror acts associated with those identified as "Islamist domestic terrorism." The joint report identified 63 incidents involving those "motivated by a theocratic political ideology espoused by such groups as ISIS. Right-wing extremists, often White supremacists, were responsible for 115 incidents within the same period. Events like Robert Dear's killing of three people at a Colorado Planned Parenthood women's health clinic in December 2015 for offering abortion services fell into this category" (Sampathkumar, 2017).
- Another report by the Investigative Fund of The Nation Institute questioned President Donald Trump's repeated claim that "radical Islamic terrorism" is the most significant threat to the U.S. homeland. Their database shows that between 2008 and 2016, far-right plots and attacks outnumber "jihadist" incidents by almost two to one (Neiwert et al., 2017). The database also reveals a serious imbalance in the way the United States confronts terrorism institutionally, from the resources federal officials devote to gathering intelligence to the investigation, prosecution, and punishment of perpetrators and their associates (Neiwert et al., 2017).
- According to the FBI, approximately 94 percent of all terrorist attacks carried out in the United States from 1980 to 2005 were carried out by non-Muslims (FBI, 2005). The FBI data means that during that 25-year time span an "American terrorist" was over nine times more likely to be a non-Muslim than a Muslim.

- Data produced by the National Consortium for the Study of Terrorism and Responses to Terrorism (START) shows that far-right wing extremists are the most likely population to target civilians in the United States. Their report "Far-right Violence in the United States: 1990–2010" reveals that far-right-wing terrorists perpetrated approximately 145 ideologically motivated homicide incidents between 1990 and 2010. In that same timeframe, the START found that Al-Qaeda affiliates, Al-Qaeda-inspired extremists, and secular Arab nationalists committed 27 homicide incidents in the United States, involving 16 perpetrators or groups of perpetrators (National Consortium For the Study of Terrorism and Responses to Terrorism, n.d.).
- A 2013 report published by West Point's Combating Terrorism Center revealed even more startling numbers than those revealed by the National Consortium for the Study of Terrorism and Responses to Terrorism. The author of the report, Arie Perliger (2012), found that the number of far-right attacks had jumped 400 percent in the first 11 years of the 21st century.

Islamic organizations across the country also have done their part to document the number and nature of terrorist attacks on American soil. In 2013, the Muslim Public Affairs Council (MPAC) (2013) tracked plots by Muslim and non-Muslim violent extremists against the United States. The MPAC report, titled "Post-9/11 Terrorism Incident Database," provides a comparison of incidents involving Muslims and non-Muslims adhering to various ideologies. Between 2001 and 2013, MPAC found a total of 135 total plots by U.S.-originated non-Muslim perpetrators against the United States, compared to 60 total plots by U.S. and foreign-originated Muslim perpetrators since 9/11 (Muslim Public Affairs Council, 2013). MPAC's report also provides additional evidence on the general rise of violent extremism across ideologies. Between 2008 and 2013, they found 88 plots by domestic non-Muslim violent extremists, compared to 36 plots by Muslim U.S. and foreign-originated extremists (Muslim Public Affairs Council, 2013).

The Anti-Defamation League (ADL), an international Jewish nongovernment organization, also reports that far-right extremists and white supremacists have been responsible for plotting the largest number of terrorist attacks in the United States over the past 25 years (Anti-Defamation League, 2017a). The ADL study analyzed 150 terrorist acts committed, attempted, and plotted by right-wing extremists over this period. More than 800 people were killed or injured in these attacks, which surged during the mid-to-late 1990s and again started in 2009 (Anti-Defamation League, 2017b). The report reveals that white supremacists (64 incidents) and antigovernment extremists, such as militia groups and sovereign citizens (63 incidents), were responsible for the vast majority of the attacks (Anti-Defamation League, 2017b). The ADL also looked at other acts of violence and determined that "from 2007 to 2016, a range of domestic extremists of all kinds were responsible for the deaths of at least 372 people [across the country]. Seventy-four percent of these murders came at the hands of right-wing extremists such as White supremacists, sovereign citizens and militia adherents" (Anti-Defamation League, 2017b). Moreover, as the ADL notes, far-right-wing extremists and white supremacists choose their targets carefully: Jews, Muslims, and—the most common racial target—African Americans (see King, 2017).

A portion of the U.S. Muslim population—Muslim immigrants and refugees—is often identified as being particularly prone to carrying out acts of terrorism. In January 2017, President Donald Trump signed the controversial executive order titled "Protecting the Nation from Foreign Terrorist Entry into the United States," which suspended entry of all refugees to the United States for 120 days. This order, also known as the "Muslim ban" or the "travel ban," barred Syrian refugees indefinitely and blocked entry into the country for 90 days for citizens of seven predominantly Muslim countries: Iran, Iraq, Libya, Somalia, Sudan, Syria, and Yemen (Corinthios, 2017). According to the executive order, the immigration policy aims to "protect the American people from terrorist attacks by foreign nationals admitted to the United States." The order added: "Numerous foreign-born individuals have been convicted or implicated in terrorism related crimes since September 11, 2001. The United States must be vigilant during the visa-assurance process to ensure that those approved for admission do not intend to harm Americans and that they have no ties to terrorism." The executive order was quickly blocked by federal judges, and the White House pivoted to a somewhat softened order that exempted lawful permanent residents and removed language suggesting that Christians from the affected countries would enjoy special treatment (*The Economist*, 2018). The second attempt to pass the "Muslim travel ban" fared no better in the minds of federal judges. As of January 2018, the Supreme Court agreed to resolve a challenge to a third version of Executive Order 13769. The case, *Trump v. Hawaii*, arises from the Ninth Circuit Court of Appeals (*The Economist*, 2018). The Supreme Court suggested in December 2017 that it was likely to uphold the contentious policy when it allowed the ban to go into full effect by a vote of 7–2.

The facts show that of the seven countries on the "Muslim ban" no deadly attacks were carried out by immigrants or refugees from the list (Corinthios, 2017). While two attacks have been carried out by individuals with ties to the seven countries—in 2006 at the University of North Carolina and in 2016 at Ohio State University—neither of those plots resulted in American deaths (Corinthios, 2017). A study by the New American Foundation (NAF) (2017), a nonpartisan think tank, also does not support Trump's argument that Muslim immigrants and refugees are a serious national security threat. The NAF identified 10 terrorist attacks that occurred on American soil since 9/11, all of which were carried out by so-called radical Muslims. Of the 12 perpetrators who participated in the attacks, all were either American citizens or in the country legally.

There have, however, been acts of terrorism planned or carried out by Muslims in the United States. Early in May 2010, Pakistani American Muslim Faisal Shahzad, a U.S. citizen, was charged with trying to detonate a car bomb in New York's bustling district of Times Square. Shahzad's actions were similar to three previous incidents in which a Muslim living in the United States acted out violently or contributed to terrorist activities (Benson, 2010). In November 2010, U.S. Army Major Nidal Malik Hasan fatally shot 13 people at Fort Hood, a military post located in Killeen, Texas. In 2010, "Colorado resident Najibullah Zazi, an Afghan national, pleaded guilty in February for conspiring to detonate explosives in the New York subway system. David Headley, [a U.S.] citizen from Chicago, Illinois, [was] accused of providing surveillance in the Mumbai, India, terrorist [attack] that killed 160 people" (Benson, 2010). In 2015, a shooting in San Bernardino, California, carried out by a married couple who had steeped themselves in the ideology of Islamic terrorists killed 14 people and injured another 22.

In response to these crimes, President Barack Obama, for the first time in U.S. history, made "homegrown terrorism" part of the U.S. National Security Strategy (Benson, 2010). The idea of including "homegrown terrorists" in the United States' efforts to combat terrorism appeared to be justified on the ground that "radical Muslims" posed the most serious threat to the safety of Americans. For example, John Brennan, President Obama's national security advisor, stated: "We've seen an increasing number of individuals here in the United States become captivated by extremist ideology or causes. We have seen individuals, including U.S. citizens armed with their U.S. passports, travel easily to extremist safe havens, return to America, their deadly plans disrupted by coordinated intelligence and law enforcement" (Benson, 2010). Brennan added that

Al-Qaeda, the militant group, recruits American Muslims to become "foot soldiers who might slip through our defense." Ultimately, Brennan's idea that U.S. "law enforcement's mass surveillance of [American] Muslim communities is a necessary, if unfortunate, counterterrorism tool rests on the empirically false notion," as journalist Matthew Harwood (2013) notes, that Muslims in the United States are more prone to terrorist violence than non-Muslim Americans (Harwood, 2013).

FURTHER READING

Anti-Defamation League. (2017a). *A Dark and Constant Rage: 25 Years of Right-Wing Terrorism in the United States.* New York, NY: Anti-Defamation League. Retrieved from https://www.adl.org/education/resources/reports/a-dark-and-constant-rage-25-years-of-right-wing-terrorism-in-the-united

Anti-Defamation League. (2017b, May 22). "ADL Report Exposes Right-Wing Terrorism Threat in the U.S." New York, NY: Anti-Defamation League. Retrieved from https://www.adl.org/news/press-releases/adl-report-exposes-right-wing-terrorism-threat-in-the-us

Benson, Pam. (2010, May 26). "Homegrown Terrorist Threat to Be Part of National Security Strategy." CNN.com. Retrieved from http://edition.cnn.com/2010/POLITICS/05/26/homegrown.terror/index.html

Corinthios, Aurelie. (2017, January 29). "How Many Terrorist Attacks in the U.S. Have Been Carried Out by Immigrants from the 7 Banned Muslim Countries?" People.com. Retrieved from http://people.com/politics/donald-trump-refugee-muslim-ban-terrorist-attack-us-statistics/

The Economist. (2018, January 23). "Donald Trump's Travel Ban Heads Back to the Supreme Court." Retrieved from https://www.economist.com/blogs/democracyinamerica/2018/01/travelling-ban

Eichenwald, Kurt. (2016, February 4). "Right-Wing Extremists Are a Bigger Threat to America Than ISIS." *Newsweek.* Retrieved from http://www.newsweek.com/2016/02/12/right-wing-extremists-militants-bigger-threat-america-isis-jihadists-422743.html

FBI. (2005). "Terrorism 2002–2005." Washington, DC: FBI. Retrieved from https://www.fbi.gov/stats-services/publications/terrorism-2002-2005

Global Terrorism Database. (2017). "Information on More Than 150,000 Terrorist Attacks." Retrieved from http://www.start.umd.edu/gtd/

Harwood, Matthew. (2013, July 10). "How Phony Fear of US Jihadist Obscures the Real Threat of Far-Right Terror." *The Guardian.* Retrieved from https://www.theguardian.com/commentisfree/2013/jul/10/fear-jihadist-threat-far-right-terror

Hasan, Mehdi. (2017, May 31). "The Numbers Don't Lie: White Far-Right Terrorists Pose a Clear Danger to Us All." TheIntercept.com. Retrieved from https://theintercept.com/2017/05/31/the-numbers-dont-lie-white-far-right-terrorists-pose-a-clear-danger-to-us-all/

Hertel, Nora G., & Anderson, Jonathan. (2017, February 8). "Sean Duffy Slammed for White Terrorism Comments." *Journal Sentinel.* Retrieved from http://www.jsonline.com/story/news/2017/02/08/sean-duffy-slammed-white-terrorism-comments/97639414/

King, Colbert I. (2017, May 26). "The U.S. Has a Homegrown Terrorist Problem—and It's Coming from the Right." *The Washington Post.* Retrieved from https://www.washingtonpost.com/opinions/the-us-has-a-homegrown-terrorist-problem--and-its-coming-from-the-right/2017/05/26/10d88bba-4197-11e7-9869-bac8b446820a_story.html?utm_term=.e17f7c621f36

Kurzman, Charles, & Schanzer, David. (2015a, June 16). "The Growing Right-Wing Terror Threat." *The New York Times.* Retrieved from https://www.nytimes.com/2015/06/16/opinion/the-other-terror-threat.html?_r=0

Kurzman, Charles, & Schanzer, David. (2015b, June 25). "Law Enforcement Assessment of the Violent Extremism Threat. Triangle Center on Terrorism and Homeland Security." Durham, NC: Triangle Center. Retrieved from https://sites.duke.edu/tcths/files/2013/06/Kurzman_Schanzer_Law_Enforcement_Assessment_of_the_Violent_Extremist_Threat_final.pdf

Muslim Public Affairs Council. (2013, April 23). "Post-9/11 Terrorism Database: A Racking of Plots by MUSLIM and Non-Muslim Violent Extremists against the United States." Los Angeles, CA: Muslim Public Affairs Council. Retrieved from https://www.mpac.org/publications/policy-papers/post-911-terrorism-database.php

National Consortium for the Study of Terrorism and Responses to Terrorism. (n.d.). "Far-Right Violence in the United States: 1990–2010." College Park, MD: University of Maryland. Retrieved from http://www.start.umd.edu/sites/default/files/files/publications/br/ECDB_Far Right_FactSheet.pdf

Neiwert, David, Ankrom, Darren, Kaplan, Esther, & Pham, Scott. (2017, June 22). "Homegrown Terror: Explore 9 Years of Domestic Terrorism Plots and Attacks." Berkeley, CA: Center for Investigative Reporting. Retrieved from https://apps.revealnews.org/homegrown-terror/

New America Foundation. (2017). *Terrorism in America after 9/11.* Washington, DC: New America Foundation. Retrieved from https://www.newamerica.org/in-depth/terrorism-in-america/

Perliger, Arie. (2012, November 2). *Challengers from the Sidelines: Understanding America's Violent Far-Right.* West Point, NY: The Combatting Terrorism Center at West Point–United States Military Academy. Retrieved from https://info.publicintelligence.net/CTC-ViolentFarRight.pdf

Perliger, Arie. (2017, May 28). "The Rising Homegrown Terror Threat on the Right." The Conversation.com. Retrieved from https://the conversation.com/the-rising-homegrown-terror-threat-on-the-right-78242

Sampathkumar, Mythili. (2017, June 23). "Majority of Terrorists Who Have Attacked America Are Not Muslim, New Study Finds." *The Independent.* Retrieved from http://www.independent.co.uk/news/world/americas/us-politics/terrorism-right-wing-america-muslims-islam-white-supremacists-study-a7805831.html

Scott, Eugene. (2017, February 8). Duffy: " 'There's a Difference' on White Terror and Muslim Terror." CNN.com. Retrieved from http://www.cnn.com/2017/02/07/politics/sean-duffy-white-terrorism-cnntv/

U.S. Government Accountability Office. (2017, April). *Countering Violent Extremism: Actions Needed to Define Strategy and Assess Progress of Federal Efforts. Report to Congressional Requesters.* Washington, DC: United States Congress. Retrieved from http://www.gao.gov/assets/690/683984.pdf

Q14. ARE THERE ACTUAL JIHAD TRAINING CAMPS LOCATED IN THE UNITED STATES?

Answer: No. The claim that there are jihad training campus run by "radical" American Muslims inside the United States has been disproven by law enforcement officials and the U.S. intelligence community.

The Facts: The claim that jihad camps exist across the United States relates back to a single 2005 report from the National White Collar Crime Center (NWCCC), a congressionally funded nonprofit corporation that trains state and local law enforcement agencies to combat cyber crimes. In this report, titled "Identifying the Links between White Collar Crime and Terrorism," the NWCCC discussed a group called *Jamaat ul-Fuqra*, a Muslim group that they alleged had conducted terrorist activities and had terrorist training camps across the nation (Kane & Wall, 2005). The group's leader—a first-generation Pakistani cleric named Mubarik Ali Shah Gilani—urged American Muslims to leave metropolitan areas during the 1980s to establish rural communities centered on "Islamic life" (Kearney, 2015). The Jamaat ul-Fuqra is best known for its "headquarters" in Islamberg, a "hamlet" within the town of Tompkins, New York, that now claims to have 22 such "Islamic villages" across the United States.

The "jihad camp" claim appeared again in 2009 when CBS News discussed *Homegrown Jihad: The Terrorist Campus around the U.S.*, a documentary film produced by PRB Films in association with the Christian Action Network. The documentary allegedly exposes 35 Muslim jihad camps in various parts of the country (Orr, Wassef, & Delargy, 2009). National security experts described the film to CBS News as "sensationalistic" and without any real foundation on facts. According to one official, who went unnamed by CBS for security reasons, "homegrown jihad" is designed to upset and inflame people to perceive American Muslims in a negative manner. As such, the film does not present a true picture of any so-called homegrown jihad threat (Orr, Wassef, & Delargy, 2009).

The Clarion Project, an organization that makes and distributes anti-Muslim films that portray the threat of "Islamism" as akin to Nazism, claims that the abundance of "jihad camps" like Islamberg is a serious threat to U.S. national security. As part of its efforts to expose the threat of "Islamic extremism," the Clarion Project created a website called Fuqra Files, which the organization refers to as "the most comprehensive non-governmental data about the *Jamaat ul-Fuqra* organization led by Sheikh Mubarak Ali Gilani" (The Fuqra Files, n.d.).

The idea of jihad camps around the United States has also been publicized by other conservative and far-right-wing media outlets and advocacy groups (Bertrand, 2015). In January 2015, for example, Fox News host Bill O'Reilly hosted Ryan Mauro, a self-proclaimed "national security analyst" for the Clarion Project. Mauro told O'Reilly that the FBI knew of at least 22 paramilitary Islamic communities in the United States run by the Jamaat ul-Fuqra, with the most dangerous one located in Tompkins, New York (Islamberg)—about 145 miles from Manhattan (WorldNet-Daily.com, 2015b). Mauro also showed O'Reilly a video reportedly given to him by a law enforcement source that shows Muslims marching with rifles in apparent guerilla warfare training (Fox News, 2015).

As of early 2018, no current U.S. intelligence or law enforcement agency believes in the threat connected to the alleged existence of jihad camps. Law enforcement officials near Islamberg are on record stating there is no evidence of Muslim communities preparing for guerilla warfare in the United States. In 2014, Sheriff Deputy Craig Dumont called the accusation "perplexing" and added, "We just don't find any of that to be valid at this time. . . . There are not active threats" (WorldNetDaily.com, 2015a). Thomas Mills, the sheriff of Delaware County near Islamberg, also publicly rejected the accusation. Sheriff Mills commented: "We haven't really had any big issues with them." Michelle Phoenix, a town clerk in nearby Tompkins, said her exchanges with the Muslims of "Islamberg" have been friendly (Kearney, 2015).

When CBS News visited Islamberg in 2015, Islamberg-leader Hussain Adams insisted that there was nothing sinister about their community and that far from "hating America," the Muslims of Islamberg valued their U.S. citizenship (Novaic, 2015). Adams stated: "We are very fortunate to live our lifestyle and practice our religion freely within the United States. We have actually been protected because of the freedoms that the United States affords to Muslims" (Novaic, 2015).

Reuters, the media corporation, also visited Islamberg in 2015. They observed an organized community where women tended to vegetables, "while young girls in head scarves and boys in knitted caps played nearby" (Kearney, 2015). Muslims of Islamberg told Reuters they do not live in complete isolation from their neighbors. Most of the adult residents commute daily to nearby towns or cities. Residents "own and drive cars, work, study and vote in local and national elections. Children are home-schooled, [but] engage in sports and social activities in nearby towns." During a "dinner gathering in an Islamberg home," Reuters reported how the residents dismissed the "idea that they are training for a holy war" or engage in violence of any sort (Kearney, 2015). "They condemned tactics used by [ISIS] . . . and said they did not consider the group to be true Muslims," Reuters noted.

Despite the fact checking and fieldwork of journalists, right-leaning news sites warned of imminent attacks from "jihad camp" cells. In July 2017, the Freedom Daily blog published an article with a sensational-sounding title: "Trump Sends Feds in to Raid NY'S Islamberg after 2 *Decades*—Uncover America's *Worst* Nightmare" (Holly, 2017). The article publicized "rumors" that "infidels [or non-Muslims] have been prohibited from entering, as anyone attempting to enter will be 'greeted' by armed Muslims patrolling a guard shack at the compound's entry gate." The article concluded: "It's absolutely ridiculous that Muslims in this country are allowed to have their own freaking jihadi compounds, where they're actively training their residents on the necessary tactics to carry out terror attacks!" (Holly, 2017).

The conspiracy theory surrounding the Islamberg "jihad camp" prompted a foiled terrorist attack by a far-right white extremist named Robert Doggart. In the spring of 2015, the FBI arrested Doggart, a Tennessee man, who was plotting to lead a militia to kill Muslims in Islamberg (Fisher, 2015). A one-time congressional candidate from Tennessee, Doggart believed the community was a "Muslim jihadist training camp," according to a post he made on his website (Fisher, 2015). Doggart explained in the post: "Given the recent beheading of an American journalist by the treacherous ISIS group, the Islamic networking that is underway in America, and the threats directed at us, there is no choice but to engage this topic, face-to-face, on location" (Fisher, 2015). In wire-tapped phone calls and in meetings with FBI informants, Doggart called for a militia to attack Islamberg, saying he intended to destroy its mosque and gun down residents who tried to stop him (Kearney, 2015). Doggart also told FBI informants that he planned to take an assault rifle, armor-piercing ammunition, and other weapons, including a machete, to attack Muslims (Kearney, 2015). In February 2017, Doggart was found guilty of plotting to round up militia and burn down the Islamberg mosque, school, and cafeteria. He was convicted in the U.S. District Court in Chattanooga, Tennessee, on solicitation to commit arson and violate civil rights, as well as of making a threat in interstate commerce, the U.S. Department of Justice said in a written statement (Reuters, 2017).

There is only one case in U.S. history that does indicate that at one time, there did exist a potential "jihad camp" on U.S. soil. In 1999, James Ujaama, a 31-year-old American Muslim who converted from Catholicism, arrived in the rural southern Oregon town of Bly with a convoy of cars carrying about a dozen Muslims from the Dar us Salaam mosque in Seattle, Washington. Settling on a 16-acre plot, Ujaama planned to establish a "jihad camp" for guerilla warfare training (Hirschkorn, 2014). Ujaama became the central figure in a 2003 11-count indictment, in which he pleaded guilty to aiding the Taliban. He was arrested as a fugitive in Belize in early 2006 after fleeing the United States and violating his parole (Carter, 2006).

Spreading the myth of "jihad camps" is not the only way the Islamophobia industry exacerbates misunderstanding of the term jihad, which has become widely associated with "holy war" and the most vulgar images of religious fanaticism. Jihad is an Arabic word that means "striving," "effort," or "struggle" and refers specifically to the effort to follow the teachings of Islam (Considine, 2017: 185). Within the Islamic tradition, there are two basic theological understandings of the word jihad: The "greater jihad" is the struggle to purify one's heart, to do good, and to avoid evil and make oneself a better person. The "lesser jihad" is an outward struggle that often results in violence through self-defense. Jihad, in short, is not "holy war." The form of jihad that involves fighting and warfare requires specific conditions under which it is ethically permissible to fight, including rules of engagement and the requirement to protect noncombatants (El Fadl, 2002).

As of January 2018, there are no reports from any law enforcement or intelligence agencies that "jihad camps" exist in the United States.

FURTHER READING

Bertrand, Natasha. (2015, September 19). "Donald Trump Gave Credence to a Major Right-Wing Conspiracy Theory about Muslim 'Training Camps.'" *Business Insider*. Retrieved from http://www.businessinsider.com/donald-trump-muslim-training-camps-2015-9

Bump, Philip. (2015, September 18). "Donald Trump and the 'Terrorist Training Camps' Conspiracy Theory, Explained." *The Washington Post*. Retrieved from https://www.washingtonpost.com/news/the-fix/wp/2015/09/18/donald-trump-and-the-terrorist-training-camps-conspiracy-theory-explained/?utm_term=.0561d4dee77e

Carter, Mike. (2006, December 20). "Fugitive Ujaama Arrested in Belize." *The Seattle Times*. Retrieved from https://www.seattletimes.com/seattle-news/fugitive-ujaama-arrested-in-belize/

Carter, Mike, & Bowermaster, David. (2007, August 14). "Ujaama Admits to Terror Charges." *The Seattle Times*. Retrieved from http://www.seattletimes.com/seattle-news/ujaama-admits-to-terror-charges/

Considine, Craig. (2017). *Islam, Race, and Pluralism in the Pakistani Diaspora*. London and New York, NY: Routledge.

El Fadl, Khaled A. (2002). *The Place of Tolerance in Islam*. Boston, MA: Beacon Press.

Fisher, Max. (2015, September 18). "Here's the Terrifying Anti-Muslim Conspiracy Theory That Trump's Supporter Was Citing." Vox.com. Retrieved from https://www.vox.com/2015/9/18/9351903/trump-muslims-camps-supporter

Fox News. (2015, January 14). "Video: Muslims Training for Guerilla Warfare in New York." Retrieved from http://nation.foxnews.com/2015/01/14/video-muslim-training-guerilla-warfare-new-york

The Fuqra Files. (n.d.). "About." The Clarion Project. Retrieved from http://www.fuqrafiles.com/about/

Gilbert, Jason O. (2016, December 7). "Inside the Wild Conspiracy Theory That Obama Is Protecting 22 Secret ISIS Compounds." Mic.com. Retrieved from https://mic.com/articles/161405/terrorist-camps-in-america-obama-secret-islamic-isis-compounds-to-attack-donald-trump#.EEzTXwo2N

Hirschkorn, Phil. (2014, May 7). "The Terror Camp That Wasn't." *Politico*. Retrieved from http://www.politico.com/magazine/story/2014/05/the-terror-camp-that-wasnt-106446

Holly, Prissy. (2017, July 18). "Trump Sends Feds in to Raid NY's Islamberg after 2 DECADES—Uncover America's WORST Nightmare." FreedomDaily.com. Retrieved from http://web.archive.org/web/20170718224025/http://freedomdaily.com/trump-sends-feds-raid-nys-islamberg-2-decades-uncover-americas-worst-nightmare/

Kane, John, & Wall, April. (2005, April). *Identifying the Links between White-Collar Crime and Terrorism*. Washington, DC: U.S. Department of Justice. Retrieved from https://www.ncjrs.gov/pdffiles1/nij/grants/209520.pdf

Kearney, Laila. (2015, June 1). "A Tranquil Muslim Hamlet in the Catskills—until the Attack Plot." Reuters. Retrieved from http://www.reuters.com/article/us-usa-islamberg-insight-idUSKBN0OH1D920150601

Kilgannon, Trish. (2017, June 14). "Cache of High-Powered Weapons Leads to Arrest of Johnson City Man." *Spectrum Local News*. Retrieved from http://spectrumlocalnews.com/nys/binghamton/news/2017/06/14/johnson-city-gun-bust

The Muslims of America, Inc. (n.d.). "TMOA." Retrieved from http://www.tmoamerica.org/news/pr/fake-fox-news/

Novaic, Ines. (2015, July 16). "Muslim Enclave in U.S. Battles Suspicion, Alleged Threats." CBSNews.com. Retrieved from http://www.cbsnews.com/news/inside-islamberg/

Orr, Bob, Wassef, Khaled, & Delargy, Christine. (2009, February 11). "'Homegrown Jihad' Documentary Trailer." CBSNews.com. Retrieved from http://www.cbsnews.com/news/homegrown-jihad-documentary-trailer/

Reuters. (2017, February 16). "Tennessee Man Convicted of Plot to Attack Muslim Community." Retrieved from https://www.reuters.com/article/us-usa-islamberg/tennessee-man-convicted-of-plot-to-attack-muslim-community-idUSKBN15V2SC

Snopes. (n.d.). "Did President Trump Send Feds to Raid Islamberg, New York?" Snopes.com. Retrieved from http://www.snopes.com/islamberg-raid/

WorldNetDaily.com. (2015a, January 25). "Local Police Speak Out about Islamberg." WorldNetDaily.com. Retrieved from http://www.wnd.com/2015/01/local-police-speak-out-about-islamberg/

WorldNetDaily.com. (2015b, January 15). "O'Reilly Jumps on WND Terror-Training Camp Report." WorldNetDaily.com. Retrieved from http://www.wnd.com/2015/01/oreilly-jumps-on-wnd-terror-training-camp-report/

Q15. HAVE U.S. POLITICIANS INTRODUCED LEGISLATION CALLING FOR A BAN ON ISLAMIC LAW (SHARIA) IN THE AMERICAN JUSTICE SYSTEM?

Answer: Yes. Anti-sharia legislation has been introduced at both the state and national levels despite the fact that no U.S. Islamic organization is calling for the implementation of sharia. Although the anti-sharia movement is a recent phenomenon, U.S. courts have long recognized sharia and other forms of religious law.

The Facts: Before examining anti-sharia legislation in the United States, it is important to define what sharia is and is not. The term *sharia* literally means "the path" (Considine, 2017: 187) or "the way to a water source" (Rashid, 2014). Sharia, or Islamic law, is derived from the Qur'an. Prophet Muhammad's *Sunnah* and *Hadith* serve as persuasive authority in interpreting the Qur'an, which is binding and always held as superior to the *Sunnah* and *Hadith* (Rashid, 2014). The term Sunnah is the Arabic word referring to the normative practice of the behavior of Prophet Muhammad (Considine, 2017: 187). Hadith is the Arabic word that refers to a narrative report of Muhammad's sayings and actions (Considine, 2017: 187).

According to Awad (2012), sharia is "a complex system of moral codes that governs all aspects of Muslim life." More than simply as a *law*, he refers to sharia as "the methodology through which Muslims engage with foundational religious texts to search for the divine will." For devout Muslims, sharia governs everything from the way a Muslim eats to how a Muslim treats animals, protects the environment, conducts business, and deals with both marriage and estate disputes (Awad, 2012). Sharia represents how practicing Muslims can lead their daily lives in accordance with God's divine guidance, as has been interpreted by Muslim scholars over the centuries (Interfaith Alliance & First Amendment Center, n.d.). Although the emergence of the nation-state did away with the premodern methodology of sharia, its current manifestations are either a source of legislation or actual state law in [some] Muslim-[majority] countries around the world (Esposito, 1998). Throughout history, Islamic law has remained central to Muslim identity and practice, for it constitutes the ideal social blueprint for the "good society" (Esposito, 1998).

Sharia is a topic of interest in the minds of many Americans, especially politicians who fear an infiltration of sharia in the U.S. political system. Many of the fears surrounding sharia in the United States orbit around the idea that Muslims want to make Islamic law the basis of the American legal system, and that all U.S. laws would give way to Islamic religious doctrine. Following a July 2016 attack in Nice, France, former House of Representatives speaker Newt Gingrich called for deporting everyone in the United States with a Muslim background who believes in sharia. "Western civilization is in a war. We should frankly test every person here who is of a Muslim background and if they believe in sharia they should be deported," Gingrich told Fox News's Sean Hannity. "*Sharia* is incompatible with Western civilization" (Etehad, 2016).

Legal experts say, though, that Gingrich's proposal "would violate scores of First and Fourteenth Amendment-based Supreme Court rulings that together bar discriminating on the basis of religion, favoring one religion over another by the government and restricting freedom of expression and belief" (Etehad, 2016). The Council of American-Islamic Relations' (CAIR) National Executive Director Nihad Awad, meanwhile, charged that "[Gingrich] plays into the hands of terror recruiters and betrays the American values he purports to uphold" (Council on American-Islamic Relations, 2016).

The fear of sharia infiltrating the U.S. courts is not novel. One hundred twenty anti-sharia bills have been introduced in 42 states since 2010 (Southern Poverty Law Center, 2017). In 2017 alone, 13 states introduced an anti-sharia law bill, with Texas and Arkansas enacting the legislation (Southern Poverty Law Center, 2017). Congress proposed several bills banning federal courts from considering foreign law from 2004 to 2009 (Boyer, 2013). These measures were driven largely by the fear that the judicial systems are turning toward international law rather than the U.S. Constitution. The anti-sharia movement gained steam in Oklahoma during November 2010 with the introduction of State Question 755 (SQ755), a ballot measure that would have amended Oklahoma's constitution to forbid judges from considering Islamic principles (sharia) or international law when making a ruling (Council on American-Islamic Relations, 2015). After an aggressive campaign in support of the measure, Oklahoman voters overwhelmingly approved (70 percent) a constitutional amendment that banned the consideration of sharia principles in court (Elliot, 2011). The day after the ballot measure was passed, the Executive Director of CAIR's Oklahoma chapter filed a lawsuit in federal court to address the dangerous and unconstitutional elements of the bill (Council on American-Islamic Relations, 2015). A federal judge agreed with CAIR's argument and put a temporary hold on SQ755 (Council on American-Islamic Relations, 2015). In striking down the legislation in 2012, the U.S. Court of Appeals for the Tenth Council noted that proponents of the bill did "not identify any actual problem the challenged amendment sought to solve" (U.S. Court of Appeals, 2012).

The nearby state of Kansas continued the anti-sharia momentum when Republican governor Sam Brownback signed legislation prohibiting judges in the state from considering foreign laws in their rulings (Awad, 2012). On May 21, 2012, Governor Brownback signed into law Senate Bill 79, of which Article 51 plainly prohibits "any law, legal code or system of a jurisdiction outside of any state or territory of the United States" (Boyer, 2013). In cases such as *Soleimani v. Soleimani* in Kansas, a ban against foreign law adopted by state lawmakers in 2012 had negative ramifications. A Muslim woman had signed an Islamic agreement with her husband that guaranteed her a sum of US$677,000 in case of death or divorce. The jury, however, chose not to factor the contract into its final ruling, and the woman ended up getting a substantially lower sum (Boyer, 2013). According to Republican state senator Chris Steineger, the real target of the law—Muslims—goes unnamed. "This [bill] doesn't say 'sharia law,' but that's how it was marketed back in January and all session long" (Awad, 2012).

The anti-sharia movement was particularly active in 2011 and 2012, when 78 such bills or amendments were introduced in the legislatures of 29 state legislatures, as well as the U.S. Congress (Saylor, 2014). Seventy-three of these bills were introduced by Republicans, while one bill, in Alabama, was introduced by a Democrat. Between 2011 and 2012, three anti-sharia bills at the state level were bipartisan (Kansas, South Carolina, South Dakota). Anti-sharia bills were subsequently signed into law in Arizona, Kansas, South Dakota, and Tennessee over the same period (Saylor, 2014). According to the Institute for Social Policy and Understanding, a research institute that tracks the anti-sharia movement and hate crimes against Muslims in the United States, approximately 80 percent of U.S. legislators who sponsor this type of legislation also sponsor bills restricting the rights of other minorities and marginalized communities. As of 2016, at least thirty-two states across the United States had introduced and debated anti-sharia or anti-foreign law bills (Rifai, 2016). At least nine states have passed "foreign law" statutes banning sharia in U.S. courts—even though no U.S. court has ever issued a ruling based on sharia (Quraishi-Landes, 2016).

The anti-sharia movement insists that Islamic law is encroaching on the U.S. justice system and represents a threat to the "American way of life" (Gay, 2011). The calls to ban sharia stem largely from concerns raised about a single New Jersey case, *S.D. v. M.J.R.* In June 2011, Herman

Cain, then a Republican presidential candidate, cited it as proof that "there have been instances in New Jersey . . . where Muslims did try to influence court decisions with *sharia* law" (Mariano, 2011). In *S.D. v. M.J.R.*, "a wife sought a restraining order against her husband, alleging that he repeatedly beat and sexually assaulted her" (Awad, 2012). The judge denied her request on the grounds that the husband was treating her according to his Islamic beliefs. "The ruling was wrong—both under state law and sharia—and, not surprisingly, the New Jersey Appellate Court reversed it in 2010" (Awad, 2012). *S.D. v. M.J.R.* and more court cases that are cited as symptoms of some kind of "Muslim threat" actually show the opposite (Gay, 2011). A report called *Nothing to Fear* by the American Civil Liberties Union (ACLU) (2011) debunked the myth that sharia is "creeping" into the U.S. judicial system. The ACLU notes that U.S. courts "treat lawsuits that are brought by Muslims or that address the Islamic faith in the same way that they deal with similar claims brought by people of other faiths or that involve no religion at all." These cases, the ACLU added, show that sufficient protections already exist in the U.S. justice "system to ensure that courts do not become impermissibly entangled with religion or improperly consider, defer to, or apply religious law where it would violate basic principles of U.S. or state public policy" (American Civil Liberties Union, 2011).

The legal consideration of sharia in U.S. courts is not a new phenomenon. Islamic law has long been considered by American judges in "everything from the recognition of foreign divorces and custody decrees to the validity of marriages, the enforcement of money judgments and the awarding of damages in commercial disputes and negligence matters" (Awad, 2012). In one particular court case, *Odatalla*, involving Islamic law, "a state judge declined to recognize a Syrian court order that would have transferred the custody of a child to her father because of the mother's remarriage. The judge reasoned that remarriage alone is not sufficient to transfer custody. Far from deferring to judgments from foreign countries, [U.S.] courts regularly refuse to recognize such orders due to the constitutional and due-process implications. Had an anti-sharia ban been in place, [the wife] in *Odatalla* [would not] have been able to enforce her marriage contract" (Awad, 2012). The sharia ban proposed by U.S. politicians would have stripped the U.S. judge's ruling on *Odatalla* of his ability to fully and fairly consider this case.

Anti-Muslim activists are responsible for much of the misinformation surrounding sharia. In June 2017, Brigitte Gabriel, the president and founder of ACT! for America, a nonprofit, nonpartisan grassroots national security organization, organized "March against Sharia" rallies in more than 29 cities across the United States. These rallies opposed what protestors described as the threat posed by Islamic law, which they say includes oppression of women, honor killings, homophobic violence, female genital mutilation, and other abuses (Doubek, 2017). Christopher Mathias (2017), a national reporter for the *Huffington Post* covering hate and extremism in American society, referred to the "March against Sharia" rallies as an "unholy alliance of Islamophobic hate group members, neo-Nazis, white supremacists and armed anti-government militia members." These rallies were denounced for exacerbating fear of Islam and hate of Muslims (Osman, 2017). The ACT marches were met with counter protestors in California, Georgia, Illinois, Michigan, New York, and Washington state, among other locations. The Anti-Defamation League, Amnesty International, and 129 additional organizations also sent letters to mayors in the 29 cities where the marches were scheduled, calling on them to reject ACT's "bigotry" and to "issue an official statement to reiterate to the people of your city that every person is welcome" (Mathias, 2017).

Critics claim that the anti-sharia movement has no purpose in the United States other than to vilify Muslims. The ACLU notes that prohibiting courts from considering sharia serves the purpose of barring Muslims from having the same rights and access to the courts as any other individuals in American society (Gay, 2011). Aside from the unconstitutionality of banning sharia, experts also point out that sharia, as an Islamic legal system, is not interpreted the same way by Muslim judges and scholars. Though only one version of the Qur'an exists, sharia is not recorded as a single canon (Rashid, 2014). On the contrary, four different schools of *fiqh*, or Islamic jurisprudence, interpret sharia in different ways (Rashid, 2014). These four schools consist of Hanafi, Hanbali, Maliki, and Shafi. By analogy, consider the U.S. Supreme Court justices who often interpret the U.S. Constitution in different manners. Sharia is no exception.

The true story of sharia in U.S. courts is not one of a plot for imminent takeover but rather another part of the tale of globalization (Awad, 2012). Marriages, divorces, corporations, and commercial transactions are global, meaning that the U.S. judicial system must consistently interpret and apply foreign laws such as sharia (Awad, 2012). The ground reality of case-by-case decision making contradicts the "creeping *sharia*" movement (Kutty, 2014). In 2012, Faisal Kutty, a leading U.S. legal expert and professor at the Law School of Valparaiso University, wrote that there have been a whopping seven cases (over the last 35 years) in which some "foreign law" was honored, and not enough information even to tell if something truly unjust happened in any of the seven" (Franck, 2012). In the other 13 cases in which sharia was involved, "Islamic legal principles were rejected either at trial or on appeal" (Franck, 2012).

FURTHER READING

American Civil Liberties Union. (2011, May). *Nothing to Fear: Debunking the Mythical "Sharia Threat" to Our Judicial System.* New York, NY: American Civil Liberties Union. Retrieved from https://www.aclu.org/files/assets/Nothing_To_Fear_Report_FINAL_MAY_2011.pdf

Arab American News. (2017, June 18). "Anti-Sharia Law Rallies in Michigan Draw Counter-Protests." ArabAmericanNews.com. Retrieved from http://www.arabamericannews.com/2017/06/18/anti-sharia-law-rallies-in-michigan-draw-counter-protests/

Awad, Abed. (2012, June 14). "The True Story of Sharia in American Courts." *The Nation.* Retrieved from https://www.thenation.com/article/true-story-sharia-american-courts/

Boyer, Ryan H. (2013, June 1). " 'Unveiling' Kansas's Ban on Application of Foreign Law." *Kansas Law Review*, 61(5): 1061–1087.

Council on American-Islamic Relations. (2015, March 11). "Anti-Sharia Legislation Campaign." Washington, DC: Council on American-Islamic Relations. Retrieved from https://www.cair.com/anti-sharia-legislation-campaign.html

Council on American-Islamic Relations. (2016, July 15). "CAIR Condemns Terror Attack in France, Newt Gingrich's Call to 'Test' and Deport American Muslims." Washington, DC: Council on American-Islamic Relations. Retrieved from http://myemail.constantcontact.com/CAIR-Condemns-Terror-Attack-in-France--Newt-Gingrichs-Call-to--Test--and-Deport-American-Muslims.html?soid=1103010792410&aid=TIbtI65CDWU

Doubek, James. (2017, June 11). " 'Anti-Sharia' Marchers Met with Counter-Protests around the Country." NationPublicRadio.com. Retrieved from http://www.npr.org/sections/thetwo-way/2017/06/11/532454216/anti-sharia-marchers-met-with-counter-protests-around-the-country

Elliot, Andrea. (2011, July 30). "The Man behind the Anti-Shariah Movement." *The New York Times.* Retrieved from http://www.nytimes.com/2011/07/31/us/31shariah.html

Esposito, John. (1998). *Islam: The Straight Path*, 3rd ed. New York, NY, and: Oxford University Press.

Etehad, Melissa. (2016, July 15). "After Nice, Newt Gingrich Wants to 'Test' Every Muslim in the U.S. and Deport Sharia Believers."

Washington Post. Retrieved from https://www.washingtonpost.com/news/morning-mix/wp/2016/07/15/after-nice-newt-gingrich-wants-to-test-every-american-muslim-and-deport-those-who-believe-in-sharia/?utm_term=.5a8066fec047

Franck, Matthew J. (2012, June 15). "A Solution in Search of a Problem." *The National Review*. Retrieved from http://www.nationalreview.com/bench-memos/303028/solution-search-problem-matthew-j-franck

Gay, Alicia. (2011, August 1). "ACLU Lens: The Truth Behind the Anti-Sharia Movement." New York, NY: American Civil Liberties Union. Retrieved from https://www.aclu.org/blog/aclu-lens-truth-behind-anti-sharia-movement

Interfaith Alliance & The First Amendment Center. (n.d.). *What Is the Truth about American Muslims?* Washington, DC: Interfaith Alliance. Retrieved from http://interfaithalliance.org/americanmuslimfaq/

Kutty, Fasial. (2014, October 28). "Creeping Sharia or Conspicuous Islamophobia." *Journal of International Affairs of Columbia University*. Retrieved from https://jia.sipa.columbia.edu/online-articles/creeping-sharia-or-conspicuous-islamophobia

Mariano, Willoughby. (2011, June 20). "Cain Claims Muslims Tried to Influence Sharia Law in NJ and OK." *Politifact*. Retrieved from http://www.politifact.com/georgia/statements/2011/jun/20/herman-cain/cain-claims-muslims-tried-influence-sharia-law-nj-/

Mathias, Christopher. (2017, June 10). "The 'March against Sharia' Protests Are Really Marches against Muslims." *The Huffington Post*. Retrieved from http://www.huffingtonpost.com/entry/march-against-sharia-anti-muslim-act-for-america_us_5939576ee4b0b13f2c67d50c

Osman, Abdulaziz. (2017, June 16). "Midwestern Muslims Fearful after Anti-Sharia Rallies." VoiceofAmerica.com. Retrieved from https://www.voanews.com/a/midwestern-us-muslims-fearful-after-anti-sharia-rallies/3904368.html

Quraishi-Landes, Asifa. (2016, July). "5 Myths about Sharia Law Debunked by a Law Professor." *Dallas News*. Retrieved from https://www.dallasnews.com/opinion/commentary/2016/07/19/asifa-quraishi-landes-5-myths-shariah-law

Rashid, Qasim. (2014, July). "America's Muslim Problem: Anti-Shariah Laws and the Threat to American Civil Rights." *Claremont Journal of Religion*, 3(2), 18–72.

Rifai, Ryan. (2016, June 24). "Report: Islamophobia Is a Multimillion-Dollar Industry." AlJazeera.com. Retrieved from http://www.aljazeera.com/indepth/features/2016/06/report-islamophobia-multi-million-dollar-industry-160623144006495.html

Saylor, Cory. (2014, Spring). "The U.S. Islamophobia Network: Its Fund-
    ing and Impact." *Islamophobia Studies Journal*, 2(1), 99–118 Retrieved
    from http://crg.berkeley.edu/sites/default/files/Network-CSaylor.pdf
Southern Poverty Law Center. (2017, August 8). "Anti-Sharia Law Bills
    in the United States." Montgomery, AL: Southern Poverty Law Cen-
    ter. Retrieved from https://www.splcenter.org/hatewatch/2017/08/08/
    anti-sharia-law-bills-united-states
U.S. Court of Appeals. (2012, January 10). "Awad vs. Ziriax." USCourts.
    gov. Retrieved from http://www.ca10.uscourts.gov/opinions/10/10-6273
    .pdf

Q16. DO MUSLIMS IN AMERICAN SOCIETY PREFER TO BE GOVERNED BY THE U.S. CONSTITUTION RATHER THAN SHARIA?

Answer: Yes. Public opinion polls consistently show that American Muslims prefer to be governed by laws of the U.S. Constitution rather than
sharia or other forms of religious law. American Muslims tend to regard
sharia as a personal and religious obligation governing the practice of
Islam as revealed by God to Muhammad, the prophet of Islam, and not as
some legal system to be implemented at the national level.

The Facts: Following the January 2017 terrorist attack that killed more
than 80 people in Nice, France, former speaker of the House of Representatives and conservative voice Newt Gingrich issued a call for American
Muslims to be "tested" and deported if they "believe in *sharia*" (Kuruvilla,
2017). "Sharia is incompatible with Western civilization," Gingrich told
Fox News hours after the attack. In an earlier speech during his 2012
presidential campaign, Gingrich had called sharia "a mortal threat to the
survival of freedom in the United States and in the world as we know it."
In a similar fashion to Gingrich, Allen West—a former representative of
Florida—alleged in 2012 that "there is an infiltration of the *sharia* practice
into all of our operating systems in our country as well as across Western
civilization. So we must be willing to recognize that enemy." Moreover, in
May 2016, Republican representative Joe Heck of Nevada claimed that
Muslims in Michigan "have tried to implement their version of *sharia*
law in the United States" (McDermott, 2016). These claims suggest that
Muslims in the United States want to manipulate sharia into U.S. legislation and that a coordinated "creeping sharia" program threatens the U.S.
judicial system.

In reality, however, there has been no coordinated attempt by American Muslims to incorporate sharia law into America's legal system—and most American Muslims are actually opposed to any such hypothetical proposals. According to a 2016 report produced by The Institute for Social Policy and Understanding, approximately 55 percent of American Muslims oppose using sharia as even a single source of many for U.S. laws. Despite this finding, the Public Religion Research Institute found in September 2012 that the number of Americans who feel that Muslims are working to subvert the Constitution rose from 23 percent in February 2012 to 30 percent in September 2012, during the height of the anti-sharia movement (Saylor, 2014).

The sharia myth continues to sweep across America despite the fact that Islamic law and other religious laws have long been recognized by U.S. courts. The U.S. judicial system, in fact, "has an established tradition of allowing people of faith to make agreements and resolve disputes within the parameters of their religion, as long as any resulting contract complies with U.S. law" (Council on American-Islamic Relations, 2013).

While there is no national Muslim organization that has ever called for sharia to supersede the U.S. Constitution, the Council on American-Islamic Relations, the United States' primary Muslim civil rights organization, has repeatedly been accused of masterminding a plot to infiltrate the U.S. government and subvert the Constitution through the use of sharia (Council on American-Islamic Relations, 2013). These accusations have been routinely condemned by leaders of CAIR. Cyrus McGoldrick, CAIR-NY's civil rights manager, told the New York Senate Standing Committee on Veterans, Homeland Security and Military Affairs in 2011 that "the Constitution is the law of the land and CAIR likes it that way. Our organization expends enormous legal and advocacy energy defending its principles" (Council on American-Islamic Relations, 2013). Corey Saylor, the national legislative director of CAIR, mirrored McGoldrick's words in a 2011 blog post discussing the role of sharia in the United States. Saylor states that the U.S. Constitution "is the law of the land" and that allowing Muslims to enter into agreements based on Islamic principles is "reasonably common" (Saylor, 2011). However, as Saylor clarifies, "any such agreement must comply with U.S. law." As noted in Q15, Muslims in the United States already operate in a sharia-compliant manner so long as their resulting transactions or contracts fit within the boundaries of the U.S. Constitution.

One of the most successful far-right groups in promoting the idea that America is threatened by the imposition of sharia law is the Center for Security Policy (CSP), a neo-conservative think tank. In July 2016, the

CSP released a survey of 6,000 Muslims in the United States. The main finding of the poll, according to a headline on the CSP website, was that "ominous levels of support" existed for " 'Islamic Supremacists' Doctrine of Shariah, Jihad." Specifically, the CSP reported that a majority (51 percent) of American Muslims believe that they should have the choice of being governed according to sharia. More than half (51 percent) of the poll's respondents reportedly asserted that they should have the choice of U.S. courts over sharia courts, or that they should have their own tribunals to apply Islamic law. Nearly a quarter of the American Muslims surveyed by CSP agreed that it was legitimate to use violence to punish those who offend Islam by, for example, portraying the Prophet Muhammad in a negative manner. According to the CSP, nearly one fifth of the American Muslim respondents stated that the use of violence in the United States is justified in order to make sharia the law of the land in this country. The CSP's results suggest that roughly 300,000 Muslims living in the United States believe that sharia is "The Muslim God Allah's law that Muslims must follow and imposed worldwide by jihad." In December 2015, Republican presidential candidate Donald Trump turned to the CSP poll to justify his proposal to temporarily ban all Muslims from entering the United States (Carroll & Jacobson, 2015).

Critics of the CSP poll, however, say that it was profoundly flawed and should not be taken seriously (Lean & Denari, 2016). In terms of its methodology, which is questionable, the poll was a non-probability-based, opt-in online survey (Lean & Denari, 2016). According to the American Association for Public Opinion Research (AAPOR), a professional organization of more than 2,000 public opinion professionals, the data from opt-in surveys cannot be generalized to the wider population. The AAPOR states that non-probability-based, opt-in online surveys such as those created by the CSP "do not have such a 'ground statistical tie' to the [overall] population" under consideration. In short, "[the CSP] survey does not represent the views of American Muslims. It only represents the views of the 600 Muslims that it polled" (Lean & Denari, 2016). The design of the survey questions is also flawed because the questions are "imbued with assumptions and replicate, in an interrogative form" statements that the CSP has declared as "facts" (Lean & Denari, 2016). For example, a question on "characterizing *sharia*" does not allow the respondent to unpack the meaning of sharia. As noted in Q15, sharia is digested, interpreted, and implemented in different ways both in the United States and around the "Muslim world."

David Yerushalmi is the leading voice of the anti-sharia movement in the United States. He is the author of "American Laws for American

Courts," the template for many anti-sharia bills introduced across the nation (Saylor, 2014) and another bill for the American Public Policy Alliance (APPA). The APPA bill has been used at the state level by groups like ACT! For America, the Eagle Forum, and to a lesser extent Stop the Islamization of America (Saylor, 2014). A total of 62 of the 78 anti-sharia bills that were introduced in state legislatures in 2011 and 2012 contained language extracted directly from Yerushalmi's bills. The American Bar Association passed a resolution in 2011 opposing this type of legislation, noting that it is "duplicative of safeguards that are already enshrined in federal and state law. . . . Initiatives that target an entire religion or stigmatize an entire religious community, such as those explicitly aimed at 'Sharia law,' are inconsistent with some of the core principles and ideals of American jurisprudence" (American Bar Association, 2011).

The Interfaith Alliance and the First Amendment Center (n.d.) highlight three types of cases in which U.S. courts already take notice of sharia:

> The first is a case in which a party alleges that some government practice interfered with the ability to practice his or her faith by *sharia*. Such a Free Exercise claim is identical to claims that government practice violates Jewish law, canon [Catholic] law or other religious laws. Courts decide only whether the claim is sincere and whether the government action violates the person's rights. The second is an arbitration agreement providing for arbitration under *sharia*. These can be enforced by courts if voluntary and not in violation of public policy. The third, and least common case, is one in which a foreign country's law governs a dispute (e.g., an accident that occurred abroad) and the country's law includes *sharia*. In general, the same rules apply: U.S. courts will not interpret religious law and will not apply foreign law in violation of basic public policies. The rules are no different for Islamic law than for canon [Catholic] law, *Halakha* (Jewish law) or other religious laws.

Catholic canon law and Jewish *Halakha* are the most frequently cited examples in the context of incorporating Islamic practices through sharia (Saylor, 2014). The Founding Fathers designed the Constitution in a manner that made it illegal for courts to apply religious law in deciding contract disputes and divorce or child custody cases and even in refereeing disputes over control of houses of worship (Interfaith Alliance & First Amendment Center, n.d.). The Establishment and Free Exercise Clauses of the First Amendment prohibit courts or other governance agencies from substituting religious law for civil law (Interfaith Alliance and the First Amendment Center, n.d.).

The anti-sharia movement across the United States is ironic considering that Prophet Muhammad is honored by the U.S. Supreme Court as one of the greatest lawgivers of the world. Inside the Supreme Court chamber, the highest court in the country, there is a frieze of "a person holding a copy of the [Qur'an] Islamic holy book. It is intended to recognize Muhammad as one of the greatest lawgivers in the world, along with Moses, Solomon, Confucius and Hammurabi" (Mujahid, n.d.). Here is what the Supreme Court's website says about this frieze:

> *Muhammad* (c. 570–632) The Prophet of Islam. He is depicted holding the *Qur'an*. The *Qur'an* provides the primary source of Islamic law. Prophet Muhammad's teachings explain and implement Qur'anic principles. The figure above is a well-intentioned attempt by the sculptor, Adolph Weinman, to honor Muhammad, and it bears no resemblance to Muhammad. Muslims generally have a strong aversion to sculptured or pictured representations of their Prophet.

The frieze, erected in 1935 by President Franklin D. Roosevelt while Charles Evans was the chief justice, is a symbol of the Supreme Court's respect and admiration for the teachings of the Prophet and the Qur'an. "Unfortunately, the brutal and often biased implementation of criminal law in some Muslim countries has given *sharia* a bad name" (Mujahid, n.d.).

The fact of the matter is that there is no meaningful Muslim support for a sharia takeover in the United States. American Muslims do not want sharia to supersede the U.S. Constitution, and not a single national Islamic organization is calling for the implementation of foreign law in the country (Saylor, 2014). As the Jewish Anti-Defamation League stated in 2012 while responding to an anti-sharia bill proposed in Florida, "[there] simply is no documentation or unconstitutional application of foreign law in our judicial system" (Saylor, 2014).

FURTHER READING

American Bar Association. (2011, August 8–9). "Resolution." American Bar Association. Retrieved from https://www.americanbar.org/con tent/dam/aba/directories/policy/2011_am_113a.authcheckdam.pdf.

Aslan, Reza, & Zaffar, Harris. (2012, February 29). "Those Defending US Constitution from Sharia Must Have Failed High School Civics." *Christian Science Monitor.* Retrieved from https://www.csmonitor.com/Commentary/Opinion/2012/0229/Those-defending-US-Constitution-from-sharia-must-have-failed-high-school-civics

Carroll, Lauren, & Jacobson, Louis. (2015, December 9). "Trump Cites Shaky Survey in Call to Ban Muslims from Entering US." *Politifact.* Retrieved from http://www.politifact.com/truth-o-meter/statements/2015/dec/09/donald-trump/trump-cites-shaky-survey-call-ban-muslims-entering/

Center for Security Policy. (2015, June 23). "Poll of U.S. Muslims Reveals Ominous Levels of Support for Islamic Supremacists' Doctrine of Shariah, Jihad." Washington, DC: Center for Security Policy. Retrieved from https://www.centerforsecuritypolicy.org/2015/06/23/nationwide-poll-of-us-muslims-shows-thousands-support-shariah-jihad/

Council on American-Islamic Relations. (2013, May). "Top Internet Misinformation and Conspiracy Theories about CAIR." Washington, DC: Council on American-Islamic Relations. Retrieved from https://www.cair.com/about-us/dispelling-rumors-about-cair.html

Council on American-Islamic Relations. (2016, January 29). "CAIR: South Carolina Assembly Asked to Drop Unconstitutional Anti-Islam Legislation." Washington, DC: Council on American-Islamic Relations. Retrieved from https://www.cair.com/press-center/press-releases/13363-cair-south-carolina-assembly-asked-to-drop-unconstitutional-anti-islam-legislation.html

Interfaith Alliance & The First Amendment Center. (n.d.). *What Is the Truth about American Muslims?* Washington, DC: InterfaithAlliance.org. Retrieved from http://interfaithalliance.org/americanmuslimfaq/

Kuruvilla, Carol. (2017, January 31). "5 Things You Need to Know about Sharia Law." *The Huffington Post.* Retrieved from http://www.huffingtonpost.com/entry/5-facts-you-need-to-know-about-sharia-law_us_5788f567e4b03fc3ee507c01

Lean, Nathan, & Denari, Jordan. (2016, July 7). "Here's Why You Shouldn't Trust the Latest Poll on American Muslims." *The Huffington Post.* Retrieved from http://www.huffingtonpost.com/nathan-lean/heres-why-you-shouldnt-trust-the-latest-poll-on-american-muslims_b_7688204.html

McDermott, Nathan. (2016, June 20). "Joe Heck Falsely Claims Muslims in Michigan Have Tried to Implement Sharia Law." Buzzfeed.com. Retrieved from https://www.buzzfeed.com/natemcdermott/joe-heck-falsely-claims-muslims-in-michigan-have-tried-to-im?utm_term=.ajbJVBRjj#.tv8oQ8rvv

Mujahid, Abdul M. (n.d.). "Prophet Muhammad Honored by the U.S. Supreme Court as One of the Greatest Lawgivers of the World in 1935." Sharia101.org. Retrieved from http://www.sharia101.org/proph et-muhammad-honored-by-us-supreme-court.php

Saylor, Cory. (2011, July 11). "Islam, U.S. Courts and State Sponsored Discrimination." CoreySaylor.blogspot.com. Retrieved from http:// coreysaylor.blogspot.com/2011/07/islam-us-courts-and-state-spon sored.html

Saylor, Cory. (2014, Spring). "The U.S. Islamophobia Network: Its Fund-ing and Impact." *Islamophobia Studies Journal*, 2(1), 99–118 Retrieved from http://crg.berkeley.edu/sites/default/files/Network-CSaylor.pdf

Q17. IS THE COUNCIL ON AMERICAN-ISLAMIC RELATIONS AN ACTUAL "TERRORIST ORGANIZATION"?

Answer: No. There is no proof that the Council on American-Islamic Relations (CAIR) itself either supports or actually contributes to terrorist activities in the United States or around the world. The CAIR consistently denounces terrorist acts carried out by Muslims in the name of Islam. The CAIR also appreciates "American values" and works to improve relations between Muslims and non-Muslims in the United States.

The Facts: Like other religious populations in the United States, American Muslims have institutions of their own. There are many long-established Islamic organizations in the country, perhaps none more important than the CAIR. Headquartered in Washington, D.C., the CAIR is a nonprofit organization with offices around the United States. It was established in 1994 to defend Muslims against discrimination and def-amation. According to its website, the CAIR defines its vision and mis-sion as "to enhance understanding of Islam, encourage dialogue, protect civil liberties, empower American Muslims, and build coalitions that pro-mote justice and mutual understanding" (Council on American-Islamic Relations, n.d.). Since the attacks on 9/11, the organization has sought with some success to position itself as the "go to" American Muslim civil rights organization in the United States. On that day, the CAIR issued a statement declaring that "we condemn in the strongest terms possible what are apparently vicious and cowardly acts of terrorism against inno-cent civilians."

The CAIR's critics often accuse the organization of hiring "employ-ees and board members who have been arrested, convicted, deported or otherwise linked to terrorism-related charges and activities" (Council on American-Islamic Relations, 2013). The CAIR came under specific fire during the Holy Land Foundation (HLF) case. In December 2001, the U.S. government designated the HFL a "terrorist organization," confiscated its assets, and shut down the organization. According to the FBI, the CAIR worked with the Holy Land Foundation for Relief and Development, which used the guise of charity to raise and funnel millions of dollars to the infrastructure of Hamas, a Palestinian organization branded as a "terrorist organization" by the U.S. Department of State (FBI, 2008). District Judge Jorge A. Solis sentenced the HLF and five of its leaders following their conviction by a federal jury in November 2008 on charges of providing material support to Hamas. The trial ended with guilty verdicts on all charges against the HLF, including a 65-year sentence for Ghassan Elashi, the founder and chairman of the HLF and former member of the founding board of directors of the Texas branch of the CAIR (Anti-Defamation League, n.d.). The case focused on four individuals: Ismail Royer, Dr. Bassem El-Khafagi, Rabid Haddad, and Ghassan Elashi. In January 2004,

> Royer pled guilty to weapons charges, but he did not plead guilty to any charge of "terrorism." Any criminal action to which he pleaded guilty was done when Royer was no longer employed with CAIR and it was certainly not at CAIR's direction. El-Khafagi was never an employee of CAIR and was never convicted on terrorism charges. According to an Associated Press article announcing his plea, federal officials stated that [El-Khafagi] was charged with writing bad checks [not engaging in terrorism-related activities] in February and June of 2001. El-Khafagi was only an independent contractor for CAIR, effective November 2, 2001, the actions of which he was accused occurred before any relationship with CAIR had commenced and without any knowledge by CAIR's of any wrongdoing on his part. (Council on American-Islamic Relations, 2013)

The third individual, Rabid Haddad, who was deported for overstaying his tourist visa, was never an employee or fundraiser of the CAIR. Haddad's only association with the organization was as a speaker at a single CAIR chapter event. Ghassan Elashi was convicted of terrorism-financing crimes related to financial transactions with Hamas, a Palestinian organization based in the Gaza Strip. Elashi, however, was never an employee or officer of the CAIR. The fact that Elashi was once briefly associated with one of the CAIR's more than 30 regional chapters has no legal significance to the organization since any actions he took were outside the scope and chronology of his association with one of the CAIR's chapters (Council on American-Islamic Relations, 2013).

The Center for Security Policy (CSP), which the Southern Poverty Law Center (SPLC) refers to as an "extremist group" (Southern Poverty Law Center, n.d.), claims that the HLF case proves that the CAIR "is an entity founded by the Muslim Brotherhood's Palestinian franchise" (Center for Security Policy, 2016). The SPLC, however, states that the CSP "has gone from a respected hawkish think tank focused on foreign affairs to a conspiracy-oriented mouthpiece for the growing anti-Muslim movement in the United States" (Southern Poverty Law Center, n.d.). Frank Gaffney, the founder of the CSP, is also recognized by the SPLC as an individual who exacerbates the myth that the CAIR is a terrorist organization.

There is no evidence to support the CSP's accusation that the CAIR is a "terrorist organization," and no U.S. court has found links between the CAIR and the Muslim Brotherhood. To date, the CAIR or any of its employees have not been found to be sponsors or even supporters of terrorism or terrorist organizations.

Because the CAIR advocates for the integration of Muslims into American society, a vocal group of anti-Muslim bigots has made the CAIR the focus of their misinformation campaign (Council on American-Islamic Relations, 2013). Writing for the website Front Page Magazine, Daniel Pipes, president of the Middle East Forum and a well-known critic of "political Islam," claimed that the CAIR is an organization founded by "Hamas supporters" and that it has proven links to "Islamic terrorists" (Pipes & Chadha, 2005). U.S. intelligence officials, however, disagreed with Pipes's characterization of the CAIR. Michael Rolince, a retired FBI official who directed counterterrorism in the Washington field office from 2002 to 2005, acknowledged that there is a lot of speculation about the CAIR in the intelligence agencies, but he stated that "when you ask people for cold hard facts, you get blank stares" (MacFarquhar, 2007). The *New York Times* article that quoted Rolince reported that government officials in Washington said they were not aware of any criminal investigation of the CAIR. More than one government official described the standards used by critics to link the CAIR to terrorism as akin to McCarthyism, essentially "guilt by association" (MacFarquhar, 2007).

The FBI and the CAIR are said to have a productive relationship. In April 2009, reports claimed that the FBI suspended contact with the CAIR because of evidence introduced during the HLF trial. That material suggested that the CAIR and its founders were linked to a group set up by the Muslim Brotherhood to support Hamas in the occupied Gaza Strip (Anti-Defamation League, n.d.). However, the *New York Times* reported in 2001 that Robert S. Mueller III—the then FBI director—said that the Bureau had no "formal relationship" with the CAIR but that the organization's officials and chapters regularly worked with FBI officials on investigations and related matters in a constructive manner (Shane, 2011). While the CAIR has no official partnership with the FBI, it does work regularly with law enforcement officials to improve Muslim community relations. As a civil rights organization, the CAIR frequently calls on the FBI to investigate acts of hate directed at Muslims in the United States (Council on American-Islamic Relations, 2013).

In addition to the CAIR, several organizations are working to combat misunderstanding and intolerance of American Muslims and Islam. The American-Arab Anti-Discrimination Committee has emerged as the premier Arab-American civil and human rights organizations, working to combat discrimination at home and to promote human rights for Arabs overseas (Nimer, 2005). Since 1990, the American Muslim Council has also worked to increase Muslim participation in the political process (Nimer, 2005). Other organizations, including Muslim Advocates, Muslims for Progressive Values, the Islamic Networks Group, and the Muslim Legal Fund of America, are Islamic-based entities that advocate social justice and equality for all.

Rather than committing or abating terrorism, the CAIR actually condemns terrorist groups by name. In 2007, CAIR executive director Nihad Awad joined 137 other Muslim leaders and scholars in sending a first-of-its-kind open letter—"A Common Word between Us and You"—designed to condemn acts of violence in the name of religion and promote understanding between Muslims and Christians (Council on American-Islamic Relations, 2013). On March 11, 2009, on the fifth anniversary of the tragic Madrid, Spain, attacks, CAIR issued another statement saying, "We unequivocally condemn all acts of terrorism, whether carried out by [Al-Qaeda], the Real IRA, FARC, Hamas, ETA, or any other group designated by the U.S. Department of State as a 'Foreign Terrorist Organization' " (Council on American-Islamic Relations, 2009). Years later, in 2015, the CAIR published a press release titled "CAIR's Condemnation of Terrorism." In the release, the CAIR notes it had issued more than 100 press releases condemning terrorism between the period of 1994 and 2015 (Council on American-Islamic Relations, 2015a).

The CAIR describes itself as an organization that works consistently and tirelessly to promote positive images of both Islam and American Muslims (Council on American-Islamic Relations, 2015b). The core principles of the organization include the following: supporting "free enterprise, freedom of religion and freedom of expression, protecting the civil rights of all Americans, regardless of faith; [supporting] domestic policies that promote civil rights, diversity and freedom of religion; [and opposing] domestic policies that [limit] civil rights, permit racial, ethnic or religious profiling, infringe on due process, or that prevent Muslims and others from participating fully in American civic life" (Council on American-Islamic Relations, n.d.).

The CAIR's condemnation formula of terrorism is simple: the organization condemns it "whenever it happens, wherever it happens, whoever commits it" (Council on American-Islamic Relations, 2015a). The organization added that it is a "natural enemy of violent extremists" and that it spoke out against torture and detainee abuse when majority public opinion in the United States was not in favor of the CAIR's position (Council on American-Islamic Relations, 2015a).

FURTHER READING

Anti-Defamation League. (n.d.). "Council on American Islamic Relations (CAIR)." New York, NY: Anti-Defamation League. Retrieved from https://www.adl.org/education/resources/profiles/the-council-on-american-islamic-relations-cair

Center for Security Policy. (2016, December 2). "C.A.I.R. Is HAMAS: How the Federal Government Proved That the Council on American Islamic Relations Is a Front for Terrorism." Washington, DC: Center for Security Policy. Retrieved from https://www.centerforsecuritypol icy.org/2016/12/02/c-a-i-r-is-hamas/

Council on American-Islamic Relations. (2009, March 11). "CAIR Reaffirms Repudiation of Terror on Anniversary of Madrid Bombings." Washington, DC: Council on American-Islamic Relations. Retrieved from https://www.cair.com/press-center/press-releases/3239-cair-reaffirms-repudiation-of-terror-on-anniversary-of-madrid-bombings.html

Council on American-Islamic Relations. (2013, May). "Top Internet Misinformation and Conspiracy Theories about CAIR." Washington, DC: Council on American-Islamic Relations. Retrieved from https://www.cair.com/about-us/dispelling-rumors-about-cair.html

Council on American-Islamic Relations. (2015a, December 22). "CAIR's Condemnation of Terrorism." Washington, DC: Council on American-Islamic Relations. Retrieved from https://www.cair.com/about-us/cair-anti-terrorism-campaigns.html

Council on American-Islamic Relations. (2015b, March 11). "CAIR: Who We Are." Washington, DC: Council on American-Islamic Relations. Retrieved from https://www.cair.com/about-us/cair-who-we-are.html

Council on American-Islamic Relations. (n.d.). "Vision, Mission, Core Principles." Washington, DC: Council on American-Islamic Relations. Retrieved from https://www.cair.com/about-us/vision-mission-core-principles.html

FBI. (2008, November 25). "No Cash for Terror: Convictions Returned to Holy Land Case." Washington, DC: FBI. Retrieved from https://archives.fbi.gov/archives/news/stories/2008/november/hlf112508

MacFarquhar, Neil. (2007, March 14). "Scrutiny Increases for a Group Advocating for Muslims in U.S." *The New York Times*. Retrieved from http://www.nytimes.com/2007/03/14/washington/14cair.html

Nimer, A. (2005, May 11). *Muslims in the United States: Identity, Influence, Innovation*. Washington, DC: Woodrow Wilson International Center for Scholars.

Pipes, Daniel, & Chadha, Sharon. (2005, July 28). "CAIR Founded by 'Islamic Terrorists.'" *Front Page Magazine*. Retrieved from http://www.danielpipes.org/2811/cair-founded-by-islamic-terrorists

Shane, Scott. (2011, March 11). Congressional Hearing Puts Muslim Civil Right Group in the Hot Seat Again. *The New York Times*. Retrieved from http://www.nytimes.com/2011/03/12/us/politics/12muslims.html

Southern Poverty Law Center. (n.d.). "Center for Security Policy." Montgomery, AL: Southern Poverty Law Center. Retrieved from https://www.splcenter.org/fighting-hate/extremist-files/group/center-security-policy

U.S. Department of Justice. (2009, May 27). "Federal Judge Hands Down Sentences in Holy Land Foundation Case." Washington, DC: U.S. Department of Justice. Retrieved from https://www.justice.gov/opa/pr/federal-judge-hands-downs-sentences-holy-land-foundation-case

Q18. DO MUSLIMS IN THE UNITED STATES CONDEMN THE RADICAL BELIEFS AND ACTIONS OF MILITANT GROUPS SUCH AS ISIS AND AL-QAEDA?

Answer: Yes. According to data and expert opinion, the overwhelming majority of Muslims in the United States reject the beliefs and actions of groups such as ISIS and Al-Qaeda. Specifically, American Muslims routinely condemn the use of suicide bombings, the indiscriminate killing of civilians, and the persecution of gay people. Muslims in the United States also distance themselves from the idea that only Muslims will be granted eternal life in heaven, a belief held by radical Muslim ideologues. Islamic organizations across the United States have consistently condemned and distanced themselves from ISIS and Al-Qaeda by issuing public statements denouncing the activities and beliefs of so-called radical Muslims.

The Facts: American Muslims have frequently been accused of being sympathetic to—or outright supportive of—the beliefs and actions of radical Islamic groups such as ISIS and Al-Qaeda. In an op-ed for *USA Today* in July 2016, U.S. evangelical leader Franklin Graham claimed that "tens of thousands of Muslims in America . . . are not bashful about justifying suicide bombings in the name of Islam" (Graham, 2016). Echoing Graham, Brigitte Gabriel, the president and founder of the Islamophobic group ACT! for America, remarked in June 2014 in a speech delivered at the conservative Heritage Foundation that "radical Muslims" make up 15 to 25 percent of the global Muslim population (Gabriel, 2014). On a separate occasion, according to the Southern Poverty Law Center, Gabriel also stated that a practicing Muslim who prays five times a day and believes in the teachings of the Qur'an "cannot be a loyal citizen to the United States of America" (Southern Poverty Law Center, n.d.).

On the basis of empirical evidence, Graham and Gabriel are wrong. American Muslims condemn the beliefs or actions of ISIS, Al-Qaeda, or their sympathizers. In fact, American Muslims may be even more concerned than non-Muslims about these groups and their extremism in the name of Islam. According to a 2017 Pew Research Center survey, 8 in 10 Muslims (82 percent) say they are either very concerned (66 percent) or somewhat concerned (16 percent) about extremism in the name of Islam around the world. This is similar to the percentage of the U.S. general public that shares these concerns (83 percent), although Muslims are more likely than U.S. adults overall to say they are very concerned about extremism in the name of Islam around the world (66 percent vs. 49 percent) (Pew Research Center, 2017).

While American Muslim concern about extremism in the name of Islam has risen in recent years, perceptions within the American Muslim community about attitudes toward extremism in their communities have remained stable. Essentially, American Muslims express confidence that their communities are full of loyal Americans fiercely opposed to extremism. The 2017 Pew poll found that nearly three quarters of U.S. Muslims (73 percent) say there is little or no support for extremism among American Muslims, while about one in six say there is either a "fair amount" (11 percent) or a "great deal" (6 percent) of support for extremism within the U.S. Muslim community (Pew Research Center, 2017). An earlier Pew Research Center (2011) survey found a significant majority (79 percent) of American Muslims to say that "extremism" is not found within their communities. A minority of Muslim participants in the 2011 survey said that there is a great deal (6 percent) or a fair amount (15 percent) of support for extremism in their Muslim community. Moreover, according to a 2009 poll conducted by the Pew Research Center, approximately 6 in 10 (61 percent) American Muslims were worried about the potential rise of Islamic extremism in the United States, although this figure is lower than the overall concern among the general public (78 percent) in the country (Wike & Smith, 2009). The same 2009 Pew poll found that many American Muslims share the concerns of the global Muslim population as it concerns Islamic extremism. Roughly three quarters (76 percent) of American Muslim respondents in the 2009 survey were "very concerned" or "somewhat concerned" about the activities of groups such as Al-Qaeda. Out of the entire American Muslim population, African American Muslims were the least likely to condemn Al-Qaeda completely, although only 9 percent of African American Muslims gave the organization a favorable view (Wike & Smith, 2009).

The most prominent Islamic organizations in the United States have issued statements that clearly condemn the actions and beliefs of ISIS. In August 2014, the Muslim Public Affairs Council (MPAC), an organization dedicated to strengthening the political profile of American Muslims, condemned "the extreme and repugnant principles and actions of the Islamic State of Iraq and Syria (ISIS)," adding that the rise of ISIS "is an imminent cause for concern for not only local civilians facing their deadly threats, but also for regional and international stability." The MPAC also harshly condemned ISIS's "brutal oppression" of religious minority populations including Shia Muslims, Christians, and Yazidis in the Middle East (Muslim Public Affairs Council, 2014). Additionally, the Fiqh Council of North America issued a fatwa, an authoritative legal opinion or learned interpretation of Islam, to refute the ideology of ISIS (Shah, 2014). The ruling stated that killing the innocent, declaring people non-Muslims, mistreating Jews and Christians, torturing and enslaving people, and denying women their rights are all forbidden in Islam.

In terms of suicide bombings, surveys have found a tiny fraction of support in the American Muslim community for this action. In a 2013 Pew poll, more than 8 in 10 (81 percent) American Muslims said suicide bombings and other forms of violence against civilian targets are never justified and 10 percent said they are rarely justified (Pew Research

Center, 2013). Only 1 percent of American Muslims and a median of 3 percent of Muslims worldwide said suicide bombings and other violence against civilian targets are often justified (Pew Research Center, 2013). The Pew Research Center (2009) found that support for suicide bombing is rare among U.S. Muslims—less than 1 percent of American Muslims said that suicide bombings can ever be justified (Wike & Smith, 2009). These figures reveal that American Muslims are among the most likely Muslim populations in the world to reject suicide bombing (Wike & Smith, 2009).

Of all major religious groups in the United States, U.S. Muslims are some of the staunchest opponents of military attacks on civilians. When asked whether targeting and killing civilians can be justified to further a political, social, or religious cause, 84 percent of U.S. Muslims say such tactics can rarely (8 percent) or never (76 percent) be justified, while 12 percent say such violence can sometimes (7 percent) or often (5 percent) be justified (Pew Research Center, 2017). In an earlier Abu Dhabi Gallup Center poll, American Muslims (78 percent) emerged as the staunchest opponents of military attacks on civilians (Naurath, 2011). The respondents from other faith groups in the Gallup poll, particularly American Mormons (64 percent), are more likely to say that military attacks on civilians are "sometimes justified" than "never justified." The Gallup data also highlighted that 92 percent of American Muslims think that Muslims in the United States do not sympathize with Al-Qaeda (Naurath, 2011). In the 2009 Pew Research poll, very few American Muslims held positive opinions of "radical Islamic groups"—only 5 percent gave Al-Qaeda a favorable rating, while 68 percent expressed an unfavorable view with the terrorist group, including 58 percent who described their view as very unfavorable (Wike & Smith, 2009).

American Muslims also distance themselves from groups like ISIS and Al-Qaeda on whether religions other than Islam can lead to eternal life. The Qur'an, like other sacred books, states that human life does not come to an end with death. In short, there exists another world where human beings will be rewarded or punished according to their deeds (Al Islam, n.d.). Only 20 percent of Muslims worldwide believe that other religions can lead to eternal life, compared to 56 percent of Muslims in the United States who believe so (Pew Research Center, 2014). The findings from a 2014 Pew Research Center study compares with an earlier 2008 Pew study—a slight majority of non-Muslims (52 percent) polled said that Islam can lead to eternal life, meaning that American Muslims' views on eternal life mirrors non-Muslims' views on the same subject (Pew Research Center, 2008). Fifty-five percent of American Muslims also believe that the Qur'an should not be a source of legislation and governance, compared to just 15 percent around the "Muslim world" (Pew Research Center, 2014). From 2007 to 2014, there was even an 8 percent decline—from 50 percent to 42 percent—in the share of Muslims in the United States who believe that the Qur'an should be interpreted "literally" (Bier, 2017).

Although American Muslims overwhelmingly reject "Islamic extremism," an analysis of legal documents and social media accounts by scholars at George Washington University show that authorities arrested more than 50 people in 2015 alone for activities related to ISIS (Vivino & Hughes, 2015). Up until 2015, 71 individuals had been charged by American authorities with ISIS-related activities (Vivino & Hughes, 2015). The George Washington report also stated there were roughly 900 active investigations against ISIS sympathizers in all 50 states (Vivino & Hughes, 2015). There also have been several relatively high-profile cases where American Muslims were charged by the FBI with providing material support for terrorism. In April 2017, for example, two men were arrested in Zion, Illinois, for agreeing to provide cell phones to be used as detonators for ISIS's improvised explosive devices (Mason, 2017).

In terms of the type of individuals attracted to ISIS, the Center on National Security (2016) states that the average age of those who conducted attacks in the United States is 29 years old. The average age overall of those indicted for ISIS-related crimes is 26 and the most common age among them is 20. Their young age contributes to lower levels of educational attainment, as many were still in high school or college at the time they were charged with the crime. Additionally, their young age coincides with their use of social media, including watching and sharing graphically violent videos. In addition to being young and overwhelmingly male (87 percent), those indicted for ISIS-related crimes in the United States are often seeking religious attachment. One third of the indicted individuals are converts to Islam, having been attracted to ISIS largely by serving the larger purpose of the Islamic caliphate, an Arabic word used by Sunni Muslims to refer to the successor of Muhammad as leader of the ummah (Considine, 2017: 184).

There is also a sense of identity crisis and alienation from society among those indicted on ISIS-related crimes. Of the 97 individuals who were either in the United States or arrested after leaving the country, nearly 80 percent of the cases indicated dissatisfaction with living in America. More than 10 percent of those indicted have been under some kind of treatment for mental health or have been diagnosed as schizophrenic or bipolar or suspected of suffering from acute anxiety disorder (Center on

National Security, 2016). A further 10 percent were alleged to have some history of recreational drug use.

As of June 2016, ninety-four individuals sympathetic to ISIS's cause were indicted in federal courts, while the remaining suspects were killed by law enforcement officials (Center on National Security, 2016). Although there were only 101 publicly known cases as of June 2016, the former director of the FBI James B. Comey noted that over 900 investigations were open and that they spanned all 50 states of the United States (Center on National Security, 2016).

FURTHER READING

Al Islam. (n.d.). "Towards Eternal Life." Al-Islam.org. Retrieved from https://www.al-islam.org/rationality-islam-ayatullah-sayyid-abulqa sim-al-khui/towards-eternal-life

Ali, Wajahat. (2011, August 29). "Exposing the Islamophobia Network in America." *The Huffington Post*. Retrieved from http://www.huffing tonpost.com/wajahat-ali/exposing-the-islamophobia_b_938777.html

Bier, David. (2017, January 25). "Trump Is Wrong: Muslim Immigration Is Reducing Radical Islamism." Washington, DC: CATO Institute. Retrieved from https://www.cato.org/blog/trump-wrong-muslim-immi gration-reducing-radical-islamism

Center on National Security. (2016). *Case by Case: ISIS Prosecutions in the United States*. Fordham University Law School. Retrieved from http:// static1.squarespace.com/static/55dc76f7e4b013c872183fea/t/577c 5b43197aea832bd486c0/1467767622315/ISIS+Report+-+Case+by+ Case+-+July2016.pdf

Council on American-Islamic Relations. (2016, June 12). "CAIR-FL to Respond to Florida Night Club Shooting, Urge Muslims to Donate Blood for Victims." Washington, DC: Council on American-Islamic Relations Florida. Retrieved from http://myemail.constantcontact.com/ Breaking--CAIR-FL-to-Respond-to-Florida-Night-Club-Shooting-- Urge-Muslims-to-Donate-Blood-for-Victims.html?soid=11030 10792410&aid=Jiag7_sUDMk

Durando, Jessica. (2016, June 12). "After Orlando Shooting, Muslim Americans Show Support for Victims." *USA Today*. Retrieved from https://www.usatoday.com/story/news/nation/2016/06/12/orlando- nightclub-muslim-reaction/85790320/

Fact Check. (2015, November 23). "Facts about the Syrian Refugees." Fact Check: The Annenberg Public Policy Center. Retrieved from http://www.factcheck.org/2015/11/facts-about-the-syrian-refugees/

Fantz, Ashley, & Brumfield, Ben. (2015, November 19). "More Than Half the Nation's Governors Say Syrian Refugees Not Welcome." CNN.com. Retrieved from http://www.cnn.com/2015/11/16/world/paris-attacks-syrian-refugees-backlash/

Farley, Robert. (2016, March 16). "Trump's False Muslim Claim." Fact Check. *Fact Check*. Retrieved from http://www.factcheck.org/2016/03/trumps-false-muslim-claim/

Gabriel, Brigitte. (2014, June 18). "Brigitte Gabriel Gives FANTAS-TIC Answer to Muslim Woman Claiming All Muslims Are Portrayed Badly." YouTube. Retrieved from https://www.youtube.com/watch?v=Ry3NzkAOo3s

Gambino, Lauren. (2016, September 2). "Trump and Syrian Refugees in the US: Separating the Facts from Fiction." *The Guardian*. Retrieved from https://www.theguardian.com/us-news/2016/sep/02/donald-trump-syria-refugees-us-immigration-security-terrorism

Graham, Franklin. (2016, July 18). "Too Many Muslims among Us Believe in Violence: Franklin Graham." *USA Today*. Retrieved from https://www.usatoday.com/story/opinion/2016/07/15/nice-attack-terror-islam-muslim-radical-lone-wolf-column/86670606/

Mason, Ian. (2017, April 12). "Two Illinois Muslim-Americans Arrested for Helping ISIS." *Breitbart*. Retrieved from http://www.breitbart.com/big-government/2017/04/12/two-illinois-muslim-americans-arrested-for-helping-isis/

Muslim Public Affairs Council. (2014, August 14). "MPAC Rejects ISIS' Repugnant Crimes against Humanity." Los Angeles, CA: Muslim Public Affairs Council. Retrieved from https://www.mpac.org/issues/national-security/mpac-rejects-isis-repugnant-crimes-against-humanity.php

Naurath, Nicole. (2011, August 2). "Most Muslim Americans See No Justification for Violence." Washington, DC: Gallup.com. Retrieved from http://www.gallup.com/poll/148763/muslim-americans-no-justification-violence.aspx

OutRight Action International. (n.d.). "Timeline of Publicized Executions for Alleged Sodomy by the Islamic State Militias." New York, NY: OutRight. Retrieved from https://www.outrightinternational.org/content/timeline-publicized-executions-alleged-sodomy-islamic-state-militias

Pew Research Center. (2007, May 22). *Muslim Americans: Middle Class and Mostly Mainstream*. Washington, DC: Pew Research Center. Retrieved from http://www.people-press.org/2007/05/22/muslim-americans-middle-class-and-mostly-mainstream/

Pew Research Center. (2008, December 18). "Many Americans Say Other Faiths Can Lead to Eternal Life." Washington, DC: Pew Research Center. Retrieved from http://www.pewforum.org/2008/12/18/many-americans-say-other-faiths-can-lead-to-eternal-life/

Pew Research Center. (2009, December 18). *Many Americans Say Other Faiths Can Lead to Eternal Life*. Washington, DC: Pew Research Center. Retrieved from http://www.pewforum.org/2008/12/18/many-americans-say-other-faiths-can-lead-to-eternal-life/#1

Pew Research Center. (2011, August 30). *Muslim Americans: No Signs of Growth in Alienation or Support for Extremism*. Washington, DC: Pew Research Center. Retrieved from http://www.people-press.org/2011/08/30/muslim-americans-no-signs-of-growth-in-alienation-or-support-for-extremism/

Pew Research Center. (2013, April 30). Appendix A: U.S. Muslims— Views on Religion and Society in a Global Context. Washington, DC: Pew Research Center. Retrieved from http://www.pewforum.org/2013/04/30/the-worlds-muslims-religion-politics-society-app-a/

Pew Research Center. (2014). *Religious Landscape Study: Muslims*. Washington, DC: Pew Research Center. Retrieved from http://www.pewforum.org/religious-landscape-study/religious-tradition/muslim/

Pew Research Center. (2017, July 26). "U.S. Muslims Concerned about Their Place in Society, but Continue to Believe in the American Dream." Washington, DC: Pew Research Center. Retrieved from http://www.pewforum.org/2017/07/26/findings-from-pew-research-centers-2017-survey-of-us-muslims/

Shah, Zulifqar A. (2014, September 24). "Muslim Leaders Refute ISIS Ideology." The Fiqh Council of North America. Retrieved from http://fiqhcouncil.org/node/69

Sola, Katie. (2015, November 20). "Why Syrian Refugees Aren't a Threat to America: The Numbers." *Forbes*. Retrieved from https://www.forbes.com/sites/katiesola/2015/11/20/syria-refugees/#17c7e4db508b

Southern Poverty Law Center. (n.d.). "Act for America." Montgomery, AL: Southern Poverty Law Center. Retrieved from https://www.splcenter.org/fighting-hate/extremist-files/group/act-america

Stedman, Chris. (2013, April 2). "Stop Trying to Split Gays and Muslims." *Salon*. Retrieved from https://www.salon.com/2013/04/02/stop_trying_to_split_gays_and_muslims/

Talev, Margaret. (2015, November 18). "Bloomberg Politics Poll: Most Americans Oppose Syrian Refugee Resettlement." *Bloomberg*. Retrieved from https://www.bloomberg.com/news/articles/2015-11-18/bloomberg-poll-most-americans-oppose-syrian-refugee-resettlement

Tharoor, Ishaan. (2016, June 13). "The Islamic State's Shocking War on Gays." *The Washington Post.* Retrieved from https://www.washington post.com/news/worldviews/wp/2016/06/13/the-islamic-states-shock ing-war-on-homosexuals/?utm_term=.fc84c326af72

Vivino, Lorenzo, & Hughes, Seamus. (2015, December). *ISIS in America: From Retweets to Raqqa.* Washington, DC: Program on Extremism at the George Washington University. Retrieved from https://cchs.gwu .edu/sites/cchs.gwu.edu/files/downloads/ISIS%20in%20America%20- %20Full%20Report.pdf

Wike, Richard, & Smith, Greg. (2009, December 17). "Little Support for Terrorism among Muslim Americans." Washington, DC: Pew Research Center. Retrieved from http://www.pewforum.org/2009/12/17/little- support-for-terrorism-among-muslim-americans/

Q19. DO MUSLIM IMMIGRANTS AND MUSLIM REFUGEES POSE A THREAT TO U.S. NATIONAL SECURITY?

Answer: No. Muslim immigrants and refugees do not pose a serious threat to American national security. In fact, data compiled by national security and law enforcement agencies indicate that they are far less likely to commit acts of terrorism than other populations in the United States.

The Facts: Muslim immigrants and refugees emerged as a political flashpoint during the 2016 presidential election. In August of that year, Republican candidate Donald Trump outlined a hardline approach toward Muslim immigration and American national security, particularly the war in Syria and the resettlement of Syrians to American soil. Trump recommended that Syrians and Muslim refugees, before being accepted into the United States' refugee resettlement program, in general should be subject to an "ideological test" that would ensure that those who are allowed entry to the United States "share our values and love our people" (Gambino, 2016). In linking Muslim refugees and migrants to "radical Islam" and to militant groups such as ISIS, Trump tapped into the anxieties of Americans and the "threat" of so-called foreign Muslims to strike in the United States.

Following Trump's remarks in January 2017, former New York City mayor Rudy Giuliani appeared on Fox News to defend the president's decision to ban Syrian refugees from American soil and suspend visas for potential immigrants from seven Muslim-majority countries.

According to Giuliani, Trump's proposal did not amount to a "Muslim ban." "What we did was, we focused on, instead of religion, *danger*. Which is a factual basis, not a religious basis . . . It's based on places where there are substantial evidence that people are sending terrorists into our country," Giuliani stated (Friedman, 2017). President Trump and Rudy Giuliani are right to be concerned about the threat posed by ISIS, but the facts regarding actual terrorist attacks on American soil do not align with their assertion that Muslim immigrants and refugees from Iran, Iraq, Libya, Somalia, Sudan, Syria, and Yemen pose a grave security threat to Americans.

Since 2014, the majority of individuals charged in the United States with ISIS-related offenses have been U.S. citizens (58 percent) or permanent U.S. residents (6 percent) (Vidino & Hughes, 2015). According to Alex Nowrasteh (2017) of the CATO Institute, a conservative think tank based in Washington, D.C., Muslim immigrants and refugees from the seven countries listed in Executive Order 13769 killed zero people in terrorist attacks on American soil between 1975 and 2015. Nowrasteh's study, titled "Little National Security Benefit to Trump's Executive Order on Immigration," also found that between 1975 and 2015, the "annual chance of being murdered by somebody other than a foreign-born terrorist was 252.9 times greater than the chance of dying in a terrorist attack committed by a foreign-born terrorist" (Nowrasteh, 2017). Echoing Nowrasteh's findings, journalist Uri Friedman reported that over the last 40 years, 20 out of 3.25 million refugees welcomed to the United States have been convicted of attempting or committing terrorism on American soil, and only 3 Americans have been killed in attacks committed by refugees—all by Cuban refugees in the 1970s (Friedman, 2017). The *New York Times* also pointed out that more ISIS fighters in the Middle East actually come from Saudi Arabia, Turkey, Russia, Egypt, and China, none of which were nations listed on Trump's ban (Smith & Goldman, 2016).

The question of whether Syrian refugees might be ISIS sympathizers or "terrorists" was a topic that came up repeatedly during the 2016 presidential race between Hillary Clinton and Donald Trump. In the days following the Paris attacks, the governors of 31 U.S. states refused to accept Syrian refugees, citing security fears (Fantz & Brumfield, 2015). Their sentiments are shared by Americans: only 28 percent of U.S. citizens supported settling Syrian refugees in the United States; 53 percent of U.S. citizens wanted to reject every Syrian refugee, while 11 percent favored admitting only Christians (Talev, 2015).

Far from being terrorists or terrorist sympathizers, Syrian refugees are mainly women, children, religious minorities, and victims of violence and torture who suffered under the rules of ISIS and Bashar Al-Assad, the Syrian president. Only 2 percent of Syrian refugees to America were males of military age (Sola, 2015). Fifty percent were children, and 25 percent were above the age of 65 (Sola, 2015). President Obama added that the "overwhelming numbers" of Syrian refugees referred to the United States by the United Nations have been women and children. That is true—67 percent have been children under the age of 12 and women, according to U.S. Department of State (USDOS) data (Fact Check, 2015). Supporters of refugee resettlement in America also assert that the fact that these Syrians fled their homes to escape ISIS or Assad shows they are not allied with them. Some experts also argue that by rejecting Syrian refugees the U.S. government assists ISIS by confirming the terrorist group's arguments that the United States does not care about Muslims (Gambino, 2016).

Kenneth E. Miller (2017), a psychologist and expert on refugee and war-affected populations, claims that the fear of Muslim immigrants and refugees is due to cognitive bias, misinformation, and fear mongering. In his article "Are Refugees a Threat to Americans?" in *Psychology Today*, Miller provides a sample of things more likely to kill Americans than Muslim immigrants and refugees:

1. Second-hand smoke (41,000 deaths annually)
2. Alcohol-related car crashes (10,000 deaths annually)
3. Gunshot (33,000 deaths annually)
4. Husbands/male partners (1,600 deaths annually)
5. Medical errors (250,000 deaths annually)
6. Overdose or other unintentional poisoning (22,000 deaths annually)
7. Child abuse or neglect (1,600 deaths annually)
8. Bicycle accidents (over 800 deaths annually)

In addition to these numbers, toddlers living in the United States pose a more serious threat of deadly violence than Muslim refugees. Twenty-three people have been shot by toddlers on American soil since the start of 2016—exactly 23 more than have been shot by Muslim refugees over the same period (McKay, 2016). Despite this evidence, Samantha Smith of the Pew Research Center noted that 46 percent of the U.S. public in January 2017 believed "a large number of refugees leaving countries such as Iraq and Syria" posed a "major threat to the well-being" of the United

States. While these figures highlight the overall level of anti-Muslim sentiment across the country, the Pew Research Center data notes that young Americans are less likely to view Muslim refugees as a major threat to the United States (Smith, 2017).

International organizations dealing with refugee resettlement and asylum seeker cases support the aforementioned findings. The United Nations High Commissioner for Refugees (UNHCR) notes that Syrians and other Muslim refugees pose little to no national security threat to the United States (Schlein, 2017). UNHCR spokeswoman Vannina Maestracci emphasized that refugees are *victims* of terrorists and those proposed for resettlement are among the most vulnerable people in the world. To quell fears, Maestracci told Voice of America that UNHCR carefully screens all refugees proposed for resettlement in the United States and more than 30 other countries around the world (Schlein, 2017).

According to the Refugee Processing Center, a computer system built by the U.S. Department of State to assist in the processing of refugees to American soil, Muslim immigrants are primarily coming as refugees and asylum seekers escaping violence and warfare. A total of 38,901 Muslim refugees entered the United States in fiscal year 2016, making up almost half (46 percent) of the nearly 85,000 refugees who entered the country in that period (Refugee Processing Center, n.d.). In 2016, only two countries—Syria (12,486) and Somalia (9,012)—were the source of more than half of fiscal 2016's Muslim refugees (O'Connor, 2016). The rest are from Iraq (7,853), Burma (Myanmar) (3,145), and Afghanistan (2,664), all of which are war-torn countries (O'Connor, 2016). It is worth noting that a significant number of U.S. citizens do not oppose the resettling of Muslim refugees and asylum seekers to American soil. In a study on America's fear and perceptions of terrorism, the Public Religion Research Institute (PRRI) found that a majority (53 percent) of U.S. citizens say they supported allowing Syrian refugees into the country in 2015. Nevertheless, the PRRI established that Americans also favor a strong vetting system and security clearance process (Cox & Jones, 2015).

The state of refugee affairs has been characterized in some quarters as a "flood" of Muslim immigrants and refugees into the United States. However, according to census figures compiled in 2015 by the Migration Policy Institute (MPI), a non-partisan think tank based in Washington, D.C., not one predominantly Muslim nation makes the list of top 10 countries of origin for legal immigrants (Siemaszko, 2015). Speaking on the origin of legal immigrants, Marc Rosenblum, deputy director of the MPI's U.S. immigration policy project, Middle Easterners and North Africans are a small share (3 percent) of the country's approximately 44 million immigrants (Cumoletti & Betalova, 2018).

In addition, the U.S. refugee vetting process is already among the most rigorous in the Western world. Potential refugees to the country are initially vetted by the United Nations' refugee agency. Prospective candidates are then referred to the United States, where members of the USDOS, the FBI, the U.S. Department of Defense, and the U.S. Department of Homeland Security carefully conduct further vetting. As an added check, the U.S. Citizenship and Immigration Services reviews the social media accounts of refugee and asylum seeker applicants who are referred for more enhanced vetting by UNHCR (Gambino, 2016).

Ilhan Omar, a Democratic member of the U.S. House of Representatives from Minnesota, is one of thousands of Muslims to have been cleared by the U.S. vetting process. Omar is a Somali American Muslim immigrant who arrived to the United States at the age of 12 after spending four years in a refugee camp in Kenya. In 2016, she became the highest-elected Somali American public official in the history of the United States. In addition to serving in the Minnesota legislature, Ilhan is a mother of three and the director of policy initiatives at Women Organizing Women, where she empowers East African women to take civic leadership roles in their communities (Omar, n.d.).

While much of the fear of Muslim immigrants is grounded in the attacks of 9/11 and isolated mass-killing events by Muslims, like the 2015 shooting in San Bernardino, California, which killed 14 people and injured another 22, American Muslim leaders have also blamed these views on fearmongering. Ibrahim Hooper, the national communications director for the Council on American-Islamic Relations, the largest civil rights and advocacy organization for American Muslims, asserted that America's well-coordinated Islamophobia industry "promotes fear and ignorance about Muslims. . . . There have been numerous studies that have shown that more people in America were killed by right-wing extremists. But you would be hard pressed to find anybody who knows that fact" (Siemaszko, 2015).

FURTHER READING

Cox, Daniel, & Jones, Robert P. (2015, December 10). *Nearly Half of Americans Worried That They or Their Family Will Be a Victim of Terrorism.* Washington, DC: Public Religion Research Institute. Retrieved from https://www.prri.org/research/survey-nearly-half-of-americans-worried-that-they-or-their-family-will-be-a-victim-of-terrorism/#.VmmkWPkrJ2Q

Cumoletti, Mattea, & Batalova, Jeanne. (2018, January 10). "Middle Eastern and North African Immigrants in the United States." Washington, DC: Migration Policy Institute. Retrieved from https://www.migrationpolicy.org/article/middle-eastern-and-north-african-immigrants-united-states

Fact Check. (2015, November 23). "Facts about the Syrian Refugees." Fact Check: The Annenberg Public Policy Center. Retrieved from http://www.factcheck.org/2015/11/facts-about-the-syrian-refugees/

Fantz, Ashley, & Brumfield, Ben. (2015, November 19). "More Than Half the Nation's Governors Say Syrian Refugees Not Welcome." CNN.com. Retrieved from http://www.cnn.com/2015/11/16/world/paris-attacks-syrian-refugees-backlash/

Friedman, Uri. (2017, January 30). "Where America's Terrorists Actually Come From." *The Atlantic*. Retrieved from https://www.theatlantic.com/international/archive/2017/01/trump-immigration-ban-terrorism/514361/

Gambino, Lauren. (2016, September 2). "Trump and Syrian Refugees in the US: Separating the Facts from Fiction." *The Guardian*. Retrieved from https://www.theguardian.com/us-news/2016/sep/02/donald-trump-syria-refugees-us-immigration-security-terrorism

McKay, Tom. (2016, May 1). "23 Reasons Why We Definitely Don't Need Any Gun Safety Reforms Ever." *Mic*. Retrieved from https://mic.com/articles/142318/23-reasons-why-we-definitely-don-t-need-any-gun-safety-reforms-ever#.GxrEifqsy

Miller, Kenneth E. (2017, February 20). "Are Refugees a Threat to Americans?" *Psychology Today*. Retrieved from https://www.psychologytoday.com/blog/the-refugee-experience/201702/are-refugees-threat-americans

Nowrasteh, Alex. (2017, January 25). "Little National Security Benefit to Trump's Executive Order on Immigration." Washington, DC: CATO Institute. Retrieved from https://www.cato.org/blog/little-national-security-benefit-trumps-executive-order-immigration

O'Connor, Phillip. (2016, October 5). "U.S. Admits Record Number of Muslim Refugees in 2016." Washington, DC: Pew Research Center. Retrieved from http://www.pewresearch.org/fact-tank/2016/10/05/u-s-admits-record-number-of-muslim-refugees-in-2016/

Omar, Ilhan. (n.d.). "Meet Ilhan." *Ilhan Omar*. Retrieved from https://www.ilhanomar.com/bio/

Refugee Processing Center. (n.d.). "Admissions and Arrivals." Arlington, VA: Refugee Processing Center. Retrieved from http://ireports.wrapsnet.org/Interactive-Reporting/EnumType/Report?ItemPath=/rpt_WebArrivalsReports/MX%20-%20Arrivals%20by%20Nationality%20and%20Religion

Schlein, Lisa. (2017, January 29). "UNHCR: Refugees Pose No Threat to US National Security." *Voice of America News*. Retrieved from http://www.voanews.com/a/unhcr-refugees-pose-no-threat-to-us-national-security/3697259.html

Siemaszko, Corky. (2015, December 10). "Mass Migration of Muslims to U.S. Mostly a Mirage." *NBC News*. Retrieved from http://www.nbcnews.com/storyline/immigration-border-crisis/mass-migration-muslims-u-s-mostly-mirage-n477306

Smith, Mitch, & Goldman, Adam. (2016, December 1). "From Somalia to U.S.: Ohio State Attacker's Path to Violence." *The New York Times*. Retrieved from https://www.nytimes.com/2016/12/01/us/from-somalia-to-us-ohio-state-attackers-path-to-violence.html

Smith, Samantha. (2017, February 3). "Young People Less Likely to View Iraqi, Syrian Refugees as Major Threat to U.S." Washington, DC: Pew Research Center. Retrieved from http://www.pewresearch.org/fact-tank/2017/02/03/young-people-less-likely-to-view-iraqi-syrian-refugees-as-major-threat-to-u-s/

Sola, Katie. (2015, November 20). "Why Syrian Refugees Aren't a Threat to America: The Numbers." *Forbes*. Retrieved from https://www.forbes.com/sites/katiesola/2015/11/20/syria-refugees/#17c7e4db508b

Talev, Margaret. (2015, November 18). "Bloomberg Politics Poll: Most Americans Oppose Syrian Refugee Resettlement." *Bloomberg*. Retrieved from https://www.bloomberg.com/news/articles/2015-11-18/bloomberg-poll-most-americans-oppose-syrian-refugee-resettlement

Vidino, Lorenzo, & Hughes, Seamus. (2015, December). *ISIS in America: From Retweets to Raqqa*. Washington, DC: Program on Extremism at George Washington University. Retrieved from https://cchs.gwu.edu/isis-in-america

Q20. ARE AMERICAN MUSLIMS OPPOSED TO SAME-SEX RELATIONSHIPS AND MARRIAGE?

Answer: Like the U.S. public as a whole, American Muslims have become much more accepting of gay people and same-sex relationships, including marriage, since the early 2000s.

The Facts: As of 2017, Muslims in the United States who say gay lifestyles should be accepted by society clearly outnumber those who say it should be discouraged (52 percent vs. 33 percent) (Pew Research Center, 2017). An earlier Pew Research Center (2014) poll revealed that an average of just 4 percent of Muslims around the world consider gay lifestyles "morally acceptable," compared to 45 percent among American Muslims. From 2007 to 2014, the share of American Muslims who agree not just that gay lifestyles should be legal but that they are "morally acceptable" rose from 27 percent to 45 percent (Bier, 2017). Furthermore, a previous 2011 Pew survey also showed that American Muslims have grown "considerably more accepting of homosexuality" since 2007. These findings shed light on present-day understandings of sexuality and sexual orientation, moving beyond the mere insistence that Islam does not unequivocally condemn same-sex relations.

The responses of Islamic organizations to the mass shooting at an Orlando, Florida, nightclub also show the changing views of American Muslims as they relate to gay lifestyles. After Omar Mateen, a U.S.-born Muslim, killed 49 people in a shooting spree at Pulse nightclub, a popular LGBTQ gathering spot, American Muslims came out in support of the LGBTQ community. The Florida chapter of the Council on American-Islamic Relations (CAIR) issued a statement that said, "We condemn this monstrous attack and offer our heartfelt condolences to the families and loved ones of all those killed or injured. The Muslim community joins our fellow Americans in repudiating anyone or any group that would claim to justify or excuse such an appalling act of violence" (Council on American-Islamic Relations, 2016). The CAIR also asked for blood donations to help those injured in the attack. The American Muslim Community Center, a mosque in Longwood, Florida, issued an additional statement that said it stands with all Americans and condemns "senseless violence" that "has no place in [Islam] or in our society" (Durando, 2016).

Prevailing perspectives among American Muslims on gay lifestyles and gay relationships differ significantly from the stances of terrorist groups such as ISIS. Across the Middle East and other parts of the "Muslim world," LGBTQ communities have faced varying degrees of oppression under ISIS, because of laws directed against its members and the wider social stigma (Tharoor, 2016). ISIS militants reported their executions of persons accused for indecent behavior, sodomy, homosexuality adultery, and other so-called morality-based crimes (OutRight Action International, n.d.). In a single day in September 2016, ISIS killed several men and a 15-year-old boy in a Syrian town who had been accused of homosexuality (Tharoor, 2016). In July, two men suffered the same fate in the Syrian city of Palmyra, then controlled by ISIS.

FURTHER READING

Bier, David. (2017, January 25). "Trump Is Wrong: Muslim Immigration Is Reducing Radical Islamism." Washington, DC: CATO Institute. Retrieved from https://www.cato.org/blog/trump-wrong-muslim-immigration-reducing-radical-islamism

Council on American-Islamic Relations. (2016, June 12). "CAIR-FL to Respond to Florida Night Club Shooting, Urge Muslims to Donate Blood for Victims." Washington, DC: Council on American-Islamic Relations Florida. Retrieved from http://myemail.constantcontact.com/Breaking--CAIR-FL-to-Respond-to-Florida-Night-Club-Shooting--Urge-Muslims-to-Donate-Blood-for-Victims.html?soid=1103010792410&aid=Jiag7_sUDMk

Durando, Jessica. (2016, June 12). "After Orlando Shooting, Muslim Americans Show Support for Victims." *USA Today*. Retrieved from https://www.usatoday.com/story/news/nation/2016/06/12/orlando-nightclub-muslim-reaction/85790320/

OutRight Action International. (n.d.). "Timeline of Publicized Executions for Alleged Sodomy by the Islamic State Militias." New York, NY: OutRight. Retrieved from https://www.outrightinternational.org/content/timeline-publicized-executions-alleged-sodomy-islamic-state-militias

Pew Research Center. (2014). "Religious Landscape Study: Muslims." Washington, DC: Pew Research Center. Retrieved from http://www.pewforum.org/religious-landscape-study/religious-tradition/muslim/

Pew Research Center. (2017, July 26). "U.S. Muslims Concerned about Their Place in Society, but Continue to Believe in the American Dream." Washington, DC: Pew Research Center. Retrieved from http://www.pewforum.org/2017/07/26/findings-from-pew-research-centers-2017-survey-of-us-muslims/

Tharoor, Ihsaan. (2016, June 13). "The Islamic State's Shocking War on Gays." *The Washington Post*. Retrieved from https://www.washingtonpost.com/news/worldviews/wp/2016/06/13/the-islamic-states-shocking-war-on-homosexuals/?utm_term=.fc84c326af72

4

❖❖❖

Islamophobia

Q21. IS ISLAMOPHOBIA ON THE RISE
IN THE UNITED STATES?

Answer: Yes. U.S. civil rights organizations and experts—from the religious to the secular—have found a steady rise in Islamophobia, which hit a high point during the 2016 presidential election, due largely to the heated rhetoric around Muslim refugees, the integration of American Muslims, the threat of ISIS, and the question of whether Muslims actually condone the views and actions of radical Islamic groups.

The Facts: According to the Runnymede Trust (1997), an independent race equality think tank based in the U.K., the term Islamophobia means the unfounded and close-minded fear and/or hatred of Islam, Muslims, or Islamic/Muslim culture. The definition identifies eight components as characteristic of Islamophobia in the following sense: (1) Islam is seen as a monolithic bloc, static and unresponsive to change; (2) Islam is seen as separate and Other. It does not have values in common with other cultures, is not affected by them, and does not influence them; (3) Islam is seen as inferior to the West. It is barbaric, irrational, primitive, and sexist; (4) Islam is seen as violent, aggressive, threatening, supportive of terrorism, and engaged in a clash of civilizations; (5) Islam is seen as a political ideology used to acquire political or military advantage; (6) criticism of the West by Muslims is rejected out of hand; (7) hostility toward Islam is used to justify discriminatory practices toward Muslims and the exclusion of Muslims from mainstream society; and (8) anti-Muslim hostility is seen as natural or normal (Runnymede Trust, 1997). Other experts conceptualize Islamophobia as an ideology, a mode of operation and an exclusionary practice (Allen, 2010: 188), as well as a form of racialized sentiment against American Muslims (Considine, 2017). The term *Islamophobia* has also been problematized by experts who question the utility of the term. Some reject the notion of Islamophobia as being a type of racism because it is "devoid of any of the biological or cultural determinism" of racist discourses (Bravo-Lopez, 2011: 559), while others have referred to it as a propaganda term coined by the Muslim Brotherhood to stifle criticism of Islam and Muslims (Semkiw, 2015).

The idea that Islamophobia is a myth and it does not exist was raised in the *National Review* by journalist Brendan O'Neill. He claimed that "the idea of Islamophobia has always been informed more by the swirling fantasies and panics of the political and media elites than by any real, measurable levels of hate or violence against Muslims" (O'Neill, 2015). As O'Neill sees it, Islamophobia is a "myth" because it cannot be empirically proven by data. Hate crimes against Muslims, however, are both real and measurable. Several major civil rights reports reveal that Islamophobic incidents in the United States have soared in the 2010s. A 2017 compilation of official Islamophobic hate crimes data by the Council on American-Islamic Relations (CAIR) shows that between 2014 and 2016, anti-Muslim incidents increased across the United States by 65 percent. In 2016 alone, reported incidents of Islamophobia rose by 57 percent (Council on American-Islamic Relations, 2017). The CAIR's findings are similar to data collected by the Center for the Study of Hate and Extremism (CSHE) at California State University–San Bernardino, which looked at Islamophobic crimes in over 20 states. The CSHE documented a total of 196 incidents in 2015 alone. These 196 incidents, which took place across 20 states, is 29 percent higher than 2014's anti-Muslim total of 154 for the *entire nation* as tabulated by the FBI (Levin, 2016) These are levels of Islamophobic hate crimes not seen since the months immediately following the attacks of 9/11, a year (2001) that recorded 481 anti-Muslim hate crimes (Lichtblau, 2016). The largest previous increase since 2001 was in 2010 when anti-Muslim hate crime rose from 107 to 160, a rise of 49.5 percent amid a controversy over the "Ground Zero mosque" in New York City (Levin, 2016). Experts also point out that the numbers of actual hate crimes against Muslims in the United States is likely higher than documented because Muslims and other hate crime victims are "often reluctant to report attacks for fear of inflaming community tensions, and because it is sometimes difficult for investigators to establish that religious, ethnic or racial hatred was a cause" (Lichtblau, 2016).

One of the most notable anti-Muslim hate crimes occurred in Chapel Hill, North Carolina. In February 2015, a man named Craig Stephen Hicks turned himself into police in the shooting deaths of a young Muslim family. All three of the victims, Deah Barakat (23), Yusor Abu-Salha (21), and Razan Abu-Salha (19), were killed in their home. Barakat was a second-year medical student in the University of North Carolina (UNC) at Chapel Hill's School of Dentistry. His wife, Yusor, was a North Carolina State University (NCSU) graduate planning to enter UNC Dentistry School, and her sister Razan was a student at NCSU majoring in architecture and environmental design. According to authorities, the three victims, aged 19–23, were killed in their home with gunshot wounds to the head in "execution style murders" (Husain, 2015). According to the *New York Times*, Hicks had a "deep dislike of all religion. On his Facebook page, nearly all of his posts expressed support for atheism, criticism of Christian conservatives or both" (Katz & Pérez-Peña, 2015). Friends of the murdered students in Chapel Hill also claim Hicks had become "obsessed" with one of his victims because of the head scarf she wore every day as a sign of her faith.

The 2016 president election has also been cited as a factor in the rise in anti-Muslim hate crimes during 2015 and 2016 (Abdelkader, 2016). During the course of 2015, Abdelkader, as part of the Bridge Initiative (a multiyear Georgetown University research project that documents Islamophobia in all its forms), found "approximately 174 reported incidents of anti-Muslim violence and vandalism, including: 12 murders; 29 physical assaults; 50 threats against persons or institutions; 54 acts of vandalism or destruction of property; 8 arsons; and 9 shootings or bombings, among other incidents" (Abdelkader, 2016). Anti-Muslim violence, as the Bridge Initiative notes

remained significantly higher in 2015 than pre-9/11 levels, with American Muslims approximately 6 to 9 times more likely to suffer such attacks. Since the start of the [2016] presidential election cycle [to May 2016], American Muslim men [were] twice as likely to be victims of physical assaults and about 11 times more likely to be the victims of murder than their female counterparts. Anti-Muslim violence remained significantly higher in 2015 than pre-9/11 levels with American Muslims approximately 6 to 9 times more likely to suffer such attacks. The number of incidents [154] in 2015 is also higher than the total number of anti-Muslim hate crimes reported in 2014. (Abdelkader, 2016)

Journalist Eric Lichtblau notes that "anti-Muslim attacks are not only rising in total numbers, but as a percentage of overall hate crimes" (Lichtblau, 2016). Additionally, as Brian Levin, author of the CSHE report, stated, "there's very compelling evidence that political rhetoric may well play a role in directing behavior in the aftermath of a terrorist attack" (Foran, 2016). Indeed, political rhetoric in the aftermath of terrorist attacks carried out by self-identified Muslims shows a correlation between incidents of hate crimes against Muslims and reactions to terrorist attacks. In his research, Levin examined incidents of hate crimes following presidential reactions to two acts of terrorism—9/11 and the 2015 San Bernardino attack. President George W. Bush responded to 9/11 by stating, "Islam is peace" and "the face of terror is not the true faith of Islam" (Bush, 2001). After San Bernardino, by contrast, Republican presidential candidate Donald Trump called for a ban on Muslims entering the United States. Levin's findings reveal a steep rise in hate crimes following Trump's remarks, and a significant drop in hate crimes after Bush's speech, relative to the number of hate crimes immediately following the initial terror attacks (Foran, 2016).

American citizens who voted for Donald Trump in the 2016 presidential election were more likely than other voters to see Muslims as threats to America and to view the nation as a Christian one (Banks, 2017). According to a Baylor Religion Survey, almost three quarters of Trump voters said Islam is a threat, compared with only 18 percent of those who voted for Hillary Clinton. An even higher percentage (81 percent) of Trump voters strongly agreed that Middle East refugees are a terror threat, compared with 12 percent of Clinton voters (Baylor Religions Survey, 2017). Another study by the Voter Study Group—comprising 20 conservative and professional survey researchers—found that most voters who switched from Barack Obama in 2012 to Trump in 2016 were motivated by their views on immigration, blacks, and Muslims. Among whites who voted for Obama in 2012 and Trump in 2016, 37 percent had a negative view of Muslims (Shepard, 2017).

Another factor in the rise of Islamophobia in the United States is what journalist Christopher Mathias described in 2017 as an "unholy alliance" of Islamophobic hate groups. This alliance consists of organizations like ACT! for America and Stop the Islamization of America, neo-Nazis, white supremacists, and armed antigovernment militia members. According to the Southern Poverty Law Center (SPLC), the convergence of anti-Muslim hate groups and other fringe organizations is a growing phenomenon in the United States. Trawling through all the local "March against Sharia" Facebook groups in June 2017, the SPLC compiled an extensive list of extremist groups and white supremacists who said they will attend the marches (Lemons, 2017). The SPLC found a slew of armed antigovernment militia groups or "Patriot" groups including the Oathkeepers, the III Percenters, and American Civil Defense (Lemons, 2017). The number of anti-Muslim groups known to be operating in the country rose from just 34 in 2015 to 101 in 2016—a 197 percent increase (Potok, 2017). The SPLC attributed this rise in radical right attacks to the candidacy of Trump.

Polls also have found a correlation between Islamophobia and the lack of exposure to American Muslims. A survey carried out by the Public Religion Research Institute (PRRI) in 2015 showed the important role that social context plays in reproducing and combatting Islamophobia. The PRRI survey highlights that relatively few Americans regularly interact with Muslims. Only 8 percent of Americans reported having had a conversation with someone who is Muslim at least once a day in the past year. About 3 in 10 (29 percent) participants report occasional interactions with someone who is Muslim, while more than 6 in 10 say they seldom (26 percent) or never (36 percent) have had such a conversation (Cooper, 2017). The PRRI also found that Americans who have had conversations with Muslims at least occasionally express much more positive views of Muslims than those who report much less regular interaction.

The lack of exposure to American Muslims and its connection to anti-Muslim sentiments in the United States is also highlighted by a joint survey carried out by the Pew Research Center. In 2014, a Pew poll revealed that only 38 percent of Americans even know a Muslim. Similarly, the findings detailed in a *Huffington Post*/YouGov poll on Americans' views of Muslims show that 55 percent of Americans had either a somewhat or very unfavorable view of Islam, while 25 percent said they were not sure how they viewed the faith (Moore, 2015). While a majority of the participants had negative views in the YouGov survey, few Americans based those judgments on direct knowledge of Muslims. One in ten said that they had never been to a mosque. Just 13 percent said that they "understand the Islamic religion" either "extremely well or very well" (Kaleem, 2015).

Even before these surveys, polls indicated that U.S. citizens were largely unfamiliar with the lives and beliefs of American Muslims. In a 2005 poll, roughly two thirds of Americans (66 percent) said that they knew little or nothing about Islam and its practices, while just 5 percent said they knew a great deal about Islam. These figures are nearly identical to the findings of a similar poll published in mid-November 2001 (Keeter & Kohut, 2005). The figures of both studies suggest that those who are more knowledgeable about Islam and more likely to interact with Muslims are more tolerant of Muslims in the United States.

FURTHER READING

Abdelkader, Engy. (2016, May 2). *When Islamophobia Turns Violent: The 2016 U.S. Presidential Elections.* Washington, DC: The Bridge Initiative of Georgetown University. bridge.georgetown.edu. Retrieved from http://bridge.georgetown.edu/when-islamophobia-turns-violent-the-2016-u-s-presidential-elections/

Allen, Chris. (2010). *Islamophobia.* Farnham: Asghate.

Banks, Adelle M. (2017, September 7). "Survey: Trump Voters 'Anti-Islam, Anti-Feminist, Anti-Globalist.'" *Religion News.* Retrieved from http://religionnews.com/2017/09/07/survey-trump-voters-anti-islam-anti-feminist-anti-globalist/

Baylor Religions Survey. (2017). "American Values, Mental Health, and Using Technology in the Age of Trump." Waco, TX: Baylor University. Retrieved from http://www.baylor.edu/baylorreligionsurvey/index.php?id=942304

Bravo-Lopez, Fernando. (2011). "Towards a Definition of Islamophobia: Approximations of the Early Twentieth Century." *Ethnic and Racial Studies,* 34: 556–573.

Bush, George W. (2001, September 17). "'Islam Is Peace' Says President. The White House—President George W. Bush Archives." Washington, DC: White House Archives. Retrieved from https://georgewbush-white house.archives.gov/news/releases/2001/09/20010917-11.html

Considine, Craig. (2017). "The Racialization of Islam in the United States: Islamophobia, Hate Crimes, and 'Flying while Brown.'" *Religions,* 8(9): 1–19.

Cooper, Betsy. (2017, February 6). "Americans Who Interact with Muslims Hold More Positive Views of Muslims, Refugees." Public Religion Research Institute. Retrieved from https://www.prri.org/spotlight/social-contact-muslims-refugee-ban/

Council on American-Islamic Relations. (2017, May 9). *The Empowerment of Hate: The Civil Rights Implications of Islamophobic Bias in the U.S. 2014–2016.* Washington, DC: Council on American-Islamic Relations. Retrieved from http://www.islamophobia.org/15-reports/188-the-empowerment-of-hate.html

The Daily Mail and Associated Press. (2015, March 4). "North Caro-lina Man Who Gunned Down Three Muslim Students Was 'Obsessed' with Victim's Head Scarf . . . as Prosecutors Seek the Death Penalty." Daily Mail and Associated Press. Retrieved from http://www.dailymail .co.uk/news/article-2977680/NC-prosecutor-seeks-death-suspect-kill ing-3-Muslims.html

Foran, Clare. (2016, September 22). "Donald Trump and the Rise of Anti-Muslim Violence." *The Atlantic*. Retrieved from https://www.the atlantic.com/politics/archive/2016/09/trump-muslims-islamophobia-hate-crime/500840/

Husain, Rahat. (2015, February 11). "Muslims React Swiftly to Chapel Hill, NC, Killings." Washington, DC: Institute for Social Policy and Understanding. Retrieved from https://www.ispu.org/muslims-react-swiftly-to-chapel-hill-nc-killings/

Hussain, Amir. (2016). *Muslims and the Making of America*. Waco, TX: Baylor University Press.

Kaleem, Jaweed. (2015, April 10). "More Than Half of Americans Have Unfavorable View of Islam, Poll Finds." *The Huffington Post*. Retrieved from http://www.huffingtonpost.com/2015/04/10/americans-islam-poll_n_ 7036574.html

Katz, Jonathan M., & Pérez-Peña, Richard. (2015, February 11). "In Chapel Hill Shooting of 3 Muslims, a Question of Motive." *The New York Times*. Retrieved from https://www.nytimes.com/2015/02/12/us/ muslim-student-shootings-north-carolina.html

Keeter, Scott, & Kohut, Andrew. (2005, May 11). *Muslims in the United States: Identity, Influence, Innovation*. Washington, DC: Woodrow Wilson International Center for Scholars.

Lemons, Stephen. (2017, June 14). "Fear and Loathing of Islam on Display at ACT's March against Sharia Rally in Phoenix." Mont-gomery, AL: Southern Poverty Law Center. Retrieved from https:// www.splcenter.org/hatewatch/2017/06/14/fear-and-loathing-islam-display-act%E2%80%99s-march-against-sharia-rally-phoenix

Levin, Brian. (2016). *Special Status Report: Hate Crime in the United States (20 State Compilation of Official Data)*. San Bernardino, CA: Center for the Study of Hate and Extremism at the California State University, San Bernardino. Retrieved from https://www.documentcloud.org/doc uments/3110202-SPECIAL-STATUS-REPORT-v5-9-16-16.html

Lichtblau, Eric. (2016, September 17). "Hate Crimes against American Muslims Most since Post-9/11 Era." *The New York Times*. Retrieved from https://www.nytimes.com/2016/09/18/us/politics/hate-crimes-ameri can-muslims-rise.html

Mathias, Christopher. (2017). "The 'March against Sharia' Protests Are Really Marches against Muslims." *The Huffington Post*. Retrieved from http://www.huffingtonpost.com/entry/march-against-sharia-anti-muslim-act-for-america_us_5939576ee4b0b13f2c67d50c

Moore, Peter. (2015, March 9). "Poll Results: Islam." *YouGov*. Retrieved from https://today.yougov.com/news/2015/03/09/poll-results-islam/

O'Neill, Brendan. (2015, January 9). "Islamophobia Is a Myth." *National Review*. Retrieved from http://www.nationalreview.com/article/411371/islamophobia-myth-brendan-oneill

Pew Research Center. (2014). *Religious Landscape Study: Muslims*. Washington, DC: Pew Research Center. Retrieved from http://www.pewforum.org/religious-landscape-study/religious-tradition/muslim/

Pew Research Center. (2017, November 15). "Assaults against Muslims in U.S. Surpass 2001 Level." Washington, DC: Pew Research Center. Retrieved from http://www.pewresearch.org/fact-tank/2017/11/15/assaults-against-muslims-in-u-s-surpass-2001-level/

Potok, Mark. (2017, February 15). "The Year in Hate and Extremism." Montgomery, AL: Southern Poverty Law Center. Retrieved from https://www.splcenter.org/fighting-hate/intelligence-report/2017/year-hate-and-extremism

Runnymede Trust. (1997). "Islamophobia: A Challenge for Us All." The Runnymede Trust (UK). Retrieved from http://www.runnymedetrust.org/uploads/publications/pdfs/islamophobia.pdf

Semkiw, Marissa. (2015). "Expert: 'Islamophobia' Is a Muslim Brotherhood Invention to 'Stifle Criticism.'" *The Rebel*. Retrieved from http://www.therebel.media/u_of_t_professor_islamophobia

Shepard, Steven. (2017, June 13). "Study: Views on Immigration, Muslims Drove White Voters to Trump." *Politico*. Retrieved from https://www.politico.com/story/2017/06/13/trump-white-voters-immigration-muslims-239446

Q22. ARE MUSLIMS IN THE UNITED STATES MORE LIKELY TO BE VICTIMIZED BY HATE CRIMES THAN OTHER MINORITY POPULATIONS?

Answer: No. American Muslims face high levels of hate crimes in the United States in comparison to many other minorities, but crime data indicate that Jews and LGBTQ individuals are even more likely to be so victimized.

The Facts: In January 2015, a U.S. citizen named John David Weissinger called the San Diego office of the Council on American-Islamic Relations (CAIR) and left a terrifying voice mail: "You're gonna be in the news. It's gonna be like *Charlie Hebdo*," said Weissinger, referring to the deadly attack on the staff of the French satirical magazine. Weissinger followed up with an email to CAIR spokesman Ibrahim Hooper. "I'll show up any day, any time with plenty of firepower to kill any and everyone one of you f*****s," Weissinger wrote. "It's coming your way and Hell is coming with it" (Mathias, 2016). The CAIR reported the voice mail to San Diego police, who tracked Weissinger down and arrested him two weeks later. Weissinger plead guilty in August 2015 to felony charges of possessing an illegal firearm and making a criminal threat determined to be a hate crime. During a sentencing hearing, Weissinger's attorney advanced a peculiar argument for sentencing leniency: his client, who was drunk when he made the threats, had committed the crimes "after a week of watching Fox News over and over. . . . Fox News is a hate machine, spewing out horrible things" (Mathias, 2016).

Weissinger's actions and case have been cited as a reminder that misinformation and hateful rhetoric toward American Muslims have consequences. According to the FBI, "since 9/11, American Muslims, and those living in the United States who are perceived to be Muslims, have faced a steady rise in racially and religiously motivated hate crimes" (FBI, n.d.). According to the FBI's annual tally, 21 percent of the hate crimes the organization counted in 2016 were motivated by religious bias (FBI, n.d.). Of those religious-based incidents, 25 percent were anti-Muslim (FBI, n.d.). In 2016, there were 127 reported victims of aggravated or simple assault, compared with 91 the year before and 93 in 2001 (Kishi, 2017). There was a nearly 20 percent increase in anti-Muslim incidents in the same year, an increase not seen since the period directly following the 9/11 attacks (Mathias, 2017b).

A May 2017 report by the CAIR reported that "hate crimes against Muslims in the United States rose dramatically in 2016, just as they did in 2015" (Pitter, 2017). In 2016, the CAIR recorded "a 57 [percent] increase in anti-Muslim bias incidents over 2015, which was accompanied by a 44 [percent] increase in anti-Muslim hate crimes in the same period." Another key finding in the CAIR report highlights that Islamophobic bias continues its trend toward increasing violence (Council on American-Islamic Relations, 2017b).

But assaults are not the only form of hate crime carried out against Muslims and other religious groups (Pew Research Center, 2017). Harassment, a nonviolent or nonthreatening bias incident, was the most frequent type of abuse in 2016, accounting for 18 percent of the total number of incidents (Council on American-Islamic Relations, 2017b). Using the FBI's annual tally of hate crimes, the Pew Research Center calculated that "intimidation," or the reasonable fear of bodily harm, is the most common form of hate crime. According to Pew, anti-Muslim intimidation also increased in 2016, with 144 reported victims, compared with 120 in 2015 (Pew Research Center, 2017).

The actual number of anti-Muslim hate crime incidents in the United States is likely higher than the numbers documented in the 2016 CAIR report. American Muslims, the organization wrote, "will often not report incidents such as harassment and bullying since there is a certain level of desensitization." The CAIR added that some American Muslims often feel like "nothing can be done" when they are harassed for their faith, feeling that such incidents "have become normal" (Mathias, 2017a).

Few groups in the United States face more arson attacks and acts of vandalism against their places of worship than American Muslims. Since 9/11, mosques across the country have been subjected to an increased number of hate crime incidents. In 2017, the CAIR mapped 35 incidents that took place across 19 states from January 1 to March 27 in which mosques were targets of threats, vandalism, or arson. By comparison, during the same period in 2016, the CAIR counted just 19 incidents (Coleman, 2017). The previous high of 53 such incidents came in 2010, when controversy arose in New York City over whether or not to build an Islamic center near "ground zero" of the 9/11 terrorist attacks. This harassment can take many forms. In October 2017, for example, the CAIR called on the FBI to investigate an image tweeted by an anti-Muslim group led by conspiracy theorist John Guandolo, whose post purported to show the bombing of the CAIR headquarters in Washington, D.C. (Council on American-Islamic Relations, 2017a). The CAIR's National Litigation Director Lisa Masri wrote to the FBI's Criminal Division in Washington, noting, "Guandolo's actions constitute 'true threats' and are a violation of 18 U.S.C. 875(c) which makes it a crime to transmit in interstate commerce 'any communication containing any threat to injure the property or . . . the person of another'" (Council on American-Islamic Relations, 2017a).

Hate crimes against Muslims are more likely to occur in major U.S. cities. In 2016, hate crimes in cities rose more than 20 percent, an increase attributed to the inflamed passions during the presidential campaign and more willingness for victims to step forward (Reuters, 2017). The Center for the Study of Hate and Extremism at California State University–San

Bernardino collected numbers from police departments in nine cities and found a total of 1,037 hate crime incidents, a 23 percent increase from the previous years. The cities in question were New York; Washington; Chicago; Philadelphia; Montgomery County; Maryland; Columbus, Ohio; Seattle, Long Beach, California; and Cincinnati (Levin, n.d.). The majority (60 percent) of American Muslims reported some level of religious discrimination in 2016, significantly surpassing the rates reported by all other religious groups (ranging from 38 percent among Jews to 11 percent among Catholics) (Mogahed & Chouhoud, 2017). Young Muslims, Muslim women, and Arabs are particularly susceptible to discrimination based on religion (Mogahed and Chouhoud, 2017).

According to the FBI, Muslims are ranked third on the list of groups most likely to be targeted for hate crimes in the United States. LGBTQ people ranked first. Near a fifth of the 5,461 single-bias hate crimes reported to the FBI in 2014 were because of the target's sexual orientation, or, in some cases, the target's perceived orientation (FBI, 2015). Attention to hate crimes involving LGBTQ people intensified in June 2016, after the massacre at Pulse, an LGBTQ nightclub in Orlando, Florida. An American-born Muslim, Omar Mateen, carried out an anti-LGBTQ hate crime and then pledged allegiance to ISIS during a 911 phone call during the attack (Fantz, Karimi, & McLaughlin, 2016). Mateen's choice of target, an LGBT club, highlighted the magnitude of crimes targeting LGBTQ people in the United States (Koeze, 2016). In terms of religious groups that face hate crimes, the FBI noted that Jews are the primary victims of religious hate crimes. Fifty-seven percent of all hate crimes in 2014 were committed against Jews (Markind, 2015). For a point in comparison, anti-Muslim hate crimes in 2014 amount to 16 percent of all hate crimes (Wilensky, 2017).

The American Sikh population also suffers from hate crimes inspired by Islamophobia. Sikhs and other individuals who are erroneously perceived to be Muslims, including South Asians and Arabs of various religious practices, also have been the targets of racial and religious profiling (Considine, 2017; Tanenbaum Center, n.d.). In November 2016, the FBI released its annual report on hate crimes, which, for the very first time, included reported hate crimes committed against Sikhs. The agency reported a total of six hate crimes committed against Sikhs in 2015 (FBI, 2015). While it is difficult to know the true number of hate crimes against Sikhs, the U.S. Department of Justice has noted that, since 9/11, there have been over 800 investigations by the FBI and U.S. attorneys on bias incidents against Sikhs, Arabs, Muslims, and South Asian Americans (U.S. Department of Justice, n.d.b). In a March 2017 statement, the Sikh Coalition, America's largest Sikh civil rights group, said that Sikhs are often targeted for hate crimes in part "due to the Sikh articles of faith, including a turban and beard, which represent the Sikh religious commitment to justice, tolerance and equality" (Suri & Wu, 2017). According to many reports, anti-Muslim bigots often mistake Sikhs for Muslims, because they commonly wear turbans and grow their beards (Marans, 2016). Ethnicity and national origin were revealed as the top trigger of anti-Muslim bias incidents in 2016 (Council on American-Islamic Relations, 2017b).

Throughout American history, almost every religious group has been the target of discrimination at one point or another (American Civil Liberties Union, n.d.). Significant measures were taken by the U.S. government during the civil rights movement to tackle hate crimes. In 1968, President Lyndon Johnson signed into law the first federal hate crimes statute. The 1968 statute made it a crime to use, or threaten to use, force to willfully interfere with any person because of race, color, religion, or national origin. Roughly three decades later, Congress passed the Church Arson Prevention Act. Under this Act, it is a crime to deface, damage, or destroy religious property or interfere with a person's religious practice, in situations affecting interstate commerce.

This Act also made it illegal to deface, damage, or destroy mosques and other places of worship. Perhaps the most impactful piece of anti–hate crime legislation to be passed by the U.S. government came in 2009, when President Barack Obama signed the Matthew Shepard and James Byrd Jr. Hate Crimes Prevention Act. This Act expanded the federal definition of hate crimes, enhancing the legal toolkit available to prosecutors and increasing the ability of federal law enforcement to support local and state partners. Other governmental agencies are working to track hate crimes in a more efficient manner. In a November 2015 interview with the *New York Times*, James B. Comey, then FBI director, said that the United States needs "to do a better job of tracking and reporting hate crimes to fully understand what is happening in our communities and how to stop." He added that the FBI regards the prosecution of hate crimes under federal jurisdiction as the top priority of its civil rights branch (Lichtbalu, 2016).

American Muslims and their non-Muslim allies have joined in solidarity to oppose hate crimes against Muslims in the United States. In June 2017, a memorial to Nabra Hassanen, a 17-year-old girl who was bludgeoned to death with a baseball bat by Darwin Martinez Torres after leaving her mosque in Virginia, was created in downtown Washington, D.C.,. Abas Sherif, a spokesman for the Hassenen family, told local media that Nabra was targeted for wearing the hijab (Newton, 2017). The D.C. memorial was subsequently set on fire, an incident that was also widely believed to be a hate crime (Newton, 2017). Hassanen's death and the fire at her memorial came during a time when the American Muslim population experienced a surge in violence. Nevertheless, the Hassenen memorial in Washington, D.C., represents one of many interfaith gatherings organized by Muslims and non-Muslims to stand against anti-Muslim violence and rhetoric.

FURTHER READING

American Civil Liberties Union. (n.d.). *Protecting the Religious Freedom of Muslims.* New York, NY: American Civil Liberties Union. Retrieved from https://www.aclu.org/feature/protecting-religious-freedom-muslims

Coleman, Nancy. (2017, March 20). "On Average, 9 Mosques Have Been Targeted Every Month This Year." CNN.com. Retrieved from http://www.cnn.com/2017/03/20/us/mosques-targeted-2017-trnd/index.html

Considine, Craig. (2017). "The Racialization of Islam in the United States: Islamophobia, Hate Crimes, and 'Flying while Brown.'" *Religions,* 8(9): 1–19.

Council on American-Islamic Relations. (2017a, October 31). "CAIR Asks FBI to Probe Tweet by Anti-Muslim Group Showing Bombing of 'CAIR HQ.'" Washington, DC: Council on American-Islamic Relations. Retrieved from https://www.cair.com/press-center/press-releases .html?limitstart=0

Council on American-Islamic Relations. (2017b, May 9). *The Empowerment of Hate: The Civil Rights Implications of Islamophobic Bias in the U.S. 2014–2016.* Washington, DC: Council on American-Islamic Relations. Retrieved from http://www.islamophobia.org/15-reports/188-the-empowerment-of-hate.html

Fantz, Ashley, Karimi, Faith, & McLaughlin, Eliott C. (2016, June 13). "Orlando Shooting: 49 Killed, Shooter Pledged ISIS Allegiance." CNN .com. Retrieved from http://www.cnn.com/2016/06/12/us/orlando-night club-shooting/

FBI. (2015). "Incidents, Offenses, Victims, and Known Offenders." Washington, DC: FBI. Retrieved from https://ucr.fbi.gov/hate-crime/2015/ tables-and-data-declarations/1tabledatadecpdf

FBI. (2016). *Crime in the United States.* Washington, DC: FBI. Retrieved from https://ucr.fbi.gov/ucr-publications#Hate

FBI. (n.d.). "2016 Hate Crime Statistics." Washington, DC: FBI. Retrieved from https://ucr.fbi.gov/hate-crime/2016/topic-pages/incidentsandoffenses

Kishi, Katayoun. (2017, November 15). "Assaults against Muslims in U.S. Surpass 2001 Level." Washington, DC: Pew Research Center. Retrieved from http://www.pewresearch.org/fact-tank/2017/11/15/ assaults-against-muslims-in-u-s-surpass-2001-level/

Koeze, Ella. (2016, June 14). "Hate Crimes against LGBT People Are Sadly Common." *Five Thirty Eight*. Retrieved from https://fivethirtye ight.com/features/hate-crimes-against-lgbt-people-are-sadly-common/

Levin, Brian. (n.d.). *Special Status Reports on Hate Crimes Can Be Found Here*. San Bernardino, CA: Center for the Study of Hate and Extremism at California State University, San Bernardino. Retrieved from https://csbs.csusb.edu/hate-and-extremism-center

Lichtbalu, Eric. (2016, November 14). "U.S. Hate Crimes Surge 6 Percent, Fueled by Attacks on Muslims." *The New York Times*. Retrieved from https://www.nytimes.com/2016/11/15/us/politics/fbi-hate-crimes-muslims.html

Marans, Daniel. (2016, January 5). "Wave of Islamophobia Catches Sikh American Community in Its Crosshairs." *The Huffington Post*. Retrieved from http://www.huffingtonpost.com/entry/sikh-murdered-fresno-california_us_568c596de4b0a2b6fb6dbe36

Markind, Johanna. (2015, December 5). "Jews Are Still the Biggest Target of Religious Hate Crimes." *Forward*. Retrieved from http://forward .com/news/325988/jews-are-still-the-biggest-target-of-hate-crimes/

Mathias, Christopher. (2016, January 22). "Did Binge-Watching Fox News Inspire This Man to Threaten Muslims?" *The Huffington Post*. Retrieved from https://www.huffingtonpost.com/entry/fox-news-anti-muslim-rhetoric_us_56a12d57e4b0d8cc10991d50

Mathias, Christopher. (2017a, May 9). "2016 Election Coincided with Horrifying Increase in Anti-Muslim Hate Crimes, Report Finds." *The Huffington Post*. Retrieved from http://www.huffingtonpost.com/entry/ anti-muslim-hate-crimes-2016-council-on-american-islamic-rela tions_us_5910acf4e4b0d5d9049e96d5

Mathias, Christopher. (2017b, November 13). "Hate Crimes Rose about 5 Percent in 2016, FBI Report Says." *The Huffington Post*. Retrieved from https://www.huffingtonpost.com/entry/fbi-hate-crimes-report-2016_ us_5a08c795e4b01d21c83f46ac?ncid=engmodushpmg00000004

Mogahed, Dalia, & Chouhoud, Youssef. (2017). *American Muslim Poll 2017: Muslims at the Crossroads*. Washington, DC: The Institute for Social Policy and Understanding. Retrieved from http://www.ispu.org/ wp-content/uploads/2017/05/AMP-2017_Full-Report.pdf

Newton, Creede. (2017, June 21). "Memorial to Slain American Muslim Teen Set Ablaze." *Al Jazeera*. Retrieved from http://www.aljazeera .com/news/2017/06/hate-crime-motive-probed-muslim-teen-murder-170621221830566.html

Pew Research Center. (2017, November 15). "Assaults against Muslims in U.S. Surpass 2001 Level." Washington, DC: Pew Research Center.

Retrieved from http://www.pewresearch.org/fact-tank/2017/11/15/assaults-against-muslims-in-u-s-surpass-2001-level/

Pitter, Laura. (2017, May 11). "Hate Crimes against Muslims in US Continue to Rise in 2016." *Human Rights Watch.* Retrieved from https://www.hrw.org/news/2017/05/11/hate-crimes-against-muslims-us-continue-rise-2016

Reuters. (2017, March 14). "U.S. Hate Crimes Up 20 Percent in 2016, Fueled by Election Campaign: Report." Retrieved from http://www.nbcnews.com/news/us-news/u-s-hate-crimes-20-percent-2016-fueled-election-campaign-n733306

Southern Poverty Law Center. (2016, October 25). *A Journalist's Manual: Field Guide to Anti-Muslim Extremists.* Montgomery, AL: Southern Poverty Law Center. Retrieved from https://www.splcenter.org/20161025/journalists-manual-field-guide-anti-muslim-extremists

Suri, Manveena, & Wu, Huizhong. (2017, March 7). "Sikhs: Religious Minority Target of Hate Crimes." CNN.com. Retrieved from http://www.cnn.com/2017/03/06/asia/sikh-hate-crimes-us-muslims/index.html

Tanenbaum Center. (n.d.). *Islamophobia: Challenges and Opportunities in the Workplace.* New York, NY: Tanenbaum. Retrieved from http://www.diversitybestpractices.com/sites/diversitybestpractices.com/files/attachments/2017/02/islamophobia_paper_final.pdf

U.S. Department of Justice. (n.d.a.). "Hate Crime Laws." Washington, DC: U.S. Department of Justice. Retrieved from https://www.justice.gov/crt/hate-crime-laws

U.S. Department of Justice. (n.d.b.). "Combating Post-9/11 Discriminatory Backlash." Washington, DC: U.S. Department of Justice. Retrieved from https://www.justice.gov/crt/combating-post-911-discriminatory-backlash-6

Wilensky, Uri. (2017, February 26). The Most Hated People in the United States May Not Be Who You Think. *The Huffington Post.* Retrieved from http://www.huffingtonpost.com/uri-wilensky/the-most-hated-people-in-_b_9327362.html

Q23. DO MUSLIMS FACE A SIGNIFICANT AMOUNT OF DISCRIMINATION IN TERMS OF JOB OPPORTUNITIES AND WORKPLACE EXPERIENCES IN THE UNITED STATES?

Answer: Yes. Job discrimination is one of the more significant challenges facing American Muslims, who are more likely to be unemployed and

rejected for jobs in comparison to American Christians with similar qualifications, particularly in politically and socially conservative states. Some
Muslims in the United States also face specific challenges at their places
of employment, such as not being granted prayer times and not being free
to wear the *hijab* or other forms of Islamic veiling.

The Facts: In March 2017, the *Chicago Tribune* published an article that
focused on job discrimination against Muslims. The article focused on a
former suburban Muslim police officer, Ramtin Sabet, who had filed a federal lawsuit alleging he was fired after complaining of constant workplace
harassment for being a "practicing Muslim." Sabet, an Iranian immigrant,
sued the city of North Chicago and its former and current police officers
after he was repeatedly called a "terrorist" and an "ISIS leader working as
a police officer" by his coworkers (Eldeib, 2017). Similarly, Jose Alcantara, an American Muslim, claimed that he was fired from a Bed Bath &
Beyond in Manhattan in a case of religious discrimination (Richards,
2017). According to a suit filed in Manhattan Supreme Court, Alcantara was subjected to months of torment after he revealed to coworkers
that he was growing his facial hair in adherence with his Muslim faith
(Brown & Schapiro, 2015). His colleagues repeatedly referred to him as a
"terrorist," which, Alcantara told the *New York Daily News*, "made [him]
question everything—my religion, my beliefs, myself" (Brown and Schapiro, 2015). The cases of Sabet and Alcantara are only scratching the
surface of cases involving job discrimination against American Muslims.
Between 9/11 and March 2012, 1,040 charges were filed related to attacks
on individuals who are—or are perceived to be—Muslim, Sikh, Arab,
Middle Eastern, or South Asian (U.S. Equal Employment Opportunity
Commission, n.d.).

Negative public perceptions of American Muslims has translated into
a serious issue of anti-Muslim discrimination in business environments
and workplaces across the country. According to the Pew Research Center (2011a), discrimination (20 percent) is the second most important
problem facing Muslims in the United States, trailing only negative views
about Muslims (29 percent). While the proportion of American Muslims
who are employed in full-time jobs (41 percent) roughly mirrors the general public (45 percent), underemployment is more common among Muslims than in the general public. According to the Pew Research Center
(2011b), approximately 29 percent of Muslims are either unemployed and
looking for work or working part-time but would prefer to have full-time
employment, compared with 20 percent of adults nationwide who are
in these circumstances. Underemployment also is more common among

younger Muslim adults in comparison to the American public at large (Pew Research Center, 2011b). Pew also reported in 2011 that 37 percent of those under 30 are underemployed, compared with 23 percent of those aged 40 to 54 and 14 percent of those 55 and older (Pew Research Center, 2011b). More than 20 percent of religion-based discrimination charges brought to the U.S. Equal Employment Opportunity Commission (n.d.) between 2001 and 2011 had been filed by Muslims.

Recent studies "indicate a pattern of religious discrimination in hiring in regions of New England and the Southern United States, with Muslims being the most heavily targeted" population (Equal Rights Center, n.d.). In one 2014 study, the Equal Rights Center (ERC), a civil rights organization that identifies discrimination in housing, employment, and public accommodation, sent mock résumés to U.S. companies in an attempt to apply for entry level jobs. The resumes were comparable in every facet except for religious affiliation. Apart from the control group, which had no religious affiliation, each resume listed affiliation with some type of on-campus religious organization, such as "Muslim Student Group." In New England, the ERC researchers submitted 6,400 resumes to 1,600 jobs advertised within 150 miles of Hartford, Connecticut. Muslim applicants got 32 percent fewer emails and 48 percent fewer callbacks—overall, they received 41 percent fewer contacts (Equal Rights Center, n.d.). In the southern United States, the ERC researchers sent 3,200 resumes to 800 jobs within 150 miles of two major southern cities. Muslims got 38 percent fewer emails and 54 percent fewer callbacks than the control group.

Similar results were discovered in a 2013 survey by researchers at Carnegie Mellon. Applicants who self-identified as Muslim on their social media profiles were called back at a lower rate nationwide by prospective employers than Christians with the same exact names and qualifications (Greenberg, 2013). In the Carnegie survey, researchers created fictional resumes, professional network profiles, and social network profiles for Muslim, Christian, gay, and straight job applicants and submitted the resumes to 4,183 openings across the United States. The resumes and profiles were comparable in every facet apart from the distinguishing variables. The study found that "employers that looked into an applicant's social media presence were more biased against the Muslim candidate than the Christian candidate" (Equal Rights Center, n.d.).

The 2013 Carnegie Mellon study uncovered additional findings. In Republican-leaning states, only 2 percent of applications by the Muslim candidate received interview invitations compared to 17 percent for the Christian candidate. Employers in most Republican states also were less likely to interview job candidates whose social networking profile indicate that the applicants are Muslim. Specifically, Muslim job candidates had a 13 percent lower callback rate compared to Christian candidates. Republican states exhibited significant bias both against Muslim candidates and in favor of Christian candidates (Acquisti & Fong, 2012).

Once hired, American Muslims also experience discrimination in the workplace environment (Lakhani, 2017). Muslim workers in the United States reported a record number of complaints based on employment discrimination (Greenhouse, 2010). Muslims in U.S. workplaces report being called "terrorist" or "Osama" and being barred from completing their five daily prayers. In terms of prayer breaks during work hours, 160 Somali immigrants in Grand Island, Nebraska, were fired from working at a JBS meatpacking plant in 2008. The Somalis had demanded and were refused time to pray and break their fast during the holy month of Ramadan (Semple, 2008). Some workers requested a bathroom break and would secretly pray during the time allotted (Considine, 2008). The JBS management suspected that they went not to the bathroom but to pray—at which point many of them were fired (Martin, 2008). The Somalis reported having blood, meat, and bones thrown at them for requesting break time (Greenhouse, 2010). Several other recent workplace complaints filed with the U.S. Equal Opportunity Employment Commission were settled with companies, including Autzo, Inc. and United Parcel Services, Inc., whose Muslim employees were taunted by colleagues, were referred to as "terrorists," or were not allowed to change schedules so they could go to the mosque to pray (Hymnowitz & Green, 2016).

American Muslims also experience religious discrimination in the health care industry, one of the nation's most highly regarded professions. In a national survey of 255 American Muslim physicians published by *AJOB Empirical Bioethics*, University of Chicago researchers found that nearly half of respondents felt greater scrutiny at workplaces compared to their peers (News Medical, 2015). Nearly 25 percent of respondents said workplace religious discrimination had taken place "sometimes"—or "more often"—during their career. The same percentage (25 percent) of American Muslims who participated in the study believed they have been passed over for career advancement due to their religion (News Medical, 2015).

Islamic organizations and American Muslim leaders have called on U.S. employers to help Muslims feel more accepted and safe at work. In a 2016 interview, Ibrahim Hooper, the communications director for the Council on American-Islamic Relations (CAIR), stated that the CAIR filed complaints on behalf of 100 Muslims fired in January 2016 from Fort Morgan Cargill, a meatpacking plant, after they staged a walk-out to protest what they said were restrictions on their ability to take prayer breaks (Hymnowitz & Green, 2016). The CAIR later welcomed the rulings by Colorado's Department of Labor and Employment, stating that the Muslim workers fired from Cargill were eligible for unemployment benefits. The Colorado Department of Labor and Employment rulings repeatedly stated: "No person should be expected to choose between fidelity to their religion and their job" (Council on American-Islamic Relations, 2016). Similarly, in May 2015, the U.S. Supreme Court overwhelmingly ruled against the retailer Abercrombie & Fitch for failing to accommodate a young American Muslim woman job applicant who wore a *hijab* (Levine, 2015). The clothing chain declined to hire Samantha Elauf in 2008 as a sales associate because her *hijab* violated the company's "look policy," which at the time prohibited employees from wearing head coverings (Levine, 2015). The late conservative Justice Antoninn Scalia of the U.S. Supreme Court defended Elauf's claim by referring to Title VII of the 1964 Civil Rights Act, which demands that U.S. employers reasonably accommodate a potential employee's religious beliefs without undue hardship to the employee (Levine, 2015). Though some local, state, and national laws guarantee "reasonable accommodations" to allow for workers' religious observances, many employers are unwilling to make minor arrangements for Muslims (Lakhani, 2017).

Several major U.S. companies have taken the lead to protect American Muslims in workplace environments. JP Morgan Chase & Co., the U.S. multinational banking and financial service, has initiated various efforts to accommodate the religious practices of Muslims. In 2016, the company announced that it would provide transportation to mosques and other places of worship for Muslim employees in offices not big enough to have prayer rooms (Hymnowitz & Green, 2016). At Accenture Plc, a global management consulting and professional service, the corporate calendar has been recently organized to prevent events from conflicting with Muslim holidays, such as Ramadan, as well as those of other faiths. Moreover, Horizon Blue Cross & Blue Shield, a health insurance provider, held a company Q&A session about religion in the aftermath of a terrorist attack in Paris in 2016 (Tanenbaum Center, n.d.). Mary Baynard, a senior vice president of Horizon Blue Cross & Blue Shield New Jersey's service division and chairman of its diversity council, stated that the Q&A "was cathartic for everyone" (Hymnowitz & Green, 2016).

While serving as the president of the United States, Barack Obama spoke out against Muslim discrimination on several occasions. In responding to Republican presidential candidate Donald Trump's anti-Muslim rhetoric in July 2016, President Obama called discriminatory policies against Muslims an insult to the "values that already make our nation great." He encouraged Americans "to be bigger than fear and ignorance and recognize that every individual, regardless of religion or faith, has a right to equal opportunity in employment" (Equal Rights Center, n.d.).

FURTHER READING

Acquisti, Alessandro, & Fong, Christina M. (2012). "An Experiment in Hiring Discrimination via Online Social Networks." Social Science Research Network. Retrieved from https://papers.ssrn.com/sol3/papers.cfm?abstract_id=2031979

Brown, Stephen R., & Schapiro, Rich. (2015, November 8). "Exclusive: Muslim Man Claims He Was Fired from Bed Bath & Beyond Because of His Beard." *The New York Daily News.* Retrieved from http://www.nydailynews.com/new-york/exclusive-muslim-man-bath-fired-beard-article-1.2427007

Considine, Craig. (2008, October 16). "Somali Muslims in Grand Island, Nebraska." CNN.com. Retrieved from http://ireport.cnn.com/docs/DOC-116276

Council on American-Islamic Relations. (2016, August 8). "CAIR Welcomes Rulings Granting Benefits to Fired Muslim Cargill Workers in Colorado." Washington, DC: Council on American-Islamic Relations. Retrieved from https://www.cair.com/press-center/press-releases/13691-cair-welcomes-rulings-granting-benefits-to-fired-muslim-cargill-workers-in-colorado.html

Eldeib, Duaa. (2017, March 24). "Ex-North Chicago Cop Sues, Says He Was Harassed, Then Fired, for Being Muslim." *The Chicago Tribune.* Retrieved from http://www.chicagotribune.com/news/local/breaking/ct-muslim-police-officer-lawsuit-met-20170324-story.html

Equal Rights Center. (n.d.). *Muslim Employment Discrimination.* Washington, DC: Equal Rights Center. Retrieved from https://equalrightscenter.org/muslim-employment-discrimination/

Greenberg, Allen. (2013, December 2). "Muslim Job Candidates May Face Greater Discrimination." *Benefits Pro.* Retrieved from http://www.benefitspro.com/2013/12/02/muslim-job-candidates-may-face-greater-discriminat?slreturn=1497361840

Greenhouse, Steven. (2010, September 23). "Muslims Report Rising Discrimination at Work." *The New York Times.* Retrieved from http://www.nytimes.com/2010/09/24/business/24muslim.html?pagewanted=all

Hymnowitz, Carol, & Green, Jeff. (2016, July 27). "The Rise of Muslim-Friendly Workplaces in Corporate America." *Bloomberg.* Retrieved from https://www.bloomberg.com/diversity-inclusion/blog/rise-muslim-friendly-workplaces-corporate-america/

Lakhani, Karim. (2017, February 15). *Workplace Discrimination against Muslims*. Cambridge MA: On Labor. Retrieved from https://onlabor.org/2017/02/15/workplace-discrimination-against-muslims/

Levine, Marianne. (2015, June 1). "Supreme Court Rules against Abercrombie in Hijab Case." *Politico*. Retrieved from http://www.politico.com/story/2015/06/ambercrombie-fitch-hijab-case-supreme-court-ruling-118492

Martin, Frankie. (2008, November 21). "Hundreds of Somali Muslims Fired for Praying." *The Huffington Post*. Retrieved from http://www.huffington post.com/frankie-martin/hundreds-of-somali-muslim_b_135485.html

News Medical. (2015, December 11). "Nearly Half of Muslim Americans Face Discrimination in Health Care Workplace." Retrieved from http://www.news-medical.net/news/20151211/Nearly-half-of-Muslim-Americans-face-discrimination-in-health-care-workplace.aspx

Pew Research Center. (2011a, August 30). *Muslim Americans: No Signs of Growth in Alienation or Support for Extremism*. Washington, DC: Pew Research Center. Retrieved from http://www.people-press.org/2011/08/30/muslim-americans-no-signs-of-growth-in-alienation-or-support-for-extremism/

Pew Research Center. (2011b, August 30). *Section 1: A Demographic Portrait of Muslim Americans*. Washington, DC: Pew Research Center. Retrieved from http://www.people-press.org/2011/08/30/section-1-a-demographic-portrait-of-muslim-americans/

Rascoe, Ayesha. (2016, July 21). "Discrimination against Muslims an Affront of American Values: Obama." Reuters. Retrieved from http://www.reuters.com/article/us-obama-muslims-idUSKCN10131V

Richards, Kimberley. (2017, January 16). "Muslim Man Fired from Bed Bath & Beyond Says He Was Called 'Terrorist.'" *The Huffington Post*. Retrieved from http://www.huffingtonpost.com/entry/muslim-man-fired-bed-bath-beyond_us_5640aed2e4b0b24aee4add11

Sahgal, Neha. (2013, November 26). "Study: Muslim Job Candidates May Face Discrimination in Republican States." Washington, DC: Pew Research Center. Retrieved from http://www.pewresearch.org/fact-tank/2013/11/26/study-muslim-job-candidates-may-face-discrimination-in-republican-states/

Semple, Kirk. (2008, October 15). "A Somali Influx Unsettles Latino Meatpackers." *The New York Times*. Retrieved from http://www.nytimes.com/2008/10/16/us/16immig.html?pagewanted=1&_r=1&bl&ei=5087&en=2dc94ea08df22d41&ex=1224302400

Tanenbaum Center. (n.d.). *Islamophobia: Challenges and Opportunities in the Workplace.* New York, NY: Tanenbaum. Retrieved from http://www.diversitybestpractices.com/sites/diversitybestpractices.com/files/attachments/2017/02/islamophobia_paper_final.pdf

U.S. Equal Employment Opportunity Commission. (n.d.). "What You Should Know about the EEOC and Religious and National Origin Discrimination Involving the Muslim, Sikh, Arab, Middle Eastern and South Asian Communities." Washington, DC: U.S. Congress. Retrieved from https://www.eeoc.gov/eeoc/newsroom/wysk/religion_national_origin_9-11.cfm

Q24. DO AMERICAN MEDIA AND THE U.S. ENTERTAINMENT INDUSTRY UNFAIRLY REPRESENT MUSLIMS AS VIOLENT PEOPLE?

Answer: Yes. Studies have found that the media and entertainment industry tend to depict Muslims as oppressors of women, extremists, and terrorists. These negative depictions ultimately influence how non-Muslims in the United States view Muslims in their midst. American Muslims and their allies are working to improve the image of Islam and representations of Muslims in the media and entertainment industry.

The Facts: At his first address to a session of Congress, President Donald Trump reiterated his plan to focus on "radical Islamic terrorism." In his speech, the president revealed the measures his administration had taken to protect the nation from Muslims who might be sympathetic to the cause of ISIS or Al-Qaeda. Citing data provided by the U.S. Department of Justice, Trump claimed "the vast majority of individuals convicted for terrorism-related offenses since 9/11 came here from outside of our country." A few weeks earlier, he had provided a list of terrorist attacks he claimed were underreported by the news media, a list that primarily included attacks by Muslim perpetrators (Bump, 2017; Kearns, Betus, & Lemieux, 2017a). Terrorist attacks frequently dominate news coverage in the United States as reporters and media outlets seek to provide the American public with information about the event, its perpetrators, and the victims (Kearns, Betus, & Lemieux, 2017b). Yet, not all terrorist attacks receive equal attention. Since 9/11, negative messages about Muslims have received more media attention than positive ones. Scholars have revealed that Muslims are frequently associated with political violence and terrorism in the news, and these media portrayals influence public opinion of both American Muslims and policies affecting Muslims at home and abroad (Terman, 2017).

In a study on how private organizations with pro- and anti-Islam agendas interacted with media, Christopher Bail, a sociologist at the University of North Carolina, collected 1,084 press releases from 120 organizations, including Muslim groups and Christian evangelical groups. He found that press releases that were emotional, displaying fear and anger, had the best chance of getting the media's attention (85 percent of all the press releases were unnoticed by journalists). In another study on news stories collected from LexisNexis Academic and CNN for all terrorist attacks in the United States between 2011 and 2015, researchers from Georgia State University found that news media give drastically more coverage to attacks by Muslims, particularly foreign-born Muslims, than by non-Muslim offenders—even though attacks by Muslims constitute a small overall percentage of all terrorist attacks. Attacks by Muslim perpetrators received, on average, 449 percent more coverage than attacks carried out by non-Muslims (Kearns, Betus, & Lemieux, 2017b). Erin Kearns, one of the authors of the study, told National Public Radio (2017b) in June 2017 that according to their findings, "a perpetrator who is not Muslim would have to kill on average about seven more people to receive the same amount of coverage as a perpetrator who is Muslim."

According to Media Tenor International, a research institute that studies data for NGOs and governments, news outlets such as Fox News, NBC News, and CBS News depicted Islam primarily as a source of violence between 2007 to 2013 (Media Tenor International, n.d.). In an earlier 2011 report, Media Tenor found that out of nearly 975,000 news stories from U.S. and European media outlets, networks significantly reduced coverage on events in the Middle East to actions of Muslim militants (Media Tenor International, 2011). The disparity of coverage was further discussed by John Esposito, a professor at Georgetown University, who compared media coverage of Muslims in the years 2001 and 2011. In 2001, 2 percent of all news stories in the Western media focused on Muslim militants, while just over 0.1 percent presented stories of "ordinary" Muslims—the mainstream majority. By 2011, the 2 percent of stories had risen to 25 percent on militant Muslim images and stories, while the coverage of ordinary mainstream Muslims remained at 0.1 percent (Esposito, 2016). The net result is an astonishing imbalance of coverage and an exponential increase in coverage of militants, but no increase at all over the 10-year period in the coverage of "ordinary" Muslims (Esposito, 2015).

Correctly or not, American Muslims and Muslims around the world perceive the Western media as hostile to them. Akbar Ahmed, author of *Islam Today*, argues that "the general attitude of hostility is true. Western programs about Muslims are often slanted to suggest negative images of Muslims" (Ahmed, 2002). In the case of American Muslims, they appear to be conscious of the negative images of Islam and Muslims in the news media. A 2017 Pew survey found most U.S. Muslims (60 percent) perceive media coverage of Islam and Muslims as unfair, and a similar share (62 percent) think the American people as a whole do not see Islam as part of mainstream American society. These views are largely echoed by U.S. adults overall, many of whom (53 percent) agree that media coverage of Muslims is unfair and say they personally do not see (50 percent) Islam as part of mainstream society (Pew Research Center, 2017).

The U.S. entertainment industry, which also plays a role in exacerbating Islamophobia, was a point of focus during President Barack Obama's speech at the Islamic Society of Baltimore in February 2016. In his address, President Obama encouraged films and television shows to have American Muslim characters that are unrelated to national security. "[The entertainment industry should] lift up the contributions of the Muslim-American community not when there's a problem, but all the time," Obama said. "Our television shows should have some Muslim characters that are unrelated to national security. It's not that hard to do. There was a time when there were no black people on television and you can tell good stories while still representing the realities of our communities."

Experts on the characterization of Muslims in the U.S. entertainment industry have echoed Obama's remarks, criticizing Hollywood for using Islam to drive the action in storytelling, rather than to flesh out Muslim character details (Rosenberg, 2016). In television shows and films like *Homeland*, *24*, and *Argo*, Americans come across a steady stream of stereotypes of Muslims (Harvard, 2015). American cinema, too, has historically employed a narrow set of stereotypes about Arabs and Muslims (Rose, 2016). Professor Jack Shaheen spent his entire career analyzing the way that Arabs (who are strongly associated in America with Islam) have been portrayed in U.S. films and television over the last century. His book *Reel Bad Arabs* (2004) showed how Hollywood depicts Arabs as "brute murderers, sleazy rapists, religious fanatics, oil-rich dimwits and abusers of women." Shaheen's research documented well over 1,200 films depicting Arabs and subsequently found that 932 films depict Arabs in a stereotypical or negative light. Only 12 films had a positive depiction. By his estimation, roughly 97 percent are unfavorable, colored by Orientalist myths, racist demonizing, and xenophobic paranoia. At most, three dozen or so had balance, or what Shaheen called "positive images" (Rose, 2016). In the rest of them, "Arabs are either terrorists or shady *sheikhs* or people you would not want to associate with. Those images continue to pervade our psyches" (Rose, 2016).

Shaheen cites films that portray Arabs as cold money-hungry oil Muslims or inept villainous terrorists who seek to destroy Western civilization. In the popular movie *Back to the Future*, for example, the antagonists who shoot the main character are described "as Libyan terrorists who shout Arabic gibberish as they ruthlessly gun down the protagonist" (Beydoun & Ayoub, 2015). Another case in point is *American Sniper*, a Clint Eastwood–directed picture. The protagonist of the film, a U.S. soldier from middle America, is depicted "as a lionized soldier," whereas Arabs and Muslims in Iraq are depicted as "unyieldingly wretched, menacing, and bent on the destruction of everything pure and civilized" (Beydoun & Ayoub, 2015). Following the release of *American Sniper*, the American-Arab Anti-Discrimination Committee (2014) issued a community advisory and warned of a "significant rise in violent hate rhetoric targeting the Arab and Muslim-American communities."

Other examples include *True Lies* (Arnold Schwarzenegger versus fanatical yet incompetent Palestinian terrorists, who detonate a nuclear device in Florida), *Protocol* (Goldie Hawn becomes a concubine to a lecherous oil-rich *sheikh*, so that the United States can build a military base in his country), *The Siege* (in which Arab Americans are rounded up after a New York terrorist attack), and *Rules of Engagement* (in which Samuel L. Jackson, a Marine goes on trial for massacring a crowd of Yemenis but is exonerated when it turns out they were all gun-toting evildoers, even the women and children) (Rose, 2016).

In his review of *The Siege*, starring Denzel Washington, film critic Roger Ebert wrote: "The prejudicial attitudes embodied in the film are insidious, like the Anti-Semitism that infected fiction and journalism in the 1930s" (Ebert, 1998). The screenplay caught the attention of critics for depicting Arab Muslims as blowing up New York City and killing hundreds of innocent people. While movie critics blasted *The Siege* for trafficking an anti-Arab message, Tony Shalhoub, an Arab American actor who played an FBI agent in the movie, applauded his character for showing Arab Americans in a positive light—a "really well-rounded character with a sense of humor, a professional life, a family life," as Shalhoub told CNN (Bay, 1998).

Rules of Engagement, on the other hand, was described by the Arab-American Anti-Discrimination Committee as "probably the most racist film ever made against Arabs by Hollywood" (Whitaker, 2000). Paul Clinton of the *Boston Globe* added about the film: "at its worst, it's blatantly racist, using Arabs as cartoon-cutout bad guys, and unrealistic in its depiction of a conflict in the Middle East" (Whitaker, 2000). "The reaction of Americans to the genre of action-adventure film, and its increasing use of Arabs as villains, shows how Americans' perceptions of Arab [communities] and [individuals] can be shaped and skewed" (Wilkins, 2008). Media critics assert that reinforcing stereotypes of the Middle East and Muslim communities as places peopled almost entirely by extremists and terrorists produces support for policies that have dire consequences for Arabs, Muslims, and people who are erroneously identified as Arab and Muslim (Alsultany, 2015).

Media representations of Muslim women are particularly skewed. Rochelle Terman of the Center for International Security and Cooperation at Stanford University conducted a large-scale study of the *New York Times* and the *Washington Post* coverage between 1980 and 2014. During that period, she cataloged every article in each newspaper that focused on a foreign country and contained the term *women*—more than 4,000 stories in all. She then used computational methods to analyze the coverage. Terman's research found that articles about Muslim countries tend to focus disproportionately on the ones especially bad for women (Terman, 2017). Over the 35-year period of Terman's study, the *Times* and the *Post* published articles about women in the Muslim world that are usually centered on one particular issue—namely, gender inequality—at the expense of topics like politics, art, fashion, or sports (Terman, 2017). Fixing these negative depictions in the future means that Hollywood will have to swim against anti-Muslim public sentiment and teach American audiences to regard Muslim characters in new ways (Rosenberg, 2016).

Breaking into the entertainment industry remains a difficult task for American Muslims. To date, there have not been enough members of the Muslim community in the industry to make a real change. The lack of established Muslim talent in the entertainment industry helps to explain the lack of resources for American Muslims to enter into the industry (Harvard, 2015). A 2002 study conducted by Cornell University provides evidence for the commonly held belief that Muslims often pursue careers in engineering, medicine, and business instead of entertainment. The Cornell data demonstrates how American Muslims do not pursue fields like journalism (1 percent), law (0.8 percent), and director/producer/action (0.6 percent), all of which influence public policy or public opinion (Nisar, n.d.).

Islamic organizations in the United States have responded to these negative media portrayals by expanding their own use of new media platforms. The Muslim Public Affairs Council (MPAC) uses its Hollywood Bureau to make a bridge between the Muslim community and the entertainment industry. This Bureau focuses on fostering relationships with industry professionals, consulting on film and television projects, and holding networking events to create opportunities for industry insiders to interact with Muslim filmmakers (Obeidi, 2014). In addition to their outreach in the entertainment industry, the MPAC's Hollywood Bureau also recently celebrated such projects as *Kinyarwanda*, a powerful film that highlights the role of Muslim leaders in creating a safe haven during the Rwandan genocide, The CW television network's *Aliens in America*, and Fox's *Bones*, both of which featured recurring Muslim characters in a humanizing light (Obeidi, 2014).

Other American Muslim organizations have taken measures to increase the Muslim influence and presence in the media industry. IslamInSpanish, a 501(c) organization founded and led by Latino members of the Islamic faith, educates Latinos in the United States and across the world about the beliefs and practices of Islam through media and is currently projecting ideas and images of their own culture and civilization to millions of Spanish-speaking people around the world. Their primary examples come from the legacy of Muslim Spain and the academic hypothesis of *la convivencia*, a Spanish term referring broadly to the notion of religious pluralism (IslamInSpanish, n.d.).

Given the underrepresentation of all minority groups, but particularly Muslims, within the U.S. media, greater diversity will improve coverage and help combat Islamophobic reporting. This requires greater outreach on the part of media outlets to bring in Muslims from all backgrounds through diversity programs, paid internships, and fact-track schemes to proactively close this gap (Versi, 2015).

FURTHER READING

Ahmed, Akbar. (2002). *Islam Today: A Short Introduction to the Muslim World*. New York, NY: I.B. Tauris.

Alsultany, Evelyn. (2015, November 11). "Muslims Are Facing a Civil Rights Crisis in America, and It's the Media's Fault." *The Washington Post*. Retrieved from https://www.washingtonpost.com/news/in-the ory/wp/2015/11/11/muslims-are-facing-a-civil-rights-crisis-in-america/? utm_term=.761f9b9d4bbe

American-Arab Anti-Discrimination Committee. (2014, January 20). "Community Advisor: ADC Alarmed by Increase in Hate Rhetoric." Washington, DC: American-Arab Anti-Discrimination Committee. Retrieved from http://salsa3.salsalabs.com/o/50434/t/0/blastContent .jsp?email_blast_KEY=1308189

Bay, Willow. (1998, November 10). "Director Ed Zwick Defends 'The Siege.'" CNN.com. Retrieved from http://www.cnn.com/SHOWBIZ/Movies/9811/10/siege/

Beydoun, Khaled A., & Ayoub, Abed. (2015, January 25). "Hollywood Shoots Arabs: The Movie." AlJazeera.com. Retrieved from http://www.aljazeera.com/indepth/opinion/2015/01/american-sniper-hollywood-iraq-201512552746382833.html

Bump, Philip. (2017, February 6). "President Trump Is Now Speculating That the Media Is Covering Up Terrorist Attacks." *The Washington Post*. Retrieved from https://www.washingtonpost.com/news/politics/wp/2017/02/06/president-trump-is-now-speculating-that-the-media-is-covering-up-terrorist-attacks/?utm_term=.a91e261884eb

Ebert, Roger. (1998, November 6). "The Siege." RogerEbert.com. Retrieved from http://www.rogerebert.com/reviews/the-siege-1998

Esposito, John. (2015). "Why Have We Normalized Islamophobia." *Oxford University Press*. Retrieved from https://blog.oup.com/2015/12/oiso-islamophobia/

Esposito, John. (2016). *Fear of Muslims? International Perspectives on Islamophobia*. Gewerbestrasse, Switzerland: Springer.

Harvard, Sarah. (2015, June 29). "To Combat Islamophobia, Hollywood Needs More Muslims. Here's Why." Bustle.com. Retrieved from https://www.bustle.com/articles/93708-to-combat-islamophobia-hollywood-needs-more-muslims-heres-why

IslamInSpanish. (n.d.). "Get to Know Us." Houston, TX: IslamInSpanish. Retrieved from https://www.islaminspanish.org/

Kearns, Erin M., Betus, Allison, & Lemiuex, Anthony. (2017a, March 13). "Yes, the Media Do Underreport Some Terrorist Attacks. Just Not the Ones Most People Think Of." *The Washington Post*. Retrieved from https://www.washingtonpost.com/news/monkey-cage/wp/2017/03/13/yes-the-media-do-underreport-some-terrorist-attacks-just-not-the-ones-most-people-think-of/?utm_term=.88d3b539de96

Kearns, Erin M., Betus, Allison, & Lemieux, Anthony. (2017b, March 7). "Why Do Some Terrorist Attacks Receive More Media Attention Than Others." *Social Science Research Network*. Retrieved from https://papers.ssrn.com/sol3/papers.cfm?abstract_id=2928138

Media Tenor International. (2011). *A New Era for Arab-Western Relations—Media Analysis*. New York, NY: Media Tenor.

Media Tenor International. (n.d.). "Coverage of American Muslims Gets Worse." MediaTenor.com. Retrieved from http://us.mediatenor.com/en/library/speeches/260/coverage-of-american-muslims-gets-worse

National Public Radio. (2017a, February 28). "Trump's Address to Joint Session of Congress, Annotated." NPR.com. Retrieved from http://

www.npr.org/2017/02/28/516717981/watch-live-trump-addresses-joint-session-of-congress

National Public Radio. (2017b, June 19). "When Is It 'Terrorism'? How the Media Cover Attacks by Muslim Perpetrators." NPR.com. Retrieved from http://www.npr.org/2017/06/19/532963059/when-is-it-terrorism-how-the-media-covers-attacks-by-muslim-perpetrators?utm_campaign=storyshare&utm_source=twitter.com&utm_medium=social

Nisar, Hasher. (n.d.). *Muslims Speak: An Action Project Proposal for Humanity in Action*. New York, NY: Humanity in Action. Retrieved from http://www.humanityinaction.org/files/743-ActionPlan-HasherNisar.pdf

Obeidi, Suhad. (2014, February 17). "Changing the Narrative of Muslims in Hollywood." HollywoodJournal.com. Retrieved from http://hollywoodjournal.com/industry-impressions/changing-the-narrative-of-muslims-in-hollywood/20140217/

Pappas, Stephanie. (2012, December 2). "Negative Portrayals of Muslims Get More Media Attention." NBC News. Retrieved from http://www.nbcnews.com/id/50008102/ns/technology_and_science-science/#.WTl5GxPyuT9

Pew Research Center. (2017, July 26). "U.S. Muslims Concerned about Their Place in Society, but Continue to Believe in the American Dream." Washington, DC: Pew Research Center. Retrieved from http://www.pewforum.org/2017/07/26/findings-from-pew-research-centers-2017-survey-of-us-muslims/

Rose, Steve. (2016, March 8). "'Death to the Infidels!' Why It's Time to Fix Hollywood's Problem with Muslims." *The Guardian*. Retrieved from https://www.theguardian.com/film/2016/mar/08/death-to-infidels-time-to-fix-hollywoods-problem-muslims

Rosenberg, Alyssa. (2016, February 4). "Hollywood's Problems Portraying Religion Go Far beyond Islam and Muslims." *Washington Post*. Retrieved from https://www.washingtonpost.com/news/act-four/wp/2016/02/04/hollywoods-problems-portraying-religion-go-way-beyond-islam-and-muslims/?utm_term=.da30b88c9caa.

Shaheen, Jack. (2004). *Reel Bad Arabs: How Hollywood Vilifies a People*. Petaluma, CA: Olive Branch.

Terman, Rochelle. (2017, May 5). "The News Media Offer Slanted Coverage of Muslim Countries' Treatment of Women." *The Washington Post*. Retrieved from https://www.washingtonpost.com/news/monkey-cage/wp/2017/05/05/the-news-media-offer-slanted-coverage-of-muslim-countries-treatment-of-women/?utm_term=.4d91b55c5c8d

Trump, Donald. (2017, February 28). "Full Text: Trump's Address to Congress." *Politico*. Retrieved from https://www.politico.com/story/2017/02/donald-trump-congress-speech-transcript-235526

Versi, Miqdaad. (2015, September 23). "It's Time the Media Treated Muslims Fairly." *The Guardian*. Retrieved from https://www.theguard ian.com/commentisfree/2015/sep/23/media-muslims-study

Whitaker, Brian. (2000, August 11). "The 'Towel-Heads' Take on Hollywood." *The Guardian*. Retrieved from https://www.theguardian.com/film/2000/aug/11/2

Wilkins, Karin G. (2008, December). *Home/Land/Security: What We Learn about Arab Communities from Action-Adventure Films*. Lanham, MD: Rowman & Littlefield.

Q25. DOES ISLAMOPHOBIA HELP ISIS AND ITS SYMPATHIZERS LEGITIMATE THE "RADICAL ISLAMIC AGENDA"?

Answer: Yes. While it is difficult to quantify an answer to this question, current evidence suggests that Islamophobia plays into the hands of ISIS's agenda. According to experts, ISIS wants and needs the United States and other Western countries to alienate their Muslim populations through Islamophobic rhetoric and actions so that the radical group is able to justify its anti-U.S. and anti-Western worldview and use discrimination against Muslims in the West as a recruiting tool. This is a well-documented and stated goal of ISIS leadership.

The Facts: In a March 2016 interview with Anderson Cooper of CNN, Republican presidential candidate Donald Trump stated, "I think Islam hates us." Drawing little distinction between mainstream American Muslims and ISIS, Trump argued that the United States would not allow Muslims into the country because the faith of Islam commands Muslims to hate Americans (Schleifer, 2016). Executive Order 13769, which was subsequently struck down by U.S. courts as unconstitutional, called for a suspension of the United States' refugee program and a ban on citizens from seven predominantly Muslim countries—Iran, Iraq, Libya, Syria, Somalia, Sudan, and Yemen—from entering the country on national security grounds. Some national security experts responded negatively to the ban. Harleen Gambhir, a researcher at the Institute for the Study of War, argued that Trump's policy helped ISIS achieve its plan of eliminating "neutral parties through either absorption or elimination, in preparation of eventual all-out battle with the West" (Gambhir, 2015). Polls indicate, that a majority of Americans support such a ban as a legitimate step to improve national security (Shepard, 2017; Levy, 2017; Agiesta, 2017).

ISIS has explicitly stated that one of its strategic goals is to eliminate neutrality, or what the group refers to as the "grayzone." The grayzone is the neutral space within which Muslims are accepted by citizens of Western countries. In a February 2015 edition of its online magazine *Dabiq*, ISIS published a 13-page article titled "The Extinction of the Grayzone." A passage from the article reads:

> The Grayzone is critically endangered, rather on the brink of extinction. Its endangerment began with the blessed operations of September 11th, as these operations manifested two camps before the world for mankind to choose between, a camp of Islam—without the body of Khalifah to represent at the time—and a camp of *kufr*—the crusader coalition. (*Dabiq*, 2015)

ISIS has been very clear about its objectives—use violence to achieve its goals, including to provoke an anti-Muslim backlash to help it attract new followers to prepare for a clash of civilizations (Gude, 2015) against *kafir*, an Arabic word meaning "unbeliever" or one who rejects the messages of Islam (Considine, 2017: 186). Groups such as Al-Qaeda actually rejoiced at the fact that, after the attacks of 9/11, Western countries divided the world into a fight between the good and the bad (Norton, 2016). Osama bin Laden himself, the founder of Al-Qaeda, favorably quoted former president George W. Bush's bifurcation of the world into an "us" and "them" binary (*Dabiq*, 2015).

One of the first actions of the Trump administration was to impose a travel ban on people from seven primarily Muslim-majority countries. Ritz Katz, director of SITE Intelligence Group, an organization monitoring jihadist websites, claimed that at the official level, there had been no direct mentions of the "Muslim ban" by ISIS, Al-Qaeda, or any other major "jihadi terrorist organizations" (Valverde, 2017b). Katz's claims are echoed by Charlie Winter, a senior research fellow at the International Centre for the Study of Radicalization and Political Violence, who cautioned not to draw "too linear a link" between Executive Order 13769 and whether it legitimates ISIS's agenda (Velverde, 2017b). However, according to a memo sent by the U.S. embassy in Baghdad to the U.S. Department of State, the order (titled "Protecting the Nation from Foreign Terrorist Entry into the United States") risked the United States losing critical support from the government, military, and the American-backed militias in the Middle East region (Fisher, 2017). The *Wall Street Journal* reported the memo revealed that diplomats in Baghdad, Iraq, were "blind-sided" by Trump's executive order and were worried that the fallout could assist ISIS (El-Ghobashy & Abi-Habib, 2017).

ISIS members and their sympathizers have used Islamophobic rhetoric from the Trump administration to incite attacks against Americans and recruit more terrorists to their side. In response to Executive Order 13769, some ISIS fighters hailed it as "the Blessed Ban"—saying it proves to their followers and Muslims worldwide that the United States—as well as its citizens—really do "hate" Islam (Perez, 2017). ISIS-friendly channels on the Telegram messenger service also described the ban as "blessed," echoing how the United States' 2003 invasion of Iraq was called a "blessed invasion" for reinvigorating anti-American sentiment in the Middle East (McKernan, 2017). One user greeted the news of the "Muslim ban" as "the best caller to Islam," hoping it would draw American Muslims to ISIS's radical agenda (McKernan, 2017). Several additional posts suggested that the prediction of Anwar al-Awlaki—a U.S.-born Al-Qaeda leader killed in an American drone strike in Yemen in 2011—that "the West would eventually turn against its Muslim citizens" was coming true (McKernan, 2017).

Terrorism expert Mia Bloom reiterated these views. Speaking to *Business Insider*, Bloom stated, "The [ISIS] chatrooms have been abuzz about how [the "Muslim ban"] shows that there is a clash of civilizations, that Muslims are not welcome in America" (Engel, 2017). Another terrorism expert, Renad Mansour, a fellow from the Middle East and North African Program at Chatham House in the United Kingdom, stated, "['The Muslim ban'] plays into this clash of civilizations idea, which is something that global jihadis need as fuel, to claim Americans are against them, that the West is against them . . . Trump is seen to be validating what they already claimed was happening" (McKernan, 2017). After Trump's election victory, *Politico* journalist Amarnath Amarasingam asked five ISIS fighters for their thoughts on the new president of the United States. A Canadian ISIS fighter responded that "[Trump] is good for us. We needed someone like him, who is direct" (Amarasingam, 2017).

Some members of Trump's own party have expressed concern that Executive Order 13769 could backfire. Following President Trump's executive order authorizing the ban, Senators John McCain and Lindsey Graham released a joint statement claiming that it "will become a self-inflicted wound in the fight against terrorism" (Valverde, 2017b). McCain and Graham identified the vast majority of Muslims, who rejected ISIS's apocalyptic ideology of hatred, as "the most important allies" in the fight against the radical group. The Republican senators also noted that

Executive Order 13769 sends a signal, intended or not, "that Americans do not want Muslims coming into our country." McCain and Graham ended the statement by proclaiming that "we fear this Executive Order may do more to help terrorist recruitment than improve our security." Other Republicans, however, strongly defended such a ban as a common-sense national security precaution.

A number of prominent counterterrorism officials agreed with Senators McCain and Graham. Former CIA director and U.S. Army general David Petraeus grew increasingly concerned about anti-Muslim rhetoric in the United States during the presidential campaign of 2016. He called Executive Order 13769 "totally counterproductive" and said that rather than make the United States safer, it would "compound the already grave terrorist danger to our citizens" (Petraeus, 2016). The general also elaborated on broader Islamophobic developments in American society, calling them "toxic . . . non-biodegradable" ideas that poison the American body politic. The "poison" that General Petraeus refers to paints American Muslims as enemies of the United States, an idea that ISIS sells through its propaganda channels. In one issue of its online magazine *Dabiq*, ISIS warned that "Muslims in the crusader countries [i.e., the United States and other Western nations] will find themselves driven to abandon their homes . . . as the crusaders increase persecution against Muslims living in Western lands" (Williams, 2017).

FURTHER READING

Agiesta, Jennifer. (2017, February 3). "CNN/ORC Poll: Majority Oppose Trump's Travel Ban." CNN.com. Retrieved from https://www.cnn.com/2017/02/03/politics/donald-trump-travel-ban-poll/index.html

Amarasingam, Amarnath. (2017, March 1). "What ISIS Fighters Think of Trump." *Politico*. Retrieved from http://www.politico.com/magazine/story/2017/03/what-isis-fighters-think-of-trump-214843

Anti-Defamation League. (n.d.). "What Is the 'Muslim Ban?'" New York, NY: Anti-Defamation League. Retrieved from https://www.adl.org/education/resources/tools-and-strategies/what-is-the-muslim-ban

Considine, Craig. (2017). *Islam, Race, and Pluralism in the Pakistani Diaspora*. London and New York, NY: Routledge.

Dabiq. (2015). "The Extinction of the Grayzone." ClarionProject.org. Retrieved from https://clarionproject.org/docs/islamic-state-dabiq-magazine-issue-7-from-hypocrisy-to-apostasy.pdf

El-Ghobashy, Tamer, & Abi-Habib, Maria. (2017, January 29). "Ban Could Hurt U.S.-Iraqi Ties, Diplomats Say." *The Wall Street Journal*.

Retrieved from https://www.wsj.com/articles/ban-could-hurt-u-s-iraqi-ties-diplomats-say-1485713137

Engel, Pamela. (2017, February 8). "ISIS Is Reportedly Calling Trump's Travel Ban 'the Blessed Ban.'" BusinessInsider.com. Retrieved from http://www.businessinsider.com/isis-trump-blessed-ban-2017-2

Fisher, Anthony L. (2017, January 30). "Trump's 'Muslim Ban' Hurts the Fight against ISIS, Say U.S. Diplomats in Iraq." Reason.com. Retrieved from http://reason.com/blog/2017/01/30/trumps-muslim-ban-hurts-the-fight-isis

Gambhir, Harleen. (2015). *ISIS Global Intelligence Summary: January 7– February 18*. Washington, DC: Institute for the Study of War. Retrieved from http://www.understandingwar.org/sites/default/files/INTSUM_Summary_update.pdf

Gude, Ken. (2015, November). *Anti-Muslim Sentiment Is a Serious Threat to American Security*. Washington, DC: Center for American Progress. Retrieved from https://cdn.americanprogress.org/wp-content/uploads/2015/11/25074358/ISISTrap.pdf

Hénin, Nicolas. (2015, November 16). "I Was Held Hostage by Isis. They Fear Our Unity More Than Our Airstrikes." *The Guardian*. Retrieved from https://www.theguardian.com/commentisfree/2015/nov/16/isis-bombs-hostage-syria-islamic-state-paris-attacks

Levy, Garbrielle. (2017, February 8). "Poll: Majority Support Trump's Travel Ban." US News and World Report. Retrieved from https://www.usnews.com/news/politics/articles/2017-02-08/poll-majority-support-trumps-travel-ban

McCarthy, Justin. (2015, June 22). "In U.S., Socialist Presidential Candidates Least Appealing." Washington, DC: Gallup.com. Retrieved from http://www.gallup.com/poll/183713/socialist-presidential-candidates-least-appealing.aspx

McKernan, Bethan. (2017, January 30). "ISIS Hails Donald Trump's Muslim Immigration Restrictions as a 'Blessed Ban.'" *The Independent*. Retrieved from http://www.independent.co.uk/news/world/middle-east/isis-donald-trump-muslim-ban-immigration-iraq-iran-restrictions-travel-islamic-state-us-visa-a7552856.html

Norton, Ben. (2016, March 22). "After Brussels, Far-Right Islamophobes Are Doing Exactly What ISIS Wants Them to Do: Threatening the 'Grayzone.' " Salon.com. Retrieved from http://www.salon.com/2016/03/22/after_brussels_far_right_islamophobes_are_doing_exactly_what_isis_wants_them_to_do_threatening_the_gray_zone/

Perez, Chris. (2017, February 9). "Islamic State Fighters Reportedly Calling Trump Travel Ban the 'Blessed Ban.'" *The New York Post*.

Retrieved from http://nypost.com/2017/02/08/isis-fighters-call-trumps-travel-order-a-blessed-ban/

Petraeus, David. (2016, May 13). "David Petraeus: Anti-Muslim Bigotry Aids Islamist Terrorists." *The Washington Post*. Retrieved from https://www.washingtonpost.com/opinions/david-petraeus-anti-muslim-bigotry-aids-islamist-terrorists/2016/05/12/5ab50740-16aa-11e6-924d-838753295f9a_story.html?utm_term=.11f2a30eb53a

Schleifer, Theodore. (2016, March 10). "Donald Trump: 'I Think Islam Hates Us.'" CNN.com. Retrieved from http://www.cnn.com/2016/03/09/politics/donald-trump-islam-hates-us/index.html

Shepard, Steven. (2017, July 5). "Poll: Majority of Voters Back Trump Travel Ban." *Politico*. Retrieved from https://www.politico.com/story/2017/07/05/trump-travel-ban-poll-voters-240215

Valverde, Miriam. (2017a, April 20). "Trump Stalls on Promise for 'Total and Complete Shutdown' of Muslims Entering the United States." *Politifact*. Retrieved from http://www.politifact.com/truth-o-meter/promises/trumpometer/promise/1401/establish-ban-muslims-entering-us/

Valverde, Miriam. (2017b, February 7). "No Proof ISIS Leaders Using Donald Trump's Travel Ban for Recruitment." *Politifact*. Retrieved from http://www.politifact.com/truth-o-meter/statements/2017/feb/07/seth-moulton/mostly-false-claim-isis-already-using-trumps-execu/

Walt, Stephen. (2015, November 16). "Don't Give ISIS What It Wants." *Foreign Policy*. Retrieved from http://foreignpolicy.com/2015/11/16/dont-give-isis-what-it-wants-united-states-reaction/

Williams, Jennifer. (2017, January 29). "Trump's 'Muslim Ban' Is a Huge Gift to ISIS." Vox.com. Retrieved from https://www.vox.com/world/2017/1/29/14426892/trump-muslim-immigration-refugee-ban-isis-terrorism

5

❖

American National Identity

Q26. ARE AMERICAN MUSLIMS HAPPY TO BE LIVING IN THE UNITED STATES?

Answer: Yes. Muslims are generally content with living in the United States. Research institutes and organizations have carried out surveys that show an overall positive view of U.S. society among American Muslims, as well as strong levels of personal happiness and satisfaction. Polls, however, also reveal that Muslims would like to see better living conditions in the United States and that they are particularly disquieted by hate crimes and anti-Muslim political rhetoric.

The Facts: Overall, U.S. Muslims have a generally positive view of the whole of the United States. In July 2017, the Pew Research Center published a survey that found that American Muslims "express a persistent streak of optimism and positive feelings" about the United States. Overwhelmingly, American Muslims are proud to be Americans (92 percent), believe that hard work generally brings success in the country (70 percent), and are satisfied with the way things are going in their own lives (80 percent). Seventy-percent of U.S. Muslims also continue to profess faith in the "American Dream" (Pew Research Center, 2017). Similarly, an Institute for Social Policy and Understanding (ISPU) poll on the experiences and views of U.S. Muslims found they are the religious group most satisfied with America's trajectory (Mogahed & Chouhoud, 2017). Two earlier

Pew Research Center (2007, 2011) reports found that American Muslims were overwhelmingly satisfied with the way things were going in their lives (82 percent) and they related their communities very positively as places to live (79 percent said "excellent" or "good") (Pew Research Center, 2011).

Despite the general contentment of American Muslims as found by the Pew Research Center, surveys have found different, more negative results that deserve attention. The American Muslim Poll 2017 by ISPU found that Muslims (38 percent) and Jews (27 percent) report higher levels of fear and anxiety than other faith groups, especially after the 2016 presidential election. More specifically, Muslim children report higher levels of bullying at schools, while 20 percent of Muslim women said that the 2016 election had "caused them enough stress and anxiety to believe they need the help of a mental professional" (Abbasi, 2017). Nearly 20 percent of all Muslim participants in the ISPU survey stated that they have made plans to leave the United States "if it becomes necessary" (Abbasi, 2017).

The percentage of Asian American Muslims (54 percent) expressing a positive outlook is nearly twice that of African American Muslims (28 percent), who echo the views of the larger African American community (23 percent) (Mogahed & Chouhoud, 2017). These figures show that while the American Muslim population, as a whole, is generally satisfied with their lives in the United States, there also exists a range of situations and inequalities that impact some U.S. Muslims more than others.

The rhetoric of Donald Trump about Muslims during the 2016 presidential election and during the first year of his presidency has been heavily scrutinized for its negative impact on the everyday lived experiences of American Muslims. Some observers, though, also criticized Democratic presidential nominee Hillary Clinton for remarks that she made about American Muslims in her presidential campaign. Clinton referred to American Muslims as valuable allies in the fight against terrorism—rather than referring to the simple fact that they, too, are Americans and deserve to be treated as such (Harvard, 2016). Pointedly, the Democratic nominee commented:

> [American Muslims are] on the front lines. They can provide information to us that we might not get anywhere else. They need to have close, working cooperation with law enforcement in these communities—not be alienated and pushed away as some of Donald [Trump]'s rhetoric, unfortunately, has led to.

Rafia Zakaria, a human rights attorney, responded to Clinton's statement by calling it a "tragedy" because both candidates for president generalize and castigate American Muslims (Harvard, 2016). Another influential American Muslim, Hatem Bazian of the University of California at Berkeley, added, "Eventually, this [association] leads to [American Muslims'] status being contingent upon whether or not they're good for us in the national security rather than their full participation and engagement as U.S. citizens or residents in this country" (Harvard, 2016). The problem with such rhetoric is that it defines the value of American Muslims strictly in national security terms, ignoring the wider contributions they make to the health and vitality of the nation (Harvard, 2016). Good Muslims are "moderate, rational, non-violent and progressive," who chant "Islam is a religion of peace." Bad Muslims, on the other hand, are "extremists, irrational, violent and fundamentalist," who chant "Death to America" (Islamic Insights, n.d.). This "good" versus "bad" binary has long been criticized by academics and religious leaders alike (Mamdani, 2005).

In the face of anti-Muslim developments in the United States, American Muslims have testified that their Islamic faith actually strengthens their patriotism. Debbie Almontaser, the founding principal of the Khalil Gibran International Academy, the first English Arabic public high school in Brooklyn, New York, wrote, "I love my country because it encourages and embraces the freedom of all people to practice their faiths without discrimination or threat of violence" (Almontaser, 2016). Almontaser cited the American Muslim Poll 2017 by ISPU and how its data showed that the more devoted an American Muslim reported being to his or her faith, the more likely they were to describe themselves as patriotic Americans (Mogahed & Chouhoud, 2017). In summary, Almontaser clarified, "There is no conflict between faith and patriotism. The two go hand in hand." As the Pew Research Center found in a 2017 survey, American Muslims express pride in their religious and national identities alike. Fully 97 percent agree with the statement, "I am proud to be Muslim" (Pew Research Center, 2017). Nearly as many (92 percent) say they agree with the statement, "I am proud to be an American" (Pew Research Center, 2017). In total, 89 percent agree with both statements, saying they are proud to be Muslim and proud to be American.

Author and anthropologist Akbar Ahmed, who wrote the book *Journey into America: The Challenge of Islam*, found positive sentiments among U.S. Muslims while carrying out fieldwork across 75 cities and 100 mosques. "Muslims again and again told us that America is the best place in the world to be a Muslim. There are countless examples of Muslims who are assimilated and are completely American in every sense" (Jacobson, 2016). Writing for *The Islamic Monthly*, Ahmed argued that the United States is a better place to be Muslim than Europe because it has an "identity advantage." He writes: "American identity is rooted in the vision of its Founding Fathers. This ideal is of a genuinely pluralist society rooted in human rights, civil liberties and democracy" (Ahmed, 2015).

FURTHER READING

Abbasi, Waseem. (2017, March 21). "Muslims More Satisfied with U.S. Than Any Religious Group, Poll Finds." *USA Today.* Retrieved from https://www.usatoday.com/story/news/nation-now/2017/03/21/muslims-more-satisfied-us-than-any-religious-group-poll-finds/99427254/

Ahmed, Akbar. (2011). *Journey into America: The Challenge of Islam.* Washington, DC: Brookings Institution Press.

Ahmed, Akbar. (2015, January 7). "The Best Place in the World to Be a Muslim: America or Europe?" *The Islamic Monthly.* Retrieved from http://theislamicmonthly.com/the-best-place-in-the-world-to-be-a-muslim-america-or-europe/

Almontaser, Debbie. (2016, August 3). "My Muslim Faith Makes Me an American Patriot." *Time.* Retrieved from http://time.com/4437446/muslim-faith-american-patriot/

DelReal, Jose A. (2016, June 15). "Trump Claims Assimilation among American Muslims Is 'Close' to 'Non-existent.'" *The Washington Post.* Retrieved from https://www.washingtonpost.com/news/post-politics/wp/2016/06/15/trump-claims-assimilation-among-american-muslims-is-close-to-non-existent/?utm_term=.e806e61d9147

Harvard, Sarah. (2016, September 28). "American Muslims Despise Donald Trump—But They Aren't Happy with Hillary Clinton, Either." AOL .com. Retrieved from https://www.aol.com/article/news/2016/09/28/american-muslims-despise-donald-trump-but-they-arent-happy-w/21482438/

Islamic Insights. (n.d.). "Good Muslim, Bad Muslim: Cracking the Media Code." IslamicInsights.com. Retrieved from http://www.islamicinsights .com/news/opinion/good-muslim-bad-muslim-cracking-the-media-code.html

Jacobson, Louis. (2016, June 18). "Donald Trump Wrong That 'There's No Real Assimilation' by U.S." Muslims. *Politifact.* Retrieved from http://www.politifact.com/nbc/statements/2016/jun/18/donald-trump/donald-trump-wrong-theres-no-real-assimilation-us-/

Mamdani, Mahmood. (2005). *Good Muslim, Bad Muslim: America, the Cold War, and the Roots of Terror.* Berkeley, CA: Ten Speed Press.

Mogahed, Dalia, & Chouhoud, Youssef. (2017). *American Muslim Poll 2017: Muslims at the Crossroads.* Washington, DC: The Institute for Social Policy and Understanding. Retrieved from http://www.ispu.org/wp-content/uploads/2017/05/AMP-2017_Full-Report.pdf

Pew Research Center. (2007, May 22). *Muslim Americans: Middle Class and Mostly Mainstream*. Washington, DC: Pew Research Center. Retrieved from http://www.people-press.org/2007/05/22/muslim-americans-middle-class-and-mostly-mainstream/

Pew Research Center. (2011, August 30). *Muslim Americans: No Signs of Growth in Alienation or Support for Extremism*. Washington, DC: Pew Research Center. Retrieved from http://www.people-press.org/2011/08/30/muslim-americans-no-signs-of-growth-in-alienation-or-support-for-extremism/

Pew Research Center. (2017, July 26). "U.S. Muslims Concerned about Their Place in Society, but Continue to Believe in the American Dream." Washington, DC: Pew Research Center. Retrieved from http://www.pewforum.org/2017/07/26/findings-from-pew-research-centers-2017-survey-of-us-muslims/

Ramadan, Tariq. (2010, February 12). "Good Muslim, Bad Muslim." *The New Statesmen*. Retrieved from http://www.newstatesman.com/religion/2010/02/muslim-religious-moderation

Schleifer, Theodore. (2016, March 10). "Donald Trump: 'I Think Islam Hates Us.'" CNN.com. Retrieved from http://www.cnn.com/2016/03/09/politics/donald-trump-islam-hates-us/

Q27. DID MUSLIMS ON AMERICAN SOIL CELEBRATE THE 9/11 ATTACKS IN NEW YORK CITY AND WASHINGTON, D.C.?

Answer: No. There is no proof that Muslims in the United States celebrated the 9/11 attacks. To the contrary, numerous American Muslim organizations, leaders, and citizens condemned the attacks in the strongest terms.

The Facts: In comments made during a speech in Birmingham, Alabama, on November 21, 2015, Republican presidential candidate Donald Trump claimed that he "watched in Jersey City, New Jersey, where thousands and thousands of people were cheering" as the World Trade Center collapsed on September 11, 2001, as the result of an Al-Qaeda terrorist attack (Carroll, 2015a). Asked by George Stephanopolous of ABC's *This Week* if he misspoke, Trump insisted that it was on television. He stated: "I saw it. It was well covered at the time . . . I know [Muslims] don't like to talk about it, but it was well covered at the time. There were people over in New Jersey that were watching it . . . [and] cheering as the buildings came down. Not good" (Carroll, 2015). The following weekend, during an appearance on NBC's *Meet the Press*, Trump again refused to budge from his claim. "I'm not going to take it back" (Bradner, 2015). Trump then said he watched a September 16, 2001, clip from WCBS, the New York City CBS News affiliate, that allegedly confirmed his assertion. In the clip, WCBS reporter Pablo Guzman identified a Jersey City apartment building, one that an investigator told him "was swarming" with eight suspects who were cheering on the roof when they saw the planes slam into the World Trade Center (Flores, 2015). Even if this unsubstantiated claim were true, eight is nowhere near the same thing as "thousands and thousands of people [who] were cheering" as claimed by Trump (Carroll, 2015b).

Trump's assertions that American Muslims had actually celebrated the attacks of 9/11 were examined by Politifact, a Pulitzer Prize–winning fact-checking website maintained by the *Tampa Bay Times*. The website checks the accuracy of claims by elected officials and others who speak up in American politics. Politifact conducted an exhaustive search of newspaper and television transcripts dated from September 2001 to December 2001. While Politifact found a widely broadcasted video of people in the occupied Palestinian territories celebrating, they found no evidence to confirm Trump's description of events in New Jersey (Carroll, 2015a). Politifact's research found only two uncorroborated sources. The first source, an Associated Press article dated to September 17, 2001, described "rumors of rooftop celebrations of the attacks by Muslims" in Jersey City, but the same report said that those rumors were unfounded. The second source, published by the *Washington Post* on September 18, 2001, claimed "law enforcement authorities detained and questioned a number of people who were allegedly seen celebrating the attacks and holding tailgate-style parties on rooftops while they watched the devastation on the other side of the river." The *Post* story "includes no sources for this information, and [Politifact] found no evidence that any of these allegations ever stuck." In a later statement, the *Post* issued a summary of their investigation, noting, "This is a bit like writing about the hole in the doughnut—how can you write about nothing?" (Kessler, 2015). The *Post* not only refutes Trump's assertion, but it also found that he, in the immediate aftermath of 9/11, never even made any mention of having witnessed the alleged celebrations (Kessler, 2015). Politifact, meanwhile, stated unequivocally that "there is no evidence whatsoever of any demonstrations where 'thousands and thousands of people' cheered. Nor is there any evidence Trump saw these events play out in any way, be it on TV or in person. . . . Trump's recollection of events in New Jersey in the hours after the September 11, 2001, terrorist attacks flies in the face of all the evidence we could find. We rate this statement Pants on Fire" (Carroll, 2015a).

Several high-profile politicians in the New Jersey area responded to Trump's claim. Steven Fulop, the former mayor of Jersey City, tweeted that Trump either had "memory issues" or "willfully distorts the truth." In a follow-up statement, Fulop accused Trump of "shamefully politicizing an emotionally charged issue," adding: "No one in Jersey City cheered on September 11. We were actually among the first to provide responders to help in lower Manhattan" (McDonald, 2015). Following Fulop, former New Jersey governor Chris Christie responded to Trump's assertion by stating: "I do not remember that, and so it's not something that was part of my recollection. I think if it had happened, I would remember it" (Arco, 2015). Jerry Speziale, the former police commissioner of Paterson, New Jersey, called Trump's statement "patently false. . . . That never happened. There were no flags burning, no one was dancing." Speziale also applauded the city's American Muslim community for being helpful and law-abiding in the struggle against "Islamic extremism" (Kopan, 2015).

Muslim organizations across the United States also condemned the 9/11 attacks in the strongest terms. The Council on American-Islamic Relations issued a statement that called for "the swift apprehension and punishment of the perpetrators" and encouraged members of the Muslim community "to offer whatever help they can to the victims and their families" (Abdelkarim, 2002; American Muslim Leaders, 2011). The Muslim Public Affairs Council (MPAC) issued a statement calling on all Americans to stand together to bring the perpetrators to justice (Muslim Public Affairs Council, 2016). The MPAC also offered its resources and resolve to help the victims of those violent acts.

Muslims around the world followed the lead of U.S. Muslims by unequivocally condemning the attacks. Despite Iran's rocky relationship with the United States, the Iranian president Mohamed Khatami and supreme leader Ali Khamenei condemned and denounced the heinous violence and the terrorists (Iranian Students' News Agency, 2001). The heads of state of Egypt, Indonesia, Jordan, Lebanon, Libya, Malaysia, Pakistan, Syria, and Turkey, all Muslim-majority countries, also condemned the attacks.

FURTHER READING

Abdelkarim, Riad Z. (2002, August 20). "How American Muslims Really Responded to September 11." MediaMonitors.net. Retrieved from http://www.mediamonitors.net/riadabdelkarim3.html

The Alex Jones Show. (2017, August 16). "Muslim No Go Zones Taking over Europe." InfoWars.com. Retrieved from https://www.infowars.com/muslim-no-go-zones-taking-over-europe/

American Muslim Leaders. (2001, September 11). "Muslim Americans Condemn Attack." IslamiCity.com. Retrieved from http://www.islamicity .com/articles/printarticles.asp?ref=am0109-335&p=1

Arco, Matt. (2015, November 22). "Christie on Trump Saying 'Thousands' in N.J. Cheered on 9/11: 'I Don't Recall That.'" NJ.com. Retrieved from http://www.nj.com/politics/index.ssf/2015/11/christie_on_thousands_ in_nj_cheering_on_911_i_dont.html

Bradner, Eric. (2015, November 30). "Trump on Muslim Claim: 'I'm Not Going to Take It Back.'" CNN.com. Retrieved from http://www.cnn .com/2015/11/29/politics/donald-trump-new-jersey-muslims-celebrating-9-11/index.html

Carroll, Lauren. (2015a, November 22). "Fact-Checking Trump's Claim That Thousands in New Jersey Cheered When World Trade Center Tumbled." *Politifact*. Retrieved from http://www.politifact.com/truth-o-meter/statements/2015/nov/22/donald-trump/fact-checking-trumps-claim-thousands-new-jersey-ch/

Carroll, Lauren. (2015b, December 2). "New Information Doesn't Fix Donald Trump's 9/11 Claim." *Politifact*. Retrieved from http://www .politifact.com/truth-o-meter/article/2015/dec/02/new-information-doesnt-fix-donald-trumps-911-claim/

Flores, Reena. (2015, December 2). "More Questions Emerge over Trump's 9/11 Celebrations Claim." CBSNews.com. Retrieved from http://www.cbsnews.com/news/more-questions-emerge-over-trumps-911-celebrations-claim/

Iranian Students' News Agency. (2001, November 10). "Iran's President Says Muslims Reject bin Laden's Islam." *Iranian Students' News Agency*. Retrieved from http://en.isna.ir/news/8008-04338/Iran-s-President-Says-Muslims-Reject-bin-Laden-s-Islam

Kessler, Glenn. (2015, November 22). "Trump's Outrageous Claim That 'Thousands' of New Jersey Muslims Celebrated the 9/11 Attacks." *The Washington Post*. Retrieved from https://www.washingtonpost.com/ news/fact-checker/wp/2015/11/22/donald-trumps-outrageous-claim-that-thousands-of-new-jersey-muslims-celebrated-the-911-attacks/ ?utm_term=.1158d6d2be19

Kopan, Tal. (2015, November 24). "Carson Walks Back Support for Trump's Disputed 9/11 Celebration Claim." CNN.com. Retrieved from http://www.cnn.com/2015/11/23/politics/donald-trump-new-jersey-cheering-september-11/

Madsen, Wayne. (2016, September 20). "Obama Flooding More U.S. Cities with Muslim Migrants." InfoWars.com. Retrieved from https://www .infowars.com/obama-flooding-more-u-s-cities-with-muslim-migrants/

McDonald, Terrence T. (2015, November 22). "Fulop: Trump's 'Shamefully Politicizing' 9/11 Attacks." NJ.com. Retrieved from http://www.nj.com/hudson/index.ssf/2015/11/fulop_trump_shamefully_politicizing_911.html

Media Matters. (2016, November 28). "Trump Ally Alex Jones Uses Trump's 2001 Remarks to Further 9/11 Inside Job Conspiracy." MediaMatters.com. Retrieved from https://www.mediamatters.org/video/2016/11/28/trump-ally-alex-jones-uses-trump-s-2001-remarks-further-911-inside-job-conspiracy/214631

Muslim Public Affairs Council. (2016, December). "History: Highlights from 28 Years of Service." Los Angeles, CA: Muslim Public Affairs Council. Retrieved from https://www.mpac.org/about/history.php

Right Wing Watch. (n.d.). "About." Washington, DC: RightWingWatch.org. Retrieved from http://www.rightwingwatch.org/about/

Roig-Franzia, Manuel. (2016, November 17). "How Alex Jones, Conspiracy Theorist Extraordinaire, Got Donald Trump's Ear." *The Washington Post.* Retrieved from https://www.washingtonpost.com/lifestyle/style/how-alex-jones-conspiracy-theorist-extraordinaire-got-donald-trumps-ear/2016/11/17/583dc190-ab3e-11e6-8b45-f8e493f06fcd_story.html?utm_term=.95904ae33e33

Southern Poverty Law Center. (n.d.). "Larry Klayman and Alex Jones Explore Theory That Obama Is a Muslim Conspiring to Destroy America." Montgomery, AL: Southern Poverty Law Center. Retrieved from https://www.splcenter.org/file/10519

Tashman, Brian. (2016, May 30). "58 Donald Trump Conspiracy Theories (and Counting!): The Definitive Trump Conspiracy Guide." Alternet.org. Retrieved from http://www.alternet.org/right-wing/58-donald-trump-conspiracy-theories-and-counting-definitive-trump-conspiracy-guide

White, Jamie. (2016, June 16). DHS Insider: Obama Blocking Terrorist Probes. InfoWars.com. Retrieved from https://www.infowars.com/dhs-insider-obama-blocking-terrorist-probes/

Q28. HAVE AMERICAN MUSLIMS SERVED AND DIED IN THE ARMED FORCES TO PROTECT THE NATIONAL SECURITY OF THE UNITED STATES?

Answer: Yes. Muslims have served in the armed forces throughout U.S. history and have died in every war, including the War of 1812, Civil War, World War I, World War II, Korean War, Vietnam War, Gulf War,

Afghanistan War, and Iraq War. Up to 10,000 American Muslims currently serve in the U.S. Armed Forces.

The Facts: American Muslims have always risked their lives to defend a nation that has historically perceived them with suspicion and fear (Curtis, 2016a). Muslims have served in the Continental Army, which defended the interests of the 13 U.S. colonies against British interests on American soil during the Revolutionary War. Yusuf Ben Ali, a slave known as Joseph Benenhaley—is said to have been an Arab Muslim of North African descent born in the Ottoman Empire (Curtis, 2010). Historian Edward E. Curtis (2016a) notes that Benenhaley was a scout for General Thomas Sumter in the South Carolina militia. Bampett Muhammad, a corporal who battled in Virginia, is said to have served under the direct command of General George Washington (Rothman, 2016). Peter Salem, a former slave who emerged as a hero during the Revolution, is reported to have fired the shot that killed British Major Pitcairn at the 1775 Battle of Bunker Hill in Boston. Salem's heroic efforts in Boston are pictured in John Trumbull's painting, *The Death of General Warren at the Battle of Bunker Hill,* by John Trumbull, a U.S. artist during the period of the Revolutionary War (Southwick, 2010). Salem is said to have dropped the name Buckminster, the same name of his "master," and took the name of Salem once he had been freed. Salem sometimes spelled his name "Saleem," an Arabic word for peace. A monument to Salem is currently standing in the Massachusetts town of Framingham (Southwick, 2010).

Muslims also defended American soil during the War of 1812. One such Muslim was Bilali Muhammad, a slave on Sapelo Island, Georgia, who is believed to have been a well-educated Muslim from the area of present-day Sierra Leone (Bailey, 2001). Other scholars believe that he was born in Timbo, Guinea, around 1770 to a well-educated African Muslim family. Before arriving at Sapelo Island, off the coast of Georgia, Bilali worked as a slave for 10 years on a plantation at Middle Caicos. He was purchased by Thomas Spalding and assigned as the head driver of his plantation on Sapelo Island. During the War of 1812, Bilali and his fellow Muslims on Sapelo Island helped to defend the United States from a British attack. According to the Harvard University Pluralism Project, Bilali "lived as a Muslim and was buried with his prayer rug and *Qur'an*" and left many children, whom he had given "Muslim names" (The Pluralism Project, n.d.). Upon his death in 1857, it was discovered that Bilali had written a 13-page Arabic manuscript that provided a Muslim legal treatise and part of West Africa's Islamic curriculum. The *Bilali Muhammad Document,* also known as the *Ben Ali Diary* or *Ben Ali Journal*, is referred to as the "mother text" of American Islamic literature. The manuscript is held at the Hargrett Rare Book and Manuscript Library at the University of Georgia.

Al Haj Omar Ibn Said, who also served during the War of 1812, wrote an autobiography detailing his life as a trader, soldier, and faithful Muslim who performed the *hajj* and studied the Qur'an for 25 years before being sold into slavery (The Pluralism Project, n.d.). Ibn Said wrote about his life prior to arriving to the United States, which he referred to as a "Christian country." In his native homeland, Ibn Said would walk to the mosque before daybreak, wash his face and hands and feet, pray fives time per day, and give charity every year. In his autobiography, Said mentioned he traveled to Mecca for the hajj (Arabic for pilgrimage) when he was 37 years old. He had been in the United States for 24 years prior to publishing his book (The Pluralism Project, n.d.). Today, in Fayetteville, North Carolina, the Masjid Omar Ibn Sayyid on Southern Avenue stands as a testament to Said and the legacy of the early American Muslims. An historical marker dedicated to Ibn Said can also be found in Fayetteville. The sign reads: "Omar Ibn Said (1770–1863)—Muslim slave and scholar, African-born, he penned autobiography in Arabic, 1831. Lived in Bladen County and worshipped with local Presbyterians."

Muslims served in both the Union and Confederate armies during the Civil War. Nicholas Said, also known as Mohammed Ali Ben Said, served in the Union Army from 1863 until 1865. Born in Bornou, near the modern-day borders of Libya, Chad, and Sudan around 1831, Ben Said was raised to practice African traditional religion but eventually converted to Islam (Curtis, 2010). In the 1850s, he is said to have converted to Orthodox Christianity, probably under duress from his Christian slave master (Curtis, 2010). Private Mohamed Kahn, a native of Iran who is also known as John Ammahail, immigrated to the United States from Afghanistan in 1861 and soon thereafter enlisted in the 43rd New York Infantry Regiment in the Union Army (Mersiovsky, 2017). A few days after the Battle of Gettysburg in July 1863, Kahn was separated from his unit and arrested in Hagerstown, Maryland, by a Union guard. Though Kahn tried to explain that he was a member of the 43rd New York, the guard did not believe that he could be part of the white unit of soldiers, as he was not a "white man" (Mersiovsky, 2017). Months later, Kahn joined up with the 14th New York Infantry and travelled to Philadelphia and Washington, D.C. In May 1864, he was shot in the left hand at the Battle of the Wilderness.

During World War I, the U.S. Armed Forces saw a dramatic rise in the probable number of Muslim servicemen (Curtis, 2010). Philip K. Hitti, an

American Lebanese professor and scholar at Princeton and Harvard universities, published a report in 1924 that found that 13,965 Arab Americans fighting for the United States in Europe, among which approximately 5,000 were Muslims (Arab American National Museum, n.d.). Among the more than 5,000 Muslims who fought for the United States in World War I, the name *Muhammad* was so common that it was spelled 41 different ways in military records (Muhammad, 2007). World War I veterans with "Muslim-sounding" names include Rashid Abdul, originally from Turkey; Mohamed Ali, born in Syria in 1893; and Mohammed Allah, from Arabia, born in 1892 (Curtis, 2010). One soldier, Private Omer Otmen, served in Company K and joined the first wave of the 260th Infantry's attack against German forces, including the division called the "Kaiser's favorites" (Curtis, 2016b). This was part of the Meuse-Argonne Offensive, the U.S. military's most important campaign in World War I.

For World War II, approximately 1,555 men and women with "Muslim-sounding" last names have been identified in the ranks of America's wartime armed forces (Curtis, 2016b). American Muslims served in North Africa, Europe, and the Pacific, even though their faith was not fully recognized by the U.S. Armed Forces. Military dog tags allowed "C" for Catholic, "P" for Protestant, or "H" for Hebrew (Wright, 2016). Abdullah Igram, a soldier from Cedar Rapids, Iowa, who was stationed in New Guinea, took issue with this lack of recognition of the Muslim faith (Tariq, 2010). Several years after returning home safely, he wrote a letter to President Dwight D. Eisenhower asking that the "M" option be added for military dog tags (Tariq, 2010). Abdullah received a letter from President Eisenhower's secretary thanking him for the suggestion and the "M" option was added.

John R. Omar, a native of Quincy, Massachusetts, was another prominent American Muslim of World War II. He served as a turret gunner on a B-24 Liberator. Assigned to the Eighth Air Force in Europe, Omar was part of 29 missions, including the Battle of the Bulge, and was awarded the Purple Heart after he was hit by shrapnel in his right leg (Curtis, 2015). Nazeem Abdul Karriem fought on the beaches of Normandy on D-Day, the largest sea-born invasion in history, which began the liberation of Nazi-occupied northwestern Europe (Carter, 2016). In June 2016, Karriem attended a Ramadan observance at the White House in which he was honored by Secretary of Defense Ashton Carter.

As they had done in World War I and World War II, Muslims fought and died in the U.S. Armed Forces during the Korean and Vietnam wars. During the Korean War, which lasted from 1950 to 1953, several Muslims died on the battlefield and were captured and imprisoned by North Koreans (Curtis, 2010). Corporal Wilbur C. Islam was killed in 1951. Born in Calhoun

County, California, Islam served in the 24th Infantry Division of the U.S. Army (Korean War Casualties, n.d.a). Corporal Mitchell R. Abbas, who was killed in October 1950, was a native of Washington County, Pennsylvania. He served in the 1st Cavalry Infantry Division of the U.S. Army (Korean War Casualties, n.d.b). Vietnam veteran Kayed "Edward" Hassan said he enlisted during the height of the Vietnam War in 1967 (Hanania, 2015). Ray Hanania, an Arab American Muslim, served in the U.S. Air Force—his brother was a U.S. Marine and his father George served during World War II, enlisting after the Japanese attack on Pearl Harbor (Hanania, 2015). American Muslims serving in Vietnam held military grades from private first class to sergeant (Curtis, 2010). Keith A. Rahmad, who was awarded the Joint Services Commendation Medal in April 1971, is probably the most decorated Muslim in the history of the U.S. Armed Forces (Hanania, 2015). At least 12 American Muslims died in Vietnam (National Archives & Records Administration, n.d.).

According to the U.S. Department of Defense, which offers service members the opportunity to identify their faith for inclusion in the Dependent Eligibility Enrollment System, there were 2.2. million active-duty and reserve members in the U.S. Armed Forces as of 2015 (Khan & Martinez, 2015). Of those, 5,896 (0.27 percent) self-identify as Muslims (Khan & Martinez, 2015). In many units, they number in the single digits and "often find themselves acting as representatives for the religion in their platoons, answering basic questions about the tenets of Islam" (Gibbons-Neff, 2015).

Section 60 of the Arlington National Cemetery, where those killed in Iraq and Afghanistan have been buried, includes the grave of Captain Humayun S. M. Khan, who died June 8, 2004 (Curtis, 2010). Captain Khan, a reserve officer of the 1st Infantry Division's 201st Forward Support Battalion, was killed in 2004 in Iraq "after a vehicle packed with an improvised [bomb ran] into the gate of his compound while he was inspecting soldiers on guard duty" (Rizvi, 2010). Khan and two Iraqi civilians were killed in addition to the two suicide bombers (Ryan, 2016). Brigadier General Daniel Mitchell, who "was Khan's commanding officer in 2004, said that as a force protection operations officer, Khan was playing a critical role in keeping [U.S.] soldiers safe from artillery attacks, sniper fire, and improvised explosive devices like the one that killed him" (Ryan, 2016). Khan was eventually awarded the Bronze Star and Purple Heart medals for his distinguished and heroic efforts.

Kareem Khan was another recipient of the Bronze Star Medal and the Purple Heart. According to his father, Khan was "spurred by the 9/11 attacks on the World Trade Center" to enlist in the Armed Forces because he "wanted to show that not all Muslims were fanatics and that many, like him, were willing to lay their lives down for their country" (Arlington National Cemetery, 2007). A graduate of Southern Regional High School in Manahawkin, New Jersey, Khan served in the Stryker Brigade combat team of the Army's 2nd Infantry Division. In reflecting back on his son's life, Khan's father added about his son: "[Kareem's] Muslim faith did not make him not want to go. It never stopped him. He looked at it that he's American and he has a job to do" (*The New York Times*, 2008).

Since the 1990s, several organizations have been set up to support Muslims in the U.S. Armed Forces, including the Muslim American Veterans Association (MAVA) and the American Muslim Armed Forces and Veterans Affairs Council (AMAFVAC). The MAVA was established and certified in 1997 to serve all veterans regardless of religion, race, or gender, and AMAFVAC was created in 1991. The AMAFVAC is a joint nonprofit, nonpolitical organization that serves the spiritual needs and religious welfare of Muslims who are current members or veterans of the U.S. Armed Forces.

In some instances, American Muslims have also been subjected to abuse from fellow service members because of their religious background. Sergeant Joseph Felix, for example, was found guilty of hazing and maltreatment of recruits at the Marine Corps' Parris Island, South Carolina, boot camp. The 34-year-old Iraq veteran was accused in more than three dozen criminal counts of being a central figure in an abusive group that came to light after the March 2016 suicide of one of the three American Muslim recruits Felix targeted. According to prosecutor Lieutenant Colonel John Norman, Felix was a "bully" who particularly "picked out three Muslim recruits for special abuse because of their Muslim faith." One of the soldiers Felix abused, Marine recruit Ameer Bourmeche, testified they were ordered into an industrial clothes dryer, which then was turned on as Felix demanded he renounce his Islamic faith (Al Jazeera, 2017). Felix was also accused of maltreating Raheel Siddiqui, a 20-year-old Pakistani American from Taylor, Michigan, who committed suicide in March 2016 after enduring sustained abusive treatment by Felix (Associated Press, 2017).

Recognizing the thousands of American Muslims who have served loyally in the U.S. Armed Forces, however, does not mean that instances of "homegrown terrorism" in the military can be dismissed (Goodman, 2011). Army Major Nidal Malik Hasan, who was Muslim, was sentenced to death in August 2013 for killing 13 people and wounding 32 others in a 2009 shooting rampage at Fort Hood, Texas, the worst mass murder at a military installation in the history of the United States. Hasan "shouted 'Allahu akbar!' meaning "God is great," before targeting soldiers with a high-powered, high-capacity handgun he had fitted with laser sights" (Kenber, 2013). In 2012, Army private Naser Jason Abdo was sentenced to two life sentences in federal prison for plotting to kill American soldiers and others near Fort Hood (FBI, 2012).

American military leaders emphasize, however, that individuals like Hasan and Abdo are very rare and that over 5,000 Muslim men and women are patriotically serving in the U.S. Armed Forces. The fact that Muslim soldiers lie buried in the Arlington National Cemetery, America's most sacred and hallowed ground, refutes any notion that the Islamic faith is somehow incompatible with definitions of American national identity and love of country.

FURTHER READING

Al Jazeera. (2017, November 10). "US Marine Trainer Guilty of Abusing Muslim Recruits." AlJazeera.com. Retrieved from http://www.aljazeera.com/news/2017/11/marine-trainer-guilty-abusing-muslim-recruits-171110083827520.html

American Muslim Armed Forces & Veteran Affairs Council. (n.d.). "About." American Muslim Armed Forces & Veteran Affairs Council. Retrieved from http://www.amafandvac.org/about/

American National Biography. (n.d.). "Salem, Peter." *American National Biography Online.* Retrieved from http://www.anb.org/articles/06/06-00893.html

The American War Library. (n.d.). "List of Bronze Star Recipients." American War Library. Retrieved from http://www.americanwarlibrary.com/personnel/bronze.htm

Arab American National Museum. (n.d.). "Patriots and Peace Makers: Arab Americans in Service to Our Country." Dearborn, MI: Arab AmericanMuseum.org. Retrieved from http://www.arabamericanmuseum.org/umages/PandP_brochure_for_dl.pdf

Arlington National Cemetery. (2007, August 9). "DoD Identifies Army Casualties." Arlington, VA: ArlingtonCemetery.net. Retrieved from http://www.arlingtoncemetery.net/krkhan.htm

Associated Press. (2017, November 10). "Marine Drill Instructor Abused Recruits, Targeted Muslims: Jury." CBSNews.com. Retrieved from https://www.cbsnews.com/news/marine-drill-instructor-abused-recruits-targeted-muslims-jury/

Bailey, Cornelia W. (2001). *God, Dr. Buzzard, and the Bolito Man: A Saltwater Geechee Talks about Life on Sapelo Island, Georgia.* New York, NY: Anchor.

Carter, Ashton. (2016, June 30). "Secretary of Defense Speech: Remarks at Pentagon Ramadan Iftar Observe." Washington, DC: U.S. Department of Defense. Defense.gov. Retrieved from https://www.defense.gov/News/Speeches/Speech-View/Article/824170/remarks-at-pentagon-ramadan-iftar-observance/

Curtis, Edward E., IV. (2010). *Encyclopedia of Muslim-American History*. New York, NY: Infobase Publishing.

Curtis, Edward E., IV. (2015, November 23). "Muslims Have Long Served in the Military of Western Countries [Commentary]." Syracuse.com. Retrieved from http://www.syracuse.com/opinion/index.ssf/2015/11/muslims_in_the_wests_fighting_ranks_commentary.html

Curtis, Edward E., IV. (2016a). *Muslim Americans in the Military: Centuries of Service*. Bloomington, IN: Indiana University Press.

Curtis, Edward E., IV. (2016b). "Remember Muslim-American Soldiers on Veterans Day." DetroitNews.com. Retrieved from http://www.detroitnews.com/story/opinion/2016/11/10/veterans-muslim-americans/93629490/

FBI. (2012, August 10). "Naser Jason Abdon Sentenced to Life in Federal Prison in Connection with Killeen Bomb Plot." Washington, DC: FBI. Retrieved from https://archives.fbi.gov/archives/sanantonio/press-releases/2012/naser-jason-abdo-sentenced-to-life-in-federal-prison-in-connection-with-killeen-bomb-plot

Gibbons-Neff, Thomas. (2015, December 9). "For Muslims in the U.S. Military, a Different U.S. Than the One They Swore to Defend." *The Washington Post*. Retrieved from https://www.washingtonpost.com/news/checkpoint/wp/2015/12/09/for-muslims-in-the-u-s-military-a-different-u-s-than-the-one-they-swore-to-defend/?utm_term=.cfce510e9104

Goodman, Alana. (2011, December 7). "Rep. King Releases Muslim American Military Statistics." CommentaryMagazine.com. Retrieved from https://www.commentarymagazine.com/american-society/military/rep-king-muslim-american-military-statistics/

Hanania, Ray. (2015, November 11). "American Arabs Reflect on US Military Service." AlJazeera.com. Retrieved from http://www.aljazeera.com/indepth/features/2015/11/american-arabs-reflect-military-service-151111120809075.html

Hitti, Philip K. (1924). *The Syrians in America*. New York, NY: George H. Doran Company.

Hussain, Amir. (2016). *Muslims and the Making of America*. Waco, TX: Baylor University Press.

Kenber, Billy. (2013, August 28). "Nidal Hasan Sentenced to Death for Fort Hood Shooting Rampage." *The Washington Post*. Retrieved from https://

www.washingtonpost.com/world/national-security/nidal-hasan-sen
tenced-to-death-for-fort-hood-shooting-rampage/2013/08/28/aad
28de2-0ffa-11e3-bdf6-e4fc677d94a1_story.html?utm_term=.53b812
7448d8

Khan, Mariam, & Martinez, Luis. (2015, December 8). "More Than 5,000
Muslims Serving in U.S. Military, Pentagon Says." ABCNews.com.
Retrieved from http://abcnews.go.com/US/5000-muslims-serving-us-
military-pentagon/story?id=35654904

Korean War Casualties. (n.d.a). "Wilbur C Islam—Korean War Casualty
File." KoreanWarCasualties.com. Retrieved from http://www.korean
warcasualties.org/index.php?page=directory&rec=69353

Korean War Casualties. (n.d.b). "Mitchell R Abbas—Korean War Casualty
File." KoreanWarCasualties.com. Retrieved from http://www.korean
warcasualties.org/index.php?page=directory&rec=28830

Lavender, Paige. (2016, June 14). "Mitch McConnell: There Are a Lot of
'Patriotic, Loyal American Muslims.'" *The Huffington Post*. Retrieved
fromhttp://www.huffingtonpost.com/entry/mitch-mcconnell-muslims_
us_5760190ee4b071ec19ef345d

Mersiovsky, Kate. (2017, June 23). "Private Mohammed Kahn: Civil
War Soldier." Washington, DC: U.S. National Archives. Narations
.gov. Retrieved from https://narations.blogs.archives.gov/2017/06/23/
private-mohammed-kahn-civil-war-soldier/

The Military Order of the Purple Heart. (n.d.). "History of the Order."
The Purple Heart. Retrieved from http://www.purpleheart.org/History
Order.aspx

Muhammad, A. N. (2007). *Muslim American Veterans of American Wars (The
Revolutionary War-War of 1812-Civil War-World War I-World War II)*.
Freeman Publications. Retrieved from https://books.google.com/books/
about/Muslim_Veterans_of_American_Wars.html?id=9TmdJAAACAAJ

Muslim American Veterans Association. (n.d.). "About MAVA." Muslim
American Veterans Association. Retrieved from http://mavanational-
.com/about-mava/

National Archives & Records Administration. (n.d.). "Statistical Information about Casualties of the Vietnam War." Washington, DC:
National Archives. Retrieved from https://www.archives.gov/research/
military/vietnam-war/casualty-statistics.html

The New York Times. (2008, October 19). "More on the Soldier Kareem R.
Khan." Retrieved from https://thelede.blogs.nytimes.com/2008/10/19/
more-on-the-soldier-kareem-r-khan/comment-page-11/

The Pluralism Project. (n.d.). "The First American Muslims." Harvard University. Retrieved from http://pluralism.org/religions/islam/
islam-in-america/the-first-american-muslims/

Rizvi, Salmah Y. (2010, August 30). "Muslim Americans Are Also Dying for America." *The Daily Beast*. Retrieved from http://www.thedailybeast.com/articles/2010/08/30/muslim-americans-are-also-dying-for-america

Rothman, Lily. (2016, August 3). "The Khan Family and American History's Hidden Muslim Soldiers." *Time*. Retrieved from http://time.com/4432865/khan-muslim-american-soldiers-history/

Ryan, Missy. (2016, August 2). "Capt. Humayun Khan, Whose Grieving Parents Have Been Criticized by Trump, Was 'a Soldier's Officer.'" *The Washington Post*. Retrieved from https://www.washingtonpost.com/news/checkpoint/wp/2016/08/02/slain-army-captain-at-center-of-political-storm-was-a-soldiers-officer/?utm_term=.633b629edce3

Southwick, Albert B. (2010, August 26). "Exploring Peter Salem's Roots." Retrieved from http://www.telegram.com/article/20100826/COLUMN21/8260819

Tariq, Bassam. (2010, September 7). "Day 25: Iowa, The Mother Mosque in Cedar Rapids." Washington, DC: The Council on American-Islamic Relations. Retrieved from http://www.cair-iowa.org/american-muslims/islam-in-america

Wright, Robin. (2016, August 15). "Humayun Khan Isn't the Only Muslim American Hero." *The New Yorker*. Retrieved from http://www.newyorker.com/news/news-desk/humayun-khan-isnt-the-only-muslim-american-hero

Q29. DO MUSLIMS IN THE UNITED STATES CONDEMN "ISLAMIC TERRORISM" AND TAKE ACTION TO COMBAT EXTREMISM INSIDE THEIR COMMUNITIES?

Answer: Yes. American Muslims consistently condemn terrorist attacks committed by Muslims either in the United States or around the world. Elements of the U.S. government, including intelligence agencies, confirm that American Muslims work closely with them to counter extremism and terrorism on American soil.

The Facts: A common criticism of American Muslims is that they remain silent—and therefore are essentially complicit—in the face of violence, extremism, and terrorism carried out by Muslims (Islamic Networks Group, n.d.). In a CNN interview in June 2016, Republican presidential candidate Donald Trump discussed whether Muslims in the United States report "radical Muslims" like Omar Mateen, an American

Muslim who carried out a mass shooting at Pulse nightclub in Orlando, Florida. Trump stated: "For some reason, the Muslim communities do not report people like [Mateen]" (Cooke & Ax, 2016). Writing in the *New York Daily News*, Dalia Mogahed, a prominent Muslim American scholar who was born in Egypt, stated that the accusation leveled by Trump is one that she often hears, especially during public lectures. Mogahed, however, pointed out that "anyone with an internet connection and a search engine will find that Muslims have and continue to condemn terrorism" (Mogahed, 2017).

Muslims Condemn, a website that provides "a collection of all the cases where [Muslims] have condemned wrongdoings done falsely in the name of Islam," is one example. Created in 2017 by Herra Hashmi, an American Muslim university student, Muslims Condemn began as a 712-page Google spreadsheet documenting all the instances in which Muslims around the world condemned acts of terrorism carried out in the name of Islam (Mahdawi, 2017). In an interview with the *Guardian*, Hashmi explained her motives: "I wanted to show people how weak the argument [is that Muslims don't care about terrorism]" (Mahdawi, 2017). As Muslims Condemn highlights, Muslim organizations across the United States have issued hundreds, if not thousands, of public statements condemning terrorism. These organizations have penned op-eds, written books, taken out full-page newspaper ads, and held rallies to condemn terrorism.

Examples of these condemnations are numerous. In October 2017, following a truck attack by Sayfullo Habibullaevic Saipov, an Uzbek national, on pedestrians in Manhattan, the Council on American-Islamic Relations (CAIR) issued a press release condemning the "cowardly attack" and offered "sincere condolences to the loved ones of those killed and injured" (Council on American-Islamic Relations, 2017b). After the San Bernardino attack in California, the local CAIR-Los Angeles branch issued an official statement that read: "We condemn this horrific and revolting attack and offer our heartfelt condolences to the families and loved ones of all those killed or injured." CAIR-Los Angeles executive director Hussam Ayloush added in the statement, "The Muslim community stands shoulder to shoulder with our fellow Americans in repudiating any twisted mindset that would claim to justify such sickening acts of violence" (Council on American-Islamic Relations, 2015a).

Following the bomb attacks carried out by Islamic terrorists during the Boston Marathon in April 2013, CAIR-National not only condemned "in the strongest possible terms [the] cowardly bomb attack on participants and spectators of the Boston Marathon" but also urged people of all faiths to "pray for the victims and their loved ones and for the speedy recovery of those injured" (Council on American-Islamic Relations, 2013). The CAIR also called on Muslims and others in the Boston area to donate blood through the Red Cross "as a concrete show of support for the bomb attack victims" (Council on American-Islamic Relations, 2013). The Muslim Public Affairs Council (MPAC) (2013) also condemned the Boston Marathon attack as a "horrible crime." The MPAC also asked "everyone to reach out to their faith and civic leaders to coordinate with authorities to bring resolution to this tragedy" (Council on American-Islamic Relations, 2013). The Islamic Society of Boston Cultural Center (ISBCC) joined MPAC by releasing a statement condemning the loss of life and injuries to the victims. "As Bostonians, and inspired by the values of mercy and justice central to our faith, the American Muslim community stands ready to help," the ISBCC added (Virtual Mosque, 2013).

American Muslim organizations and activists have condemned terrorist acts carried out overseas as well. In August 2017, CAIR issued a press release condemning an ISIS-inspired attack in Barcelona, Spain, which left over a dozen people dead and many more injured (Council on American-Islamic Relations, 2017a). The group issued a similar press release in November 2015 after a terrorist attack in Paris left over 125 people dead. "These savage and despicable attacks on civilians, whether they occur in Paris, Beirut or any other city, are outrageous and without justification," the group declared. "We condemn these horrific crimes in the strongest possible terms. The perpetrators of these heinous attacks must be apprehended and brought to justice" (Council on American-Islamic Relations, 2015b). Although news outlets seldom focus on CAIR's condemnations, a simple Google search will turn up all manner of condemnations of those whose actions tarnish the image of Muslims and teachings of Islam (Islamic Networks Group, n.d.).

Many of CAIR's official condemnations have focused specifically on the activities of ISIS. In March 2015, CAIR issued a press release that condemned ISIS as "un-Islamic and morally repugnant." The statement not only condemned the group's activities but also rejected ISIS's assertion that American Muslims are required to pay allegiance to Abu Bakr Al-Baghdadi, the then caliph, or leader, of ISIS. The CAIR urged American Muslim imams and other Muslim leaders in the country to continue to speak out against ISIS and Muslims traveling abroad to join sectarian militias (Council on American-Islamic Relations, 2015b). A year earlier, in 2014, the CAIR issued several statements condemning the murder of two American journalists by ISIS (Council on American-Islamic Relations, 2014). In August of that year, CAIR decried what it called the "gruesome and barbaric" killing of James Foley. "We strongly condemn this gruesome and barbaric killing as a violation of Islamic beliefs and of universally-accepted international norms mandating the protection of prisoners and journalists during conflicts" (Council on American-Islamic Relations, 2014). In September 2014, the Council on American-Islamic Relations, 2014 (2014) issued a statement concerning the murder of American journalist Steven Sotloff by ISIS that read in part: "No words can describe the horror, disgust and sorrow felt by Muslims in America and worldwide at the unconscionable and un-Islamic violence perpetrated by the terror group ISIS."

American Muslims have also served as the first line of defense in detecting and preventing terrorism (Gude, 2015; Muslim Public Affairs Council, 2012). Former FBI director James B. Comey confirmed this point in a press conference following the Pulse nightclub shooting in Orlando, Florida, during which he stated: "Some of our most productive relationships are with people who see things and tell us things who happen to be Muslim." Comey added: "It's at the heart of the FBI's effectiveness to have good relationships with [Muslims]" (Cooke & Ax, 2016). Michael Downing, deputy chief of the Los Angeles Police Department and head of its Counterterrorism and Special Operations Bureau, said the city's Muslim community has been helpful in reporting "red flags" (Cooke & Ax, 2016). Indeed, more terrorism suspects and perpetrators have been brought to the attention of law enforcement by American Muslims than were discovered by U.S. government investigations (Kurzman, 2014).

Suspecting someone of something as despicable as condoning the murder of civilians solely because they share the same race or religion "is the definition of bigotry" (Mogahed, 2017). According to Islamic scholar and activist John Andrew Morrow, asking Muslims if they support ISIS "is as idiotic as asking white Christians if they support the Trans-Atlantic slave trade, the genocide of Native Americans under the name of Manifest Destiny, segregation, Jim Crow Laws, the KKK and other white Christian supremacist groups. Christians know full-well that no true Christian would support such inhumanity" (Morrow, 2017).

FURTHER READING

Beckwith, Ryan T. (2016, June 13). "Read Donald Trump's Speech on the Orlando Shooting." *TIME*. Retrieved from http://time.com/4367120/orlando-shooting-donald-trump-transcript/

Cooke, Kristina, & Ax, Joseph. (2016). "U.S. Officials Say American Muslims Do Report Extremist Threats." Reuters. Retrieved from http://www.reuters.com/article/us-florida-shooting-cooperation-idUSKCN0Z213U

Council on American-Islamic Relations. (2013, April 15). "CAIR Urges Prayers, Blood Donations for Boston Bomb Victims." Washington, DC: Council on American-Islamic Relations. Retrieved from https://www.cair.com/press-center/press-releases/11835-cair-urges-prayers-blood-donations-for-boston-bomb-victims.html

Council on American-Islamic Relations. (2014, August 20). "CAIR Condemns Barbaric Killing of U.S. Journalist by Terror Group ISIS." Washington, DC: Council on American-Islamic Relations. Retrieved from https://www.cair.com/press-center/press-releases/12622-cair-condemns-barbaric-killing-of-american-journalist-james-foley-by-terrorist-group-isis.html

Council on American-Islamic Relations. (2015a, December 2). "CAIR-LA: California Muslims to Respond to San Bernardino Shooting, Naming of Suspect." Washington, DC: Council on American-Islamic Relations. Retrieved from https://www.cair.com/press-center/press-releases/13282-cair-la-california-muslims-to-respond-to-san-bernardino-shooting-naming-of-suspect.html

Council on American-Islamic Relations. (2015b, March 11). "CAIR Condemns ISIS Violence and Rejects Calls to Join Extremists Fighting Abroad." Washington, DC: Council on American-Islamic Relations. Retrieved from https://www.cair.com/press-center/press-releases/12551-cair-condemns-isis-violence-and-rejects-calls-to-join-extremists-fighting-abroad.html

Council on American-Islamic Relations. (2017a, August 17). "CAIR Condemns Barcelona Terror Attack, Trump's Islamophobic Twitter Reaction." Washington, DC: Council on American-Islamic Relations. Retrieved from https://www.cair.com/press-center/press-releases/14541-cair-condemns-barcelona-terror-attack-trump-s-islamophobic-twitter-reaction.html

Council on American-Islamic Relations. (2017b, October 31). "CAIR Condemns Manhattan Terror Attack." Washington, DC: Council on American-Islamic Relations. Retrieved from https://www.cair.com/press-center/press-releases.html

Gude, Ken. (2015, November). "Anti-Muslim Sentiment Is a Serious Threat to American Security." Washington, DC: American Progress. Retrieved from https://cdn.americanprogress.org/wp-content/uploads/2015/11/25074358/ISISTrap.pdf

Islamic Networks Group. (n.d.). "Global Condemnations of ISIS/ISIL." ING.org. Retrieved from https://ing.org/global-condemnations-of-isis-isil/

Islamic Society of North America. (2007, September 2). "Muslim Code of Honor." Plainfield, IN: Islamic Society of North America. Retrieved from http://www.isna.net/muslim-code-of-honor/

Kurzman, Charles. (2014, February 5). *Muslim-American Terrorism in 2013*. Chapel Hill, NC: University of North Carolina. Retrieved from https://sites.duke.edu/tcths/files/2013/06/Kurzman_Muslim-American_Terrorism_in_20131.pdf

Mahdawi, Arwa. (2017, March 26). "The 712-Page Google Doc That Proves Muslims Do Condemn Terrorism." *The Guardian*. Retrieved from https://www.theguardian.com/world/shortcuts/2017/mar/26/muslims-condemn-terrorism-stats

Mogahed, Dalia. (2017, May 24). "Don't Ask Muslims to Condemn Terror: Our Outrage at Atrocities Ought to Be a Given." *The New York Daily News*. Retrieved from http://www.nydailynews.com/opinion/don-muslims-condemn-terror-article-1.3193126

Morrow, John A. (2017, May 19). "If Muslims Are So Moderate, Why Don't They Speak Out against Terrorism." Covenantsoftheprophet .wordpress.com. Retrieved from https://covenantsoftheprophet.word press.com/2017/05/19/if-muslims-are-so-moderate-why-dont-they-speak-out-against-terrorism/

Muslim Public Affairs Council. (2012). *Data on Post-9/11 Terrorism in the United States*. Los Angeles, CA: Muslim Public Affairs Council. Retrieved from https://www.mpac.org/publications/policy-papers/post-11-terrorism-database.php

Muslim Public Affairs Council. (2013, April 15). "MPAC Condemns Heinous Terrorist Act." Los Angeles, CA: Muslim Public Affairs Council. Retrieved from https://www.mpac.org/issues/national-security/our-thoughts-and-prayers-are-with-all-those-in-boston.php

Muslims Condemn. (n.d.). "Collection of Cases." Muslimscondemn.com. Retrieved from https://muslimscondemn.com/

Virtual Mosque. (2013, April 15). "Condolences, Prayers and Support after Boston Marathon." Virtualmosque.com. Retrieved from http://www.virtualmosque.com/miscellaneous/announcements/condolences-prayers-and-support-after-boston-marathon/

Q30. HAVE AMERICAN MUSLIMS CONTRIBUTED TO THE WELL-BEING, VITALITY, AND CULTURAL ENRICHMENT OF THE UNITED STATES?

Answer: Yes. Muslims are well-integrated into American society and contribute significantly to the betterment of the United States. They are engaged in civic life and serve, in various ways, at the local, state, and national levels. Muslims in the United States contribute in the fields of science, medicine, sports, entertainment, education, and philanthropy. Many of these American Muslims talk about the significant role that Islam plays in their decision to serve their communities and country.

The Facts: In 2014, a member of the Michigan Republican National Committee, David Agema questioned the contribution of Muslims to American society in a Facebook post: "Have you ever seen a Muslim do anything that contributes positively to the American way of life?" (Oosting, 2014). Agema's comments, which were condemned by non-Islamic and Islamic organizations such as the Council on American-Islamic Relations, exacerbated stereotypes about Muslims and Islam that are all-too common in post-9/11 America.

In reality, the contributions of American Muslims run deep in the United States. American Muslims' philanthropic efforts often go unnoticed by the news media, but in reality Muslim charity groups in the United States are regularly active in relief efforts. Helping Hand for Relief and Development (HHRD), a partner organization of the Islamic Circle of North America, is one of the largest American Muslim relief organizations focused on providing services and support to projects overseas. In 2013, HHRD was selected by Charity Navigator, the U.S.'s largest and most-utilized evaluator of charities, as the sixth highest-rated charity relying on private contributions in the United States (Islamic Circle of North America, 2013). In recent years, the Islamic Relief USA, a nonprofit 501(c)(3) humanitarian agency and member of the Islamic Relief Worldwide group, was awarded four out of four stars in 2017 by Charity Navigator, the independent charity watchdog organization based in the United States. Recently, the IRUSA has worked with the Michigan Muslim Community Council to donate a combined $100,000 to the Detroit Water Fund and the Wayne Metropolitan Community Action Agency to help Detroiters pay their water bills during a water shortage crisis (Islamic Relief USA, n.d.). The Zakat Foundation of America (ZF), founded in 2001, is unique among humanitarian organizations in advancing charity as a vehicle for social change. The ZF "has differentiated itself from a traditional [U.S.-based] Muslim charity approach of exclusively supporting communities abroad and reaches poor and indigent communities within the United States as well" (Zakat Foundation of America, n.d.).

American Muslims—like Muslims everywhere—typically make a special effort to increase their charitable activities throughout Ramadan. Uzma Farooq, vice president of the Muslim Women's Coalition and director of the organization's greater Washington office, serves her community in an annual Ramadan tradition dating back to 2007. Since then, Farooq and her fellow volunteers launched the Ramadan Basket Project, which distributes basic necessities to disadvantaged women and children in the Washington, D.C., area. The project, which has become an annual event, benefits both Muslims and non-Muslims (Monsen, 2017).

Some of the most famous scientists and inventors in recent U.S. history have been Muslims. Fazlur Rahman Khan, a Bangladeshi American Muslim known as the *Einstein of structural engineering*, pioneered a new structural system of frame tubes that revolutionized the building of skyscrapers in the United States and beyond (Jeffries, 2015). Ahmed Zewail, an Egyptian-born scientist and physics professor at Caltech, won the Nobel Prize for Chemistry in 1999. He is known as the *father of femtochemisty* for pioneering the study of rapid molecular transformations. In 1963, Ayub Ommaya, a Pakistani-born Muslim neurosurgeon, invented an intraventricular catheter system that is used today for the aspiration of cerebrospinal fluid or the delivery of drugs (Jeffries, 2015). This system, also known as the *Ommaya reservoir*, is used to provide chemotherapy directly to the site for brain tumors. Before Dr. Omayya's invention, there was no effective way to deliver chemotherapy treatments for brain tumors. Ommaya served as the chief of neurosurgery at the National Institute of Neurological Disorders and Stroke as well as professor at George Washington University in Washington, D.C. (Baker, 2015).

American Muslims have assumed prominent roles in the health care system of the United States. The exact number of American Muslim physicians in the United States is not known, but it is estimated to be approximately 50,000 persons, about 5 percent of all U.S. physicians (Abu-Ras, Laird, & Senzai, 2012; University of Chicago Medical Center, 2015). Other analysts estimate that more than 10 percent of American physicians are Muslim, even though Muslims make up approximately 1 percent of the entire U.S. population (Karim, 2008). Perhaps the most famous Muslim doctor, Mehmet Oz, is host of *The Dr. Oz Show* and vice chair and professor of surgery at Columbia University. Oz was born in Ohio to Turkish Muslim parents (Winsor, 2014). He described his Islamic beliefs as a form of Islam closely associated with Sufism, a mystical movement that shares similar practices to mystics in Christianity, Judaism, Hinduism, and Buddhism (Considine, 2017: 35). The Islamic Medication Association of North America, founded in 1967, is the largest resource and network for American Muslim physicians, dentists, and other health care professionals in North America.

American Muslim physicians also played an important role in the development of special clinics and social services as early as the late 1980s. Twelve Muslim doctors in Potomac, Maryland, for example, began the Ibn Sina Clinic in the early 1990s for patients without health insurance, and two Muslim physicians in Sacramento, California, began the Shifa Clinic at the V Street Mosque for low-income Americans. In 1996, second-generation American Muslim medical students, led by Rushdie Cader, founded the University Muslim Medical Association Community Clinic to serve a primarily African-American and Latina/o communities in South Central Los Angeles (Curtis, 2010). The University Muslim Medical Association, a free health care clinic in Los Angeles founded in 1992 by American Muslim college students at UCLA and Charles Drew University, also serves a diverse inner-city community (Interfaith Alliance & First Amendment Center, n.d.).

Muslims for American Progress (MAP), a project of the Institute for Social Policy and Understanding, quantifies the contributions of American Muslims in eight areas: civics and democracy; economic development; medicine; science, technology, engineering, and mathematics (STEM); philanthropy and nonprofit organizations; arts and entertainment; sports; and education. To quantify these areas of contribution, the MAP project "counts and profiles" American Muslims' contributions to the betterment of American society with hard facts, while profiling individuals of distinction to showcase the community's diversity and give it a human face (Muslims for American Progress, 2017a).

In its first major report on the contributions of American Muslims, the MAP team conducted qualitative interviews in Michigan with 146 individuals from the 8 key areas. The study found that "Michigan Muslims contribute a tremendous amount across the entire state on the health, happiness, and well-being of their fellow Americans, despite comprising just 2.75 percent of Michigan's overall population" (Muslims for American Progress, 2017b). The findings from the 2017 report include the following:

1. Michigan Muslims comprise more than 15 percent of the state's medical doctors and more than 10 percent of the state's pharmacists.
2. Muslims in Michigan are expanding the state's STEM fields. More than 1,600 new patents have been awarded to Muslim-led teams in the state over the past five years.
3. Muslims represent Michigan constituents at every level of governance as politicians, public trustees, and lawyers. At the time of publication of the MAP Michigan report, 35 Muslim Michiganders held public office and more than 700 lawyers in the state were Muslim.
4. Muslims in Michigan are incredibly charitable. Not only was $177 million donated in 2015 for both domestic and international

causes, but Michigan Muslims also generously donated their time and expertise to other Michiganders in need.

5. Muslim Michiganders have helped to rebuild the state's economy. As of 2015, there were 38,835 Muslim-owned businesses in Michigan, making up 4.18 percent of all small businesses in the state and employing at least 103,062 Michiganders.
6. The number of licensed Muslim educators in Michigan has grown 127 percent in the last five years to more than 1,100 teachers, teaching an estimated 29,889 of the state's students

Taken together, the MAP data demonstrate that Michigan Muslims, like Muslims across the United States, make substantial contributions to the state's well-being in all eight key areas listed previously. These findings contrast starkly with the typical depiction of American Muslims in mainstream media (Muslims for American Progress, 2017a). In the future, MAP hopes to continue mapping the contributions made to the health and well-being of American society by focusing on states around the United States.

In a speech from the Oval Office in December 2015, President Barack Obama stated, "Muslim Americans are our friends and our neighbors, our co-workers, our sport heroes." Republican presidential candidate Donald Trump responded to Obama by stating, "Obama said in his speech that Muslims are our sport heroes. What sport is he talking about, and who?" Most Americans can actually name several famous American Muslims from the world of sports. Muhammad Ali is widely recognized as the greatest boxer to ever live. Kareem Abdul-Jabbar, a National Basketball Association (NBA) player who played for the Milwaukee Bucks and the Los Angeles Lakers, is the all-time leading scorer in the history of the NBA. Other prominent American Muslims to have played in the NBA are Hakeem Olajuwon (Basketball Hall of Fame inductee), Shaquille O'Neal (Basketball Hall of Fame inductee), Shareef Abdur-Rahim, Rasheed Wallace, and Larry Johnson. Other American Muslim athletes of note include Bernard Hopkins (boxer); Mike Tyson (boxer); Aqib Talib (National Football League [NFL]); Mohamed Sanu (NFL); Ahmad Rashad (NFL and sports broadcaster); Muhsin Muhammad (NFL); Ryan Harris (NFL); Kenneth Farid (NBA), and Mahmoud Abdul-Rauf (NBA).

Abdul-Rauf, like numerous athletes before him who converted to Islam, excelled in their respective sports while facing backlash from the media for their newfound beliefs. Thirty-two years after Muhammad Ali denounced his "slave name" Cassius Clay, Abdul-Rauf decided not to stand for the Star-Spangled Banner on March 10, 1996 (Maese, 2017). Abdul-Rauf was fined and briefly suspended by the NBA, though days later he struck a compromise with League officials, agreeing to stand for the anthem but close his eyes and pray (Maese, 2017). The decision had a lasting impact on his career. The media backlash turned into what many see as a "blacklisting," as Abdul-Rauf was traded around the League multiple times in his prime before finding himself playing overseas (Obee, 2016).

American Muslims are also thriving in the U.S. artistic landscape, finding a niche for themselves in the music industry. *XXL*, an American hip hop magazine, documented these Muslim artists in a 2016 articled, "22 Rappers Who Are Muslim" (Madden, 2016). Rappers such as DJ Khaled, Swizz Beats, and Q-Tip and Ali (of the group A Tribe Called Quest) have all been vocal about practicing Islam since the beginning of their careers. In a profile of seven American Muslim rappers who are shattering stereotypes about Islam, *Mic* looked at how devout followers of Islam embrace their faith through hip hop (Beaudoin, 2015). These Muslim artists include Rakim, Brother Ali, Poetic Pilgrimage, Lupe Fiasco, and Freeway. Another musician—Mos Def—was profiled by *Mic*. Also known as Yasiin Bey, Mos Def is widely considered to be a hip hop legend. After converting to Islam at the age of 19, Mos Def expressed a socially conscious message, and many of his songs begin with the Islamic prayer "Bismillah Ar-Rahman Ar-Raheem," or "In the name of God, the most gracious, the most merciful." Well-known retired rappers like Craig Mack and Ma$e have also incorporated Muslim beliefs into their craft.

The Nation of Islam (NOI) and other nontraditional sects like the Nation of Gods (NOG) and the Five Percenters have also influenced hip hop through lyrics and images dating back to the late 1970s. In the late 1980s and early 1990s, a wave of commercial Muslim hip-hop artists "used their platform to promote political awareness, community uplift and cultural self-determination. As movements, both the NOI and NGE actively engaged hip-hop artists and the communities in which the artists and their audiences lived" (Ali, 2014). In his autobiography, *Life and Def: Sex, Drugs, Money, and God*, Russell Simmons, a founding father of the rap music industry, refers to the NOG as an "important influence" in the history of hip hop (Simmons, 2001). In her study, *Five Percenter Rap: God Hop's Music, Message and Black Muslim Message*, Felicia M. Miyakawa observed, "Even in the earliest days of hip-hop, the Five Percenters were regarded as an integral part of the hip-hop scene" (Miyakawa, 2005). Rapper Kam of Watts, California, claims to have introduced rapper Ice Cube to the NOI (Harling, 2015). Today, Jay Electronica, an American hip-hop artist, is known for performing onstage with the NOI flag embroidered on his shoulders (Harling, 2015).

Several American Muslims have also emerged as leading comedians in the United States. Hasan Minhaj, a second-generation U.S. citizen of Indian descent who serves as a correspondent on the Emmy award–winning program *The Daily Show with Trevor Noah*, roasted President Donald Trump in front of reporters at the White House Correspondents' Association dinner in April 2017. Dean Obeidallah and Maysoon Zayid, two comedians who produced The Muslim Funny Fest in July 2015, have been putting together the New York Arab Comedy Festival for at least the past decade (Kuruvilla, 2015). Obeidallah, a lawyer turned writer and award-winning comedian, is the host of SiriusXM radio's daily program *The Dean Obeidallah Show*, making him the first American Muslim to host a national radio show. He is of Palestinian and Italian descent. Zayid is an actress and comedian who is also of Palestinian descent. Maz Jobrani, author of the *Los Angeles Times* best-selling book *I'm Not a Terrorist but I've Played One on TV*, is a standup comedian who has performed at the Kennedy Center in Washington, D.C., and the White House. As Amarnath Amarasingam noted in his 2010 article "Laughter the Best Medicine: Muslim Comedians and Social Criticism in Post-9/11 America," Muslim comedians are playing critical roles in "breaking down cultural barriers, promoting inter-religious and inter-cultural dialogue, as well as tackling the misperceptions about Muslim and Arab Americans in the United States" (Amarasingam, 2010).

FURTHER READING

Abu-Ras, Wahiba, Laird, Lance D., & Senzai, Farid. (2012, September). *A Window into American Muslim Physicians: Civic Engagement and Community Participation, Their Diversity, Contributions & Challenges.* Washington, DC: The Institute for Social Policy and Understanding. Retrieved from http://www.ispu.org/wp-content/uploads/2016/09/ISPU_Report_Muslim_Physicians.pdf

Ahmed, Akbar. (2002). *Islam Today: A Short Introduction to the Muslim World.* New York, NY: I.B. Tauris.

Ali, Zaheer. (2014, July 19). "Is It Nation of Islam Time Again in Hip-Hop?" *The Root.* Retrieved from http://www.theroot.com/is-it-nation-of-islam-time-again-in-hip-hop-1790876441

Amarasingam, Amarnath. (2010). "Laughter the Best Medicine: Muslim Comedians and Social Criticism in Post-9/11 America." *Journal of Muslim Minority Affairs* 30(4): 463–477.

Baker, J. W. (2015, October 15). "10 Great American Muslims and Their Contributions to the United States." XPatnation.com. Retrieved from

http://xpatnation.com/10-great-american-muslims-and-their-contri
butions-to-the-united-states/

Beaudoin, Kate. (2015, June 18). "7 Muslim Rappers Who Are Shattering Stereotypes about Islam." *Mic.* Retrieved from https://mic.com/
articles/120901/7-muslim-rappers-who-embrace-their-faith-through-
hip-hop#.bB0NaXX8O

Considine, Craig. (2017). *Islam, Race, and Pluralism in the Pakistani Diaspora.* London and New York, NY: Routledge.

Curtis, Edward E., IV. (2010). *Encyclopedia of Muslim-American History.*
New York, NY: Infobase Publishing.

Esposito, John. (1998). *Islam: The Straight Path.* New York, NY, and
Oxford: Oxford University Press.

Harling, Danielle. (2015, December 31). "Kam Recalls Introducing Ice
Cube to the Nation of Islam." Hiphopdx.com. Retrieved from https://
hiphopdx.com/news/id.36849/title.kam-recalls-introducing-ice-
cube-to-the-nation-of-islam#

Harris, Sam. (2013, October 11). "No Ordinary Violence." samharris
.org. Retrieved from https://www.samharris.org/blog/item/no-ordinary-
violence

Harvard University Press. (2013, October 21). "Does Malala Need Sav-
ing?" harvardpress.typepad.com. Retrieved from http://harvardpress
.typepad.com/hup_publicity/2013/10/does-malala-need-saving.html

Hassaballa, Hesham. (2014, January 31). "Muslims Don't Contribute to
America? Think Again." Chicagonow.com. Retrieved from http://
www.chicagonow.com/midwestern-muslim/2014/01/muslims-dont-
contribute-to-america-think-again/

Institute for Social Policy and Understanding. (n.d.). *Muslims for
American Progress.* Washington, DC: Institute for Social Policy and
Understanding. Retrieved from https://www.ispu.org/public-policy/
muslims-for-american-progress/

Interfaith Alliance & The First Amendment Center. (n.d.). *What Is the
Truth about American Muslims?* Washington, DC: Interfaith Alliance
and the First Amendment Center. Retrieved from http://interfaithalli
ance.org/americanmuslimfaq/

Islamic Circle of North America. (2013, August 10). "ICNA Partner Agency Rated among Top 10 US Charities." New York, NY:
Islamic Circle of North America. Retrieved from http://www.icna.org/
icna-partner-agency-rated-among-top-10-us-charity/

Islamic Medical Association of North America. "About Us." Lombard,
IL: Islamic Medical Association of North America. Retrieved from
https://imana.org/about-us/

Islamic Relief USA. (n.d.). "Arab American News: 'The Forgotten Philanthropy of American Muslims.'" Alexandria, VA: Islamic Relief USA. Retrieved from http://irusa.org/arab-american-news-the-forgotten-philanthropy-of-american-muslims/

Jeffries, Stuart. (2015, December 8). "The Muslims Who Shaped America—From Brain Surgeons to Rappers." *The Guardian*. Retrieved from https://www.theguardian.com/world/2015/dec/08/donald-trump-famous-muslims-us-history

Jobrani, Maz. (n.d.). "Bio." *Maz Jobrani*. Retrieved from http://www.mazjobrani.com/bio/

Karim, Talib I. (2008, May 12). "Muslim Doctors Abundant, but Muslim Hospitals Non-Existent." Themuslimlink.com. Retrieved from http://www.muslimlinkpaper.com/myjumla/index.php?option=com_content&view=article&id=1440:Muslim+Doctors+Abundant,+But+Muslim+Hospitals+Non-Existent&Itemid=17

Kuruvilla, Carol. (2015, July 20). "These Muslim Comedians Think Laughter Is the Best Medicine for Hate." *The Huffington Post*. Retrieved from http://www.huffingtonpost.com/entry/muslim-funny-fest_us_559e9c2ae4b05b1d028fd931

Madden, Sidney. (2016, June 13). "22 Rappers Who Are Muslim." *XXL Magazine*. Retrieved from http://www.xxlmag.com/news/2016/06/muslim-rappers/

Maese, Rick. (2017, August 24). "Mahmoud Abdul-Rauf on Kaepernick Controversy: 'It's a Duplicate Pretty Much.'" *The Washington Post*. Retrieved from https://www.washingtonpost.com/sports/mahmoud-abdul-rauf-on-kaepernick-controversy-its-a-duplicate-pretty-much/2017/08/24/cac9496e-890a-11e7-a94f-3139abce39f5_story.html?utm_term=.f177cdb84543

Minhaj, Hasan. (n.d.). About. *Hasan Minhaj*. Retrieved from https://hasanminhaj.com/

Miyakawa, Felicia M. (2005). *Five Percenter Rap: God Hop's Music, Message, and Black Muslim Mission*. Bloomington, IN: Indiana University Press.

Monsen, Lauren. (2017, June 21). "How American Muslims Give Back during Ramadan." share.america.gov. Retrieved https://share.america.gov/how-american-muslims-give-back-during-ramadan/

Murphy, Tim. (2011, July 26). "Rep. Allen West's (Very, Very) Stealth Jihad." Motherjones.com. Retrieved from http://www.motherjones.com/politics/2011/07/allen-west-peter-leitner-muslim-brotherhood/

Muslims for American Progress. (2017a). "About." Washington, DC: Institute for Social Policy and Understanding. Retrieved from https://www.muslimsforamericanprogress.org/about/

Muslims for American Progress. (2017b). *An Impact Report of Muslim Contributions to Michigan.* Washington, DC: The Institute for Social Policy and Understanding. muslimsforamericanprogress.org. Retrieved from https://www.muslimsforamericanprogress.org/an-impact-report-of-muslim-contributions-to-michigan#executive-summary

Obee, Maliik. (2016, June 13). "Being Muslim in America. Mahmoud Abdul-Rauf." Theodysseyonline.com. Retrieved from https://www.theodysseyonline.com/being-muslim-america-mahmoud-abdul-rauf

Obeidallah, Dean. (n.d.). "About Dean." Dean Obeidallah. Retrieved from http://deanofradio.com/about-dean/

Oosting, Jonathan. (2014, January 14). "Michigan Republican Dave Agema under Fire Again for Questioning Contributions of American Muslims." Mlive.com. Retrieved from http://www.mlive.com/politics/index.ssf/2014/01/michigan_republican_dave_agema.html

Oosting, Jonathan. (2015, January 14). "Republican National Committee Censures Dave Agema over 'Harmful and Offensive Rhetoric.'" Mlive.com. Retrieved from http://www.mlive.com/lansing-news/index.ssf/2015/01/republican_national_committee.html

Shellnut, Kate. (2017, April 30). "Meet Hasan Minhaj: The Muslim Comedian Who Roasted Trump in Front of Reporters." *The Washington Post.* Retrieved from https://www.washingtonpost.com/news/acts-of-faith/wp/2017/04/30/meet-hasan-minhaj-the-muslim-comedian-who-roasted-trump-in-front-of-reporters/?utm_term=.8a4c79319467

Simmons, Russell. (2001). *Life and Def: Sex, Drugs, Money, and God.* New York, NY: Three Rivers Press.

Suebsaeng, Asawin. (2016, December 12). "Allen West's Muslim Hate Goes Well beyond a Genocide Meme." *The Daily Beast.* Retrieved from https://www.thedailybeast.com/allen-wests-muslim-hate-goes-well-beyond-a-genocide-meme

University of Chicago Medical Center. (2015, December 11). "New Study Finds Nearly Half of American Muslim Doctors Feel Scrutinized on the Job." *Science Daily.* Retrieved from https://www.sciencedaily.com/releases/2015/12/151211145050.htm

Winsor, Ben. (2014, October 27). "9 Famous Americans You Probably Didn't Know Were Muslim." *Business Insider.* Retrieved from http://www.businessinsider.com/these-9-famous-americans-are-all-muslim-2014-10

Zakat Foundation of America. (n.d.). "What Makes Us Unique?" Zakat.org. Retrieved from https://www.zakat.org/en/about-us/

Q31. DO MUSLIMS IN THE UNITED STATES SUPPORT "AMERICAN VALUES" SUCH AS FREEDOM OF RELIGION AND FREEDOM OF SPEECH AS OUTLINED IN THE FIRST AMENDMENT?

Answer: Yes. Research carried out by several prominent organizations shows a high percentage of U.S. Muslims adhering to these American values.

The Facts: There is a debate in the United States that attracts publicity in media outlets, political circles, and religious communities. This debate pivots around whether American Muslims support cherished American values like freedom of religion, freedom of speech, and gender equality. Some people believe that they do not. Republican Alabama Senate candidate Roy Moore, for example, claimed in July 2017 that Islam is a "false religion" that teaches values that are "completely opposite with what our First Amendment stands for" (Koplowitz, 2017). Televangelist Pat Robertson, the founder of the Christian Broadcasting Network and host of the television show *The 700 Club*, suggested that Muslims are the new Nazis because they are "intent on dominating us and imposing sharia law and making us all part of a universal caliphate" (Robertson, 2011). Four years later, on an episode of *The 700 Club*, Robertson described Islam not as a religion but as a military ideology "bent on world domination" (Robertson, 2015). Studies and polls indicate, though, that in reality, the overwhelming majority of American Muslims actually support American values and the United States' democratic system.

According to Pew Research Center (2007, 2011, 2017) data, American Muslims appear to be highly integrated into American society. The overwhelming majority of American Muslims, as reported by Pew, do not see a conflict between being a devout Muslim and living in a modern society. Pew added that by overwhelming margins American Muslims "are satisfied with the way things are going in their own lives and rate their local communities as good places to live" (Pew Research Center, 2011).

Despite these findings, speculation among non-Muslim Americans persists that American Muslims do not believe in the freedom of religion for all U.S. citizens. Public opinion polls, however, indicate that a majority of American Muslims accept other faiths as spiritual equals. The Pew Research Center (2011) found that American Muslims were unique among Muslims around the world in that they rejected the idea that Islam is the only faith leading to eternal life, instead believing that many other religions can also do so.

In response to President Trump's proposed "Muslim travel ban", members of the House of Representatives in 2017 introduced the Freedom of Religion Act, which prohibits religious litmus tests for people seeking to enter the United States. The Council of American-Islamic Relations (CAIR), the nation's largest Muslim civil rights and advocacy organization, issued a press release on the Act calling on all Americans to urge their elected representative in the House of Representatives to vote in favor of this measure (Council on American-Islamic Relations, 2017a). The San Diego chapter of CAIR responded to Executive Order 13769, commonly known as the "Muslim ban," by holding a press conference to announce the creation of a Forum on Religious Freedom (Council on American-Islamic Relations, 2017c). The objective of the Forum "is to create a broad coalition and unite a group of organizations and individuals dedicated to challenging Islamophobia and the systematic attempt to marginalize the American Muslim Community." Furthermore, 300 American Muslim leaders crafted an open letter, titled "From American Muslim leaders to President-Elect Trump," which declared that Muslims in the United States share the same values as Americans of other faiths. The December 5, 2016 letter stated:

> The values we hold align with those of the overwhelming majority of Americans. According to a recent study by the Institute for Social Policy and Understanding (ISPU), Muslims are as likely as Protestants to have a strong American identity. American Muslims who view their faith as important are more likely to say being American is central to their identity. And, those who regularly attend mosques are more likely to be civically engaged. . . . Like other Americans, we love our country and are committed to preserving religious freedom, equal opportunity and equal protection under the law for all. (Muslim Letter to Trump, 2016)

The Muslim Public Affairs Council (MPAC), a public service agency working for the civil rights of American Muslims and for the integration of the Islamic faith into American pluralism, echoed the Muslim Letter to Trump. On its website, the MPAC notes that it "works in coalition with a wide variety of interfaith partners—spanning nearly a dozen faiths—to enhance interreligious understanding and support religious freedom for all Americans" (Muslim Public Affairs Council, n.d.).

In the spirit of these unequivocal statements, American Muslim politicians have spoken out publicly on the critical role that freedom of religion plays in their personal understanding of American national identity. Responding to Trump's Executive Order 13769 (titled "Protecting the Nation from Foreign Terrorist Entry into the United States"), U.S. representative Keith Ellison of Minnesota, a Muslim who signed the Freedom of Religion Act, stated, "Our country is built on religious tolerance and the freedom to worship"; he referred to the following inscription on the Statue of Liberty: " 'Give me your tired, your poor, your huddle masses yearning to breathe free.' It doesn't say anything about a person's faith" (U.S. House of Representatives, 2017). Following the signing of Executive Order 13769, Representative André Carson (D-IN), an American Muslim, requested that President Trump welcome Muslim immigrants in the name of the nation's core values. He hoped that the United States "will always be a country that welcomes people of all races, ethnicities, and religions" (U.S. House of Representatives, 2017). American Muslims have also extended their support of freedom of religion to religious minority communities around the world. In April 2017, for example, the CAIR (Council on American-Islamic Relations, 2017b) called on President Trump to demand an end to the denial of religious freedom for Christians in the "Muslim world" as well as Uighur Muslims in China.

According to Interfaith Alliance, "many American Muslim leaders, educational institutions and advocacy groups have repeatedly spoken out for freedom [of speech], and are actively involved in promoting liberty for all people both in the United States and abroad" (Interfaith Alliance & First Amendment Center, n.d.). In May 2015, over 200 prominent Canadian and American Muslims issued a statement that "unconditionally condemned any intimidation or threats of violence directed against any individual or group" exercising the rights of freedom of speech and freedom of religion, "even when that speech may be perceived as hurtful or reprehensible" (The American Muslim, 2015). The signers of the statement wrote they uphold the First Amendment of the U.S. Constitution because it provides protections that are fundamental to defending minorities from the whims of the majority. Signatories included Professor Hassan Abbas, Quaid-i-Azam chair, South Asia Institute, Columbia University; Asma Afsaruddin, professor of Islamic Studies, Indiana University; Professor Akbar Ahmed, Ibn Khaldun chair of Islamic Studies, American University; Amir Hussain, professor of theological studies, Loyala Marymount University; Arsalan Iftikhar, author, human rights lawyer, blogger— "the Muslim guy"; Safi Kaskas, president and CEO of Strategic Edge; and Haroon Moghul, writer and public speaker.

American Muslims have been accused of being enemies of freedom a speech, a civil right protected by the First Amendment of the U.S. Constitution. These accusations reached a boiling point following the *Jyllands-Posten* Muhammad cartoon controversy. On September 30, 2005, the Danish newspaper *Jyllands-Posten* published 12 cartoons that depicted Prophet Muhammad as a "terrorist." While *Jyllands-Posten* claimed that the cartoons contributed to the debate about criticism of Islam, Muslims worldwide condemned the depictions and even used violence and rioting to protest, though American Muslims did not partake in these kind of actions. The CAIR responded to the controversy by requesting a meeting with the Danish ambassador to discuss ways to defuse the tension between Muslims and non-Muslims. In his official letter to the Danish ambassador, CAIR executive director Nihad Awad stated that American Muslims value freedom of expression and the right to critical thought, but he added, "we should also use good judgment and common sense to avoid actions that will be perceived as intentionally insulting to others or that promoted hatred" (Council on American Islamic Relations, 2015).

The expression of unpopular opinions, even those that are deeply offensive to other people, was the focus of a lengthy survey on free speech and tolerance by the libertarian CATO Institute, a libertarian think tank, which collaborated with YouGov, the market research firm (Friedersdorf, 2017). The final data set was drawn from answers to scores of questions provided by 2,300 people (Friedersdorf, 2017). The CATO Institute/YouGov survey, which asked what constituted permissible public statements, found that Muslims (37 percent) were less likely to favor laws banning "offensive speech" than people who identified themselves as African Americans (46 percent), Jews (41 percent), and Hispanics (39 percent) (CATO Institute & YouGov, 2017). Moreover, Muslims (63 percent) were more likely than African Americans (54 percent), Jews (59 percent), and Hispanics (61 percent) to oppose laws banning offensive free speech in the United States (CATO Institute & YouGov, 2017).

In 2016, the fact-checking website Politifact analyzed levels of integration into U.S. society and culture among second- and third-generation American Muslims. After analyzing various sets of social science data and expert opinion, Politifact concluded that American Muslims are actually extremely motivated to integrate into mainstream American society. "There's clear evidence that, contrary to what Trump suggests, Muslims are embracing American identity and values," concluded Politifact. "Substantial evidence [also] confirms that Muslim Americans want to have an American identity and think that doing so is achievable. In fact, their preferences for self-identification mirror those of Christian Americans.

FURTHER READING

American Civil Liberties Union. (n.d.). *Protecting the Religious Freedom of Muslims.* New York, NY: American Civil Liberties Union. Retrieved from https://www.aclu.org/feature/protecting-religious-freedom-muslims

The American Muslim. (2015, May 5). "A Defense of Free Speech by American and Canadian Muslims." theamericanmuslim.org. Retrieved from http://theamericanmuslim.org/tam.php/features/articles/a_defense_of_free_speech_by_american_and_canadian_muslims

Bier, David. (2016, October 13). "Muslims Rapidly Adopt U.S. Social Values." Washington, DC: CATO Institute. Retrieved from https://www.cato.org/blog/muslims-rapidly-adopt-us-social-political-values

CATO Institute & YouGov. (2017, August 15–23). "CATO Institute 2017 Free Speech and Tolerance Survey." Washington, DC: CATO Institute. Retrieved from https://object.cato.org/sites/cato.org/files/survey-reports/topline/cato-free-speech-tolerance-toplines.pdf

Council on American-Islamic Relations. (2015, March 11). "CAIR Seeks Meeting with Danish Ambassador over Offensive Cartoons." Washington, DC: Council on American-Islamic Relations. Retrieved from https://www.cair.com/press-center/press-releases/1685-cair-seeks-meeting-with-danish-ambassador-over-offensive-cartoons.html

Council on American-Islamic Relations. (2017a, February 2). "CAIR Action Alert: Support the Freedom of Religion Act Today." Washington, DC: Council on American-Islamic Relations. Retrieved from https://www.cair.com/press-center/action-alerts/14081-cair-action-alert-support-the-freedom-of-religion-act-today.html

Council on American-Islamic Relations. (2017b, April 5). "CAIR Calls on Trump to Demand Religious Freedom for Christians, Uighur Muslims at Meeting with Chinese President." Washington, DC: Council on American-Islamic Relations. Retrieved from https://www.cair.com/press-center/press-releases/14252-cair-calls-on-trump-to-demand-religious-freedom-for-christians-uighur-muslims-at-meeting-with-chinese-president.html

Council on American-Islamic Relations. (2017c, January 30). "CAIR: San Diego Muslims to Announce Creation of 'Forum on Religious Freedom' in Response to 'Muslim Ban' Executive Order." Washington, DC: Council on American-Islamic Relations. Retrieved from https://www.cair.com/press-center/press-releases/14065-cair-san-diego-muslims-to-announce-creation-of-forum-on-religious-freedom-in-response-to-muslim-ban-executive-order.html

Friedersdorf, Conor. (2017, October 9). "America's Many Divides over Free Speech." *The Atlantic*. Retrieved from https://www.theatlantic.com/politics/archive/2017/10/a-sneak-peek-at-new-survey-data-on-free-speech/542028/

Hamilton, Matt. (2016, October 9). "Donald Trump Repeats False Claim That Neighbors Saw 'Bombs All Over' before San Bernardino Attack." *Los Angeles Times*. Retrieved from http://www.latimes.com/politics/la-na-pol-trump-debate-san-bernardino-20161009-snap-story.html

Hathout, Hassan. (1995). *Reading the Muslim Mind*. USA: American Trust Publications.

Interfaith Alliance & the First Amendment Center. (n.d.). *What Is the Truth about American Muslims?* Washington, DC: Interfaith Alliance. Retrieved from http://interfaithalliance.org/americanmuslimfaq/

Jacobson, Lauren. (2016, June 18). "Donald Trump Wrong That 'There's No Real Assimilation' by U.S. Muslims." *Politifact*. Retrieved from http://www.politifact.com/nbc/statements/2016/jun/18/donald-trump/donald-trump-wrong-theres-no-real-assimilation-us-/

Jenkins, Jack. (2016, December 6). "Muslim American Leaders to Trump: Protect Our Freedom of Religion." *Think Progress*. Retrieved from https://thinkprogress.org/muslim-american-leaders-letter-trump-3e2c561527f8

Koplowitz, Howard. (2017, July 25). "Roy Moore 'Un-American' for Calling Islam a 'False Religion,' Alabama Muslims Say." AL.com. Retrieved from http://www.al.com/news/index.ssf/2017/07/roy_moore_un-american_for_call.html

Muslim Letter to Trump. (2016, December 5). "Open Letter: From American Muslim Leaders to President-Elect Trump." *Muslim Letter to Trump*. Retrieved from http://www.muslimlettertotrump.com/

Muslim Public Affairs Council. (n.d.). "Religious Freedom." Los Angeles, CA: Muslim Public Affairs Council. Retrieved from https://www.mpac.org/issues/religious-freedom.php

Pew Research Center. (2007, May 22). *Muslim Americans: Middle Class and Mostly Mainstream*. Washington, DC: Pew Research Center. Retrieved from http://www.pewresearch.org/2007/05/22/muslim-americans-middle-class-and-mostly-mainstream/

Pew Research Center. (2011, August 2011). "Section 3: Identity, Assimilation and Community." Washington, DC: Pew Research Center. Retrieved from http://www.people-press.org/2011/08/30/section-3-identity-assimilation-and-community/

Pew Research Center. (2012, July 10). "Chapter 4. Gender Equality." Washington, DC: Pew Research Center. Retrieved from http://www.pewglobal.org/2012/07/10/chapter-4-gender-equality/

Pew Research Center. (2017, July 26). "U.S. Muslims Concerned about Their Place in Society, but Continue to Believe in the American Dream." Washington, DC: Pew Research Center. Retrieved from http://www.pewforum.org/2017/07/26/findings-from-pew-research-centers-2017-survey-of-us-muslims/

Robertson, Pat. (2011, May 31). "Robertson: Opposing Islam Just Like Opposing the Nazis." YouTube.com. Retrieved from https://www.youtube.com/watch?v=mQOujxM585w

Robertson, Pat. (2015, December 8). "RWW News: Robertson: Islam Not a Religion but a Military Group 'Bent on World Domination.'" YouTube.com. Retrieved from https://www.youtube.com/watch?v=6R5X2CUMFoE

U.S. House of Representatives. (2017, February 2). "Press Release: House Delegation Introduces Freedom of Religion Act in Response to President Trump's Muslim Ban." Washington, DC: U.S. House of Representatives. Retrieved from https://beyer.house.gov/news/documentsingle.aspx?DocumentID=495

Younis, Mohamed. (2009, March 2). "Muslim American Exemplify Diversity, Potential." Washington, DC: Gallup.com. Retrieved from http://www.gallup.com/poll/116260/muslim-americans-exemplify-diversity-potential.aspx

Index

About the Author

Craig Considine is a U.S. Catholic of Irish and Italian descent. He is the author of *Islam, Race, and Pluralism in the Pakistani Diaspora* (2017) and the film director of *Journey into America* (2008). Dr. Considine holds a Ph.D. from Trinity College, Dublin, an MSc from the University of London, and a BA from American University. He is a native of Needham, Massachusetts. As of 2018, he is based at Rice University in the Department of Sociology.